THEORIES
OF VALUE
AND P
OF ED

D0887148

DATE DUE

OCT 2 6 1994			

Demco, Inc. 38-293

READINGS IN
THE PHILOSOPHY
OF EDUCATION

GENERAL SERIES EDITOR, HARRY S. BROUDY

THEORIES OF VALUE AND PROBLEMS OF EDUCATION

EDITED BY PHILIP G. SMITH

UNIVERSITY OF ILLINOIS PRESS
URBANA, CHICAGO, LONDON

© 1970 by the Board of Trustees of the University of Illinois
Manufactured in the United States of America
Library of Congress Catalog Card No. 71-108594

Clothbound: 252 00105 2
Paperbound: 252 00106 0

130886

GENERAL SERIES PREFACE

Readings in the Philosophy of Education is a series of books each of which reprints significant articles, excerpts from books, and monographs that deal philosophically with problems in education.

The distinctive feature of this series is that the selection of materials and their organization are based on the results of a three-year project supported by the U.S. Office of Education and the University of Illinois. A team of philosophers of education with consultants from both philosophy of education and general philosophy scanned thousands of items. Their final selection was presented in a report entitled *Philosophy of Education: An Organization of Topics and Selected Sources* (Urbana: University of Illinois Press, 1967).

Unfortunately, not all college libraries are equally well stocked with the items listed in the report, and even with adequate resources, getting the appropriate materials to the student is a formidable task for the instructor.

Accordingly, several members of the original team that worked on the project agreed to bring out this series. The projected books are organized in two groups. One group will devote a separate volume to each of the following problems in education: the nature, aims, and policies of education; curriculum; and teaching-learning. The second group will be made up of a number of volumes each of which will bring together significant materials from one of the following philosophical disciplines: epistemology; metaphysics; value theory; aesthetics; and the philosophy of science. This volume belongs to the second group and deals with the import of value theory for various problem areas of education.

The first group of books will make available to the student some important and representative statements that philosophers of education, utilizing the resources of epistemology, metaphysics, value theory, logical and linguistic analysis, social philosophy, philosophy of science, and the philosophy of religion have made about problems of education. Used as a set, these volumes are appropriate for the first course in the philosophy of education whether offered to undergraduates or on the master's level. Individually or in combination they can also be used in courses in administration, methods, principles, curriculum, and related fields.

Each of the volumes in the second group approaches the problems of education from one of the standard divisions of general philosophy, and individually or in combination they are suited to advanced and specialized courses. Some instructors may wish to use both types in their courses.

Philip G. Smith, the editor of this volume, was a member of the Advisory Board of the Philosophy of Education Project and one of its consultants. He has written extensively in philosophy of education and is a past president of the Philosophy of Education Society.

HARRY S. BROUDY
General Series Editor

PREFACE

In contemporary value theory it is customary to differentiate ethics from meta-ethics, or substantive (normative) ethics from analytical ethics. When the literature concerned with values and education is viewed with this distinction in mind, one can see that it is substantive ethics that has dominated the field. There is a considerable body of literature, much of it somewhat homiletic or hortatory, that is concerned with (1) aims and objectives of education, (2) the role of the school as a social institution inextricably enmeshed in the values of the society that supports it, and (3) the issues and problems involved in moral education. By contrast, there has been little attention given to the bearing of general value theory upon the everyday valuing and evaluating that is involved in the conduct of schooling.

In this collection of readings no attempt has been made to present a representative, fair, or balanced selection with respect to the body of literature available; on the contrary, the effort has been to bring together a few selections that, taken as a whole, would seem to cast a more steady light upon the topic "theories of value and problems of education" than is afforded by the enormously variegated glint and glimmer of the full range of literature relevant in one way or another to this topic. It is to be hoped that not only the selections themselves but the way in which they are arranged under subtopics will contribute to the effort to provide a new focus for this important area in the field of philosophy of education. Finally, even though the selections are not representative of the larger body of literature from which they were drawn, I do believe that the "soft spots" and lacunae that will become apparent to a thoughtful reader represent a reasonably accurate reflection of weaknesses and omissions that exist in the larger body of literature.

P.G.S.

CONTENTS

THE NATURE OF VALUE THEORY
AND ITS RELEVANCE FOR EDUCATION

INTRODUCTION

It is frequently said that not all parts of general philosophy are equally relevant to philosophy of education. Since, however, it is generally acknowledged that education is pervaded by values, perhaps most philosophers would agree that value theory is certainly relevant to at least some of the problems of education. Beyond this, however, there is considerable disagreement (or, more accurately, lack of careful attention) concerning what aspects of value theory are relevant in what way to what kinds of educational problems.

It may be at least of passing interest to note that in the long history of philosophy, while discussions of both problems of value and problems of education have figured prominently (even two thousand years ago, for example, in Plato's *Republic*), it was only in the last century that each, in its own way, came to be recognized as an important philosophic topic. Value theory is now generally accepted as one of the fundamental topics of general philosophy distinct from, say, metaphysics or epistemology; philosophy of education is accepted as a field of philosophic study distinct from, say, social-political philosophy. Moreover, just as value theory as a *philosophic* topic is now clearly differentiated from the long history of more or less theoretical studies of the nature of value in, say, political economy, philosophy of education is no longer confused with the long history of pedagogic homiletics. But, of course, in the history of civilization a century is a short time indeed, and it is not surprising that we still find considerable confusion about the nature of value theory and its relevance for education.

One of the minor but still frustrating and confusing difficulties is the imprecise terminology and lack of standard classifications commonly found within general value theory. For example, while it is frequently said that axiology has two main branches, ethics and aesthetics, Professor Taylor delineates *eight* realms of value and notes that education can be involved in any or all of these.

In a more recent discussion of the problem of value classification, Professor Rescher concludes that there are at least six distinct principles or approaches justifiable in the classification of values, and under any one of these a very long list of categories may be generated.[1] Nevertheless, ethics (which is sometimes said to be the philosophical study of morality) tends to dominate the field and a study of the nature and structure of ethics (including study of ethical disagreements, the justification of ethical decisions or conclusions, the use of ethical terms, and the like) is sometimes called meta-ethics. Because of the dominant position of ethics among the realms of value, "meta-ethics" is sometimes used as a name for the whole field of general value theory (in contrast to some particular theory of value or to a theory about some particular kind of value, e.g., ethical theory).

Moreover, meta-ethics is sometimes said to be "analytical ethics" in contrast to "normative ethics" or "substantive ethics." This can be a source of additional confusion, for while the term "normative" means literally "of or about norms," it is often used more or less interchangeably with "prescriptive." Prescription typically stands in contrast to description and sometimes normative studies are contrasted with descriptive studies under the general rubric of a concern for what ought to be in contrast to what is. But, of course, norms or standards are involved in a great range of activities including analyzing and prescribing as well as describing (and the inferring that is typically involved in any attempt to describe the norms that seem to be operating in any given situation).

Perhaps a more fundamental distinction that lies beneath much of the above is a three-way differentiation of concerns with norms: (1) a concern to understand by making explicit in a clear and concise manner what norms seem to be governing various sorts of activities; (2) a concern to improve some activity by urging the adoption and use of certain norms; (3) a concern for the appropriateness, adequacy, and worth — in short, the *value* of — certain norms, whether presently clearly in use or proposed.

In any event, the question arises as to whether axiology or value theory consists of ethics plus aesthetics plus theories in other realms of value or whether there are more general questions and consid-

[1] Nicholas Rescher, *Introduction to Value Theory* (Englewood Cliffs, N.J.: Prentice-Hall, 1969), Chapter II.

erations that cut across these subdivisions and are either logically prior or common to the various branches. If such general considerations are possible and important, then while a study of these would not likely be an adequate substitute for a study of any one of the branches of axiology, these more general considerations may be the heart of general value theory and may be the most critical aspect of value theory for the philosophy of education. This is to say that while aesthetics may have the more direct bearing upon aesthetic education (and the aesthetic aspects of education) and ethics upon moral education (and the moral aspects of education), it may be the more general questions at the heart of value theory that are the critical ones for the philosophy of education. Since, as Professor Taylor has suggested, education is an arena in which all realms of value may be involved, one may hope that in further serious study of value theory and the problems of education light will be cast in both directions.

In "Moral Philosophy and Education," which is our first selection, Professor Aiken concludes that "both the methods and the results of contemporary analytical ethics are indispensable adjuncts of enlightened moral practice, and that their study is therefore a useful or even a necessary part of any truly humane or liberal education." In the process of reaching this conclusion he provides us with a brief review of the major developments in value theory since G. E. Moore and explicates the distinction between substantive ethics and analytical ethics. Moreover, since Professor Aiken believes "that moral ideals are not beyond the reach of reason," his article provides a gateway to disciplined study of the nature of value theory and its relevance for education.

It is obvious that in a brief collection of readings one cannot include all that would be helpful to a balanced consideration of a given topic. For example, had space limitations permitted, an article by Walter Kaufman, "Educational Development from the Point of View of a Normative Philosophy,"[2] would certainly have been included. Professor Kaufman, while not opposed to analysis, nevertheless argues that linguistic analysis is not enough to do the job that needs to be done. He proposes "a canon of method" that

[2] In George Barnett (ed.), *Philosophy and Educational Development* (Boston: Houghton Mifflin, 1966), pp. 27-45.

would bring consideration of value questions more securely into the fold of any inquiry that is rational and reasonable. Under this canon, when "one explores the ramifications of a view, both logical and practical, to determine what it means," the analysis need be neither exclusively nor primarily linguistic; other forms of analysis, e.g., historical, psychological, sociological, may feature prominently in the inquiry. A mode of meaning particularly apt for philosophic analysis concerns the implications and presuppositions involved in various value judgments or positions.

The approach of Professor Kaufman tends to emphasize the similarities between being reasonable with respect to judgments about values and being reasonable in making judgments in other domains, rather than emphasizing the differences that exist among various fields of inquiry. All this results in a less heavy-handed distinction between facts and values than is frequently assumed in general value theory — perhaps especially by those who have not "tried out" this distinction in the arena of education. Finally, Professor Kaufman's approach results in the conclusion that "analysis and 'normative philosophy' are far from being mutually exclusive."

Not only must one exclude many worthwhile selections, but there is not room for even brief comment upon each of the outstanding ones which have been excluded. In this connection, therefore, attention should be directed to the work of Harry S. Broudy et al.,[3] who have compiled a rather complete list (with brief comments) of the literature available under various topics in the philosophy of education. A glance at the table of contents should enable one to locate the sections on value theory under each of the main problem areas of education.

If being reasonable about values is similar to being reasonable about other matters, one may still ask why it is that one ought to be reasonable about values and whether there are peculiar difficulties encountered in the area of valuations in contrast to other areas of investigation. Our second selection, therefore, is an excerpt from the writing of C. I. Lewis which speaks to these two questions. Following this, Professor Taylor, in an excerpt from

---

[3] Harry S. Broudy et al., *Philosophy of Education* (Urbana: University of Illinois Press, 1967).

his *Normative Discourse,* discusses eight realms of value and then suggests a distinction between objective and subjective rationality, the point being that some values which *could* be rationally justified may, nevertheless, be accepted uncritically or irrationally. The question then arises as to whether or not a way of life that could be rationally justified should be indoctrinated or otherwise inculcated so that it will be embraced and practiced in a way that is subjectively irrational. Students of education will recognize, of course, that this question is critical not only in relation to the problem of moral education but also in relation to more general questions raised by the educational theory or position known as reconstructionism.

The next selections, by J. Donald Butler and Kingsley Price, are concerned with the general question of the relationship of value theory to education. The concluding article, by Clive Beck, was written in reaction to noncognitivist theories of value in general and to some suggestions by C. L. Stevenson in particular. But the main thrust is a proposal for the adoption of an empiricist-objectivist theory of value as being most adequate for understanding educational value statements.

MORAL PHILOSOPHY AND EDUCATION

HENRY D. AIKEN

I. Current Philosophy and Liberal Education

The advancement of learning is rarely attended by a ready understanding of its relevance to liberal education. It is not hard to see why this should be so. On the one side is the scholar's pardonable desire to get on with his job without being continually side-tracked by importunate questions about the practical relevance of his researches; on the other is the understandable reluctance of educators to range very far from the highway of received ideas. From the nature of his calling the educator is bound to rely heavily upon theories and principles lying somewhat to the rear of current inquiry. The more radical its departure from tradition, therefore, the less likely is any new development in any branch of learning to find its way immediately into the core curriculum. When first introduced, it is almost necessarily restricted to courses intended for the specialist. The result is an inevitable, but not necessarily unhealthy, tension between the concerns of productive scholarship and the more conservative obligations of the common educational process. Occasionally, however, there sets in a more serious dissociation between research and education which can be exceedingly harmful to the permanent values of both.

For some time such a situation appears to have been developing in philosophy. This is doubly unfortunate, since a widespread revival of educational interest in philosophical problems is occurring precisely at a time in which there has been a very rapid development in the methods of philosophical analysis that promises results of great value to educated men. As rarely before, there is an intense conviction on the part both of educators and of the general public that a sound education must include forms of instruction that transcend the scope of the special sciences. The phenomenal growth of general education is itself evidence of a

Reprinted, by permission, from *Harvard Educational Review*, XXV (Winter, 1955): 39-59. Copyright 1955 by President and Fellows of Harvard College.

conviction, not always clearly articulated or understood, that only studies having a philosophical dimension can overcome the cultural parochialism and the trained incompetence that are thought to be the by-products of scientific specialization. In practice this has usually meant a headlong return to the study of the great philosophical classics, with a corresponding stress upon the history of philosophy and a tendency to ignore or even to disparage more recent achievements. The latter, so far as they are considered at all, tend to be regarded as horrible examples of scholastic logic-chopping that are wholly divorced from the profounder human needs of our time. Such phrases as "symbolic logic," "philosophical analysis," and "logical positivism" conjure up in many academic minds only images of an outlandish professional jargon and a *recherche* symbolism whose meaning is intelligible, if at all, only to a few godless initiates, and whose point is understood not even by them. For all the external world knows or thinks it needs to know (and unfortunately this includes a good many teachers of philosophy), such symbol mongering is of interest only to a few monomaniacs who have made a fetish of something they call the methodology of science and who in consequence have forfeited the philosopher's ancient prerogative to speak and be heard on the primordial problems of man's fate. The only contemporary philosophical ideas that have received any really widespread attention outside the seminar are those impressionistic, semiliterary doctrines, such as existentialism, which least adequately represent the hard and sober thinking which has quietly made of our age one of the few periods of genuine creative advance in philosophy. The result has been that philosophical theories of very great relevance to general human enlightenment remain largely unknown or else are badly misrepresented, while at the same time, half-cooked ideas, whose very intelligibility is in doubt, are treated with polite respect and attention. Indeed the very classics themselves, which should be approached as precious harbingers of truth rather than as final or official statements of the views they represent, are set in prejudicial contrast to the present aims of philosophical research.

The truth is, of course, that any such opposition between the intellectual concerns of the great thinkers of the past, such as Aristotle, Locke, or Kant, and those of such original contemporaries as Russell, Wittgenstein, and Carnap is quite illusory. The present interest in problems of methodology and in the logical analysis of such concepts as meaning, truth, and value is merely a continuation of a perennial philosophical interest in the clarification of basic general ideas and techniques of inquiry that is older than Plato. If there is a difference, it lies rather in the fact that contemporary analytical philosophers have found ways of handling these ancient questions which are clearer and more exact, and which therefore hold the promise of answers upon which, for the first time, reasonable men might be expected to agree. The contemporary state of philosophy certainly leaves much to be desired; but its insistence upon clarity, order, and exactitude is all that has ever distinguished philosophy as a discipline from common-sense speculation concerning the organizing concepts by which we live.

It is my purpose in this essay to correct in some measure the prevailing lack of understanding of the humane import of analytical philosophy by showing some of the broader implications of recent findings in ethical theory. Moral philosophy in the twentieth century has entered upon a period of important theoretical advances which, when properly understood, cannot fail to have a more general significance for reflective men. In what follows I shall first indicate what some of these developments are and then say something about their relevance to ordinary human affairs.

II. Substantive Ethics and Analytic Ethics

Most analytical philosophers are now agreed that a primary source of the faltering progress of earlier moral philosophy is the general failure to distinguish clearly between two very different sorts of questions which we shall call questions of "substantive ethics" and "analytic ethics." As we shall presently see, these questions are not wholly unconnected, but even to understand how this may be so requires that at the outset they not be confused.

Substantive Ethics

The fundamental problem of moral philosophy has always been that of the good life. From the attempt to solve it arise the endless comparisons and reappraisals of specific standards of value and ways of life. Belonging to this side of the subject are such hoary but never irrelevant questions as "What, if any, is the highest good?", "What are the basic principles of right action?", and "What are the common rights and responsibilities of men?" These questions are commonly considered "normative ethics." To so speak of them, however, is perhaps question begging, and already implies a certain generic theory as to the nature of moral judgments. In order not to prejudice the discussion in advance, therefore, I shall refer to that side of moral philosophy which addresses itself to the question how we ought to live as "substantive ethics." By so doing I wish only to indicate that any other form of philosophical reflection about morals must take its rise from the fact that the problems of substantive ethics already exist. Were it not for them, the analytical questions with which we shall here be concerned would have no subject-matter.

Now the illusion prevails in certain quarters that the tasks of substantive ethics are, at bottom, not intellectual but decisional. On such a view analysis can have little or no bearing upon substantive problems. In a later portion of this paper I shall try to show how mistaken such a view is. Meanwhile it will suffice to remark that the possibility of substantive moral philosophy as a discipline seems to presuppose that moral ideals are not beyond the reach of reason. It assumes, or seems to assume, that some ideals are not merely better but also more reasonable than others. I do not doubt that the interests of substantive ethics are finally practical rather than speculative. But they would appear to rest upon the conviction that in some relevant sense practice may be informed, and that moral criticism is not just a matter of personal idiosyncracy. At the moment, however, I do not wish to stress this point. For purposes of contrast I wish rather to emphasize the point that although substantive ethics cannot dispense with rational methods, its aims are primarily deliberative and hence are incomplete until they issue forth into choice, even though the choices with which it is concerned are at a certain remove from the immediate decisions of daily life.

Analytic Ethics

The questions of substantive ethics are no longer denied relevance to the problems of liberal education. On the contrary, it is with them, I suppose, that general education is very largely concerned. It is the second sort of question, which marks the special province of analytical moral theory, that is more frequently thought to lie aside from the educational concerns of ordinary persons. Questions of this sort are the following: "What are the meanings or uses of 'ought,' 'right,' and 'value'?", "What are the roles of moral reasoning?", "What is the nature of moral disagreement and of moral justification?", "What is the relation of factual statements to moral judgments?" By calling such questions "analytic," I wish merely to indicate that they are concerned in the first instance with second-level problems of meaning and logic rather than with first-level problems of deliberation and choice. It is essential to bear in mind at the outset, however, that interest in analytical questions is not new; in fact it is nearly as old as moral philosophy itself, and seems to have arisen spontaneously the moment that reflection upon moral problems went to fundamentals. In the dialogues of Plato, for example, Socrates constantly and insistently asks of his pupils, "What is justice?" or "What is the nature of goodness?" And from Aristotle onward questions concerning the "nature" or "essence" of virtue and obligation and concerning the logic of practical reason have preoccupied most first-ranking classical moral philosophers.

Confusion of Substantive with Analytic Questions

Unfortunately, however, the import of such questions was not until fairly recently sharply distinguished from those of substantive ethics, with the result that even the greatest philosophers remained unclear as to the character of the problems to which they addressed themselves and were in consequence uncertain as to the sorts of arguments or evidence that would be relevant to their solution. Until very lately, in fact, the same tendency to confuse questions of meaning and logic with substantive ethical issues has plagued many contemporary analysts themselves. Even G. E. Moore (8), who is perhaps as responsible as anyone for setting analytical ethics upon its present course of inquiry, tended to conceal from himself the nature of his task by asking his own analytical questions in a misleading form. He intuitively recognized that there is a fundamental difference between questions of the form "What things are good?" and those which ask "What does 'good' mean?" Yet particularly in his earlier writings he constantly phrased questions of the latter sort in various confusing ways. By assimilating the question "What is the meaning or (better) use of 'good'?" to such apparently similar questions as "What is the property of goodness?" or, more simply, "What is goodness?" he was led to suppose that by solving the *analytical* questions he had put himself he would also be able, once and for all, to lay the cornerstone of a substantive "moral science." How dubious such a supposition is will be seen as we proceed.

The Linguistic Character of Analytic Problems

It is essential to clear understanding of the tasks of analytical ethics to see that all such questions are, at bottom, misleading ways of asking about the meanings or uses of words. They are objectionable because they tend to conceal from the questioner the point of his question and so obscure the sorts of answer that would be relevant to it. By asking about the *property* of goodness, it is assumed, first of all, that there *is* such a property which can be discovered by inspection of and abstraction from the observable characteristics of good things. This implies that we may by-pass all linguistic considerations regarding the usage of words and proceed at once to the important matters of fact lying behind them. This is the basic error. For until we have examined the use of "good" in discourse, we cannot know whether it functions referentially at all.[1] Moreover, even when words do function referentially, we still cannot determine what they mean by ignoring them and inspecting their supposed referents. It is a wise referent indeed that knows what it is called, and a wise observer who can tell by "inspection" that redness, say, is the property we call by the name "redness." Once we see, however, that problems of definition and meaning, in short, problems of analysis, can only be solved by study of the uses of signs, we gain at once a purchase upon the nature of our tasks. In this way we are able for the first time to delimit intelligibly the range of relevant disagreement and hence seriously to hope for a settlement of the endless disputes that for centuries have divided the various schools of ethics.

---

[1] I.e., whether there is in fact some objective quality or relation which it purports to designate; whether its purpose is, as a matter of fact, to designate, describe, or inform at all. The terms "referential," "descriptive," and "designative" are used interchangeably throughout.

At first sight problems of meaning may appear to have little relevance to the substantive problems of human conduct. The question how we are to use such words as "ought" and "good" may be of theoretical interest to the logician or semanticist, but the answer to it, as the saying goes, "butters no bread." On this point not merely the opponents of analytical philosophy but also a good many analysts have been agreed. And it must be confessed that there is some plausibility to the argument that analytic philosophy cannot have it both ways: it cannot claim the irrelevance of substantive or factual considerations to analytical questions without at the same time admitting the irrelevance of its own verbal and logical concerns to substantive or factual questions. On the face of it, moreover, it does appear implausible to suppose that problems of meaning are germane to the conduct of life.

The Human Relevance of Linguistic Analysis

Such views I take to be ill-considered, and I shall try subsequently to show that philosophical analysis is not the academic concern of a few methodolatrists and word-mongers who have turned their backs upon the pursuit of wisdom, but an indispensable means to clear thinking and relevant argument in the conduct of practical affairs. Ways of life are articulated through words. If we misunderstand the ways of the words through which they are expressed, so also will our grasp of the ways of life themselves be faltering and confused. If we misconceive the roles of moral judgment and the nature of moral reasoning, so also will we stumble in the use of moral discourse. And if we are unclear as to the meanings of the great terms that lay down the practical ends-in-view which are to guide our lives, there can be no clarity in the ends themselves and no settled direction to our conduct. In no domain of human activity is there more linguistic confusion and fallacious thinking than in the domain of morality, and in none therefore can a greater benefit be hoped for from the study of the language in which the activity is clothed.

In order to give body to these remarks, however, it will first be necessary to follow for a bit the progress of analytical moral theory in recent decades. In this way we will be better able to see more precisely how recent findings in this domain may be of practical human use.

III. The Development of Recent Analytic Ethics

Descriptivism and Its Defects

Most of the earlier proponents of analytical philosophy tended to take for granted that the primary function of language is the communication of knowledge or information. They not unnaturally assumed therefore that the task of the analyst is to fix more clearly the designata or referents of the terms with which he is concerned. Such an assumption can do relatively little harm so long as the words under analysis happen to be used descriptively, so long, that is to say, as the sentences in which they occur are employed to characterize and predict matters of fact. It is an egregious assumption which simply blocks the path of inquiry when the role of expressions is not essentially informative. As we shall see, it is fatal to the understanding of ethical terms whose primary uses are commendatory and prescriptive, and which only secondarily and in certain special circumstances serve to characterize the things on which they are predicated. And in humanities generally, it at once results in endless and futile disputation and fortifies where it does not itself produce profound confusions of value that have been endemic throughout the history of our intellectualistic and rationalistic culture. When what you want to know is the "cash value" of such words as "yellow" or "buffalo," the rule "Hunt the referent!" is sound enough advice, although even in such cases a flat-footed use of it can impede rather than advance inquiry. But where words are not used referentially, and the utterances in which they occur are not intended to express anything which "corresponds to the facts," the rule actually produces unclarity. By implication, moreover, it has the disastrous effect of creating the impression that when a referent cannot be found the word in question is senseless and its use the business only of the gullible and the foolish. Such an impression is inimical to the interests of literature and religion as well as morals; worse still, perhaps, it endangers fruitful theory formation in science itself.

The Search for a Science of Morals: Intuitionists and Naturalists

The referential dogma, as it may be called, dominated nearly all of the work which was done in analytical moral theory during the first decades of the present century. Even a cursory examination shows that it controls the direction of the analyses both of such influential "intuitionists" as G. E. Moore (8), W. D. Ross (11), and C. D. Broad (3) in England and of the more influential American "naturalists" such as John Dewey (5, 6, 7) and R. B. Perry (10). Under its influence, all of these important writers conceived the primary aim of moral philosophy to be that of reducing ethics to a science. They hoped that by means of a definition or clarification of the referent of the "primary" ethical terms, such as "good" or "value," we would be able to state precisely the conditions under which moral or value judgments, like other types of "scientific" statement, might be verified. They also believed that by defining such other ethical terms as "ought" and "right" in relation to the primary terms it could be shown that the concepts employed in various forms of valuation all have a common root. In this way they sought to reduce or eliminate altogether the necessity for appeals to special acts of "insight" or "intuition" either in determining the meaning of ethical terms or in certifying the judgments in which they occur.

Not all of these writers, certainly, found precisely what they were looking for. Some of them, like Ross (11), came to despair of reducing "right" to "good" or of defining "obligation" in relation to "value." Some, like Moore (8), were also forced to conclude that "good" is not an empirical concept at all. Still, all of them hoped that the hitherto insoluable disagreements in ethics would be capable of a rational resolution if only the methods employed in the validation of moral judgments could be shown to have the same essential logical structure as that which has enabled the natural sciences to move into the thoroughfare of cumulative knowledge. This meant, for intuitionists and naturalists alike, hunting and finding the common referents (objective qualities and relations) that are presumably designated by ethical terms. Thus, for example, Moore, in the opening pages of *Principia Ethica* (8), contrasts the hit or miss affair of ordinary "personal advice" and "exhortation" with the interest of "scientific ethics" which seeks to discover, amidst the apparently random assortment of things which men call "good" or "desirable," that common, objective quality through which we may truly know what things are really good. Subsequently he hoped to discover those objective principles of right action which would supply the objective bases of valid moral reasoning, thus removing from scientific moral deliberation that element of prejudice and vague surmise which characterizes the moral opinions of most men. Now superficially, no ethical theory would appear to lie at a further remove from Moore's than that of John Dewey. Moore was an intuitionist whose loyalty to understanding and truth is deeper than any loyalty he might have to any particular method such as that of empirical science. For Dewey the two commitments are identical, and he remained throughout his later life an intransigent naturalist and experimentalist. What science could not enable him to say, he did not care to discuss. Yet despite basic differences in their respective analyses of ethical terms, Dewey's fundamental view of the task of moral theory differs very little from that of Moore. The title of one of his most important and influential works in ethics, *The Logical Conditions of a Scientific Treatment of Morality* (5), itself suffices to indicate that, like Moore, he took it for granted that the task of philosophical analysis was to show in detail how moral discourse is reducible to the status of a science. Numerous other examples might be given, if there were space, to show the same underlying assumption that the language of morals is or ought to be an objective, scientific language, and that morality itself is or can be rendered intellectually respectable by and only by specifying the intersubjective verifying conditions of judgments of value and right action.

Beyond Descriptivism: Moore's Critique of Naturalists

Gradually, however, a very different view of the use of ethical terms and the role of moral judgments has emerged. By a curious irony, the rise of this conception was considerably due to conclusions to which Moore's own acute analyses forced him. Indeed, one of the dramatic turning points in the history of moral theory is due to the fact that despite his own professed intention to reduce ethics to a science, Moore's own arguments convinced him that any attempt to define moral notions empirically is bound to fail (8). As stated by Moore, these arguments were less conclusive than he supposed. Yet they served to convince a whole generation of moral philosophers of the essential wrong-headedness of the naturalistic program in ethics. In essence, the argument went something like this: Of any empirical characteristic which may be designated by such words as "desire," "pleasure," "satisfaction," or "adjustment" (the words, that is to say, which naturalists have most frequently and perhaps most plausibly identified with "good" or "value"), one may always seriously ask, in a way that does *not* simply beg the point at issue, "But, after all, is it really good?" This eternally "open question," Moore believed, shows that the property of goodness or value cannot be identified with any "natural" characteristic, and that the word "good," which designates this property, can never have the same meaning as any expression designating a natural characteristic. Moore held, in fact, that all attempts whatever to define ethical terms are at bottom guilty of the same "naturalistic fallacy" of confusing questions concerning the meaning of "good" with substantive problems as to the things which in fact are good. He concluded, in a way which is understandable given the premises of his analysis, that "good" must be assumed to designate a simple, unanalyzable, and (whatever that means) "non-natural" quality whose apprehension is entirely beyond the reach of our ordinary empirical faculties. It is for this reason that Moore is usually classified as an "intuitionist," even though that designation may appear to suggest a kind of philosopher very different from the common-sensical, "Let's-have-no-nonsense" sort of thinker Moore professed to be — and was. But Moore was no mystic or romantic advocate of private intuitions into what was never seen on land or sea. It was argument and logical analysis that convinced him that goodness is a nonnatural quality, not insight which he might claim as a prophet or a seer.

Beyond Descriptivism: Ogden and Richards' Emotive Theory of Ethics

Moore's conclusion, of course, was thoroughly unacceptable to empirically oriented philosophers, even when they were impressed by his arguments. And to many of them his analysis seemed to imply the failure of his whole program of "moral science." Negatively, his insistence upon the indefinability of "good" and upon the irreducible logical difference between "natural" and "moral" facts suggested that "moral facts" might not be facts at all. Evidently what was wanted was a more flexible conception of the roles of language that was not committed in advance to the dogma that all significant uses of signs depend upon the fact that signs are designative. Such a conception was first developed in recent times by C. K. Ogden and I. A. Richards (9), the pioneers of the now flourishing discipline of semantics. In effect, Moore was compelled to invent a realm of "non-natural" entities in order to have something for his indefinable ethical terms to refer to. Ogden and Richards, on the other hand, rejected altogether Moore's underlying descriptivistic assumptions and so were free to draw an entirely different conclusion from Moore's own arguments. Such words as "good," they contended, are nondesignative. They serve not as names, but as emotive expressions of attitude and as imperative prods to action. Accordingly the utterances in which such words occur are not statements which might be verified as true or false. Even to raise the question as to the method of their verification involves at the outset a complete misconception of their linguistic function.

Beyond Descriptivism: The Logical Positivists' Approach to Ethics

In a very different quarter this view received support from a new generation of philosophers who were uncompromisingly empirical in their approach to the method of human knowledge, but were more impressed than the older empiricists had been with the potentialities of the new logic as a tool for the analysis of propositions and for the construction of a more exact or "ideal" language for the formation and transformation of scientific statements. They accepted the directive that all "meaningful" statements must be capable in principle of reformulation in terms of an ideal language of science through which their verifying conditions would be more precisely expressed. At first, indeed, they contended that the method of their verification is literally constitutive of the meaning of all significant propositions, although in recent years they have been compelled to abandon so stringent a condition of descriptive meaning. It may appear from this that the "logical positivists" or "logical empiricists," as they alternatively called themselves, were still subtly under the spell of descriptivism; and so indeed they were. Hence it might be supposed that they would follow the lead of the naturalists in trying to reconstruct the language of morals or valuation in such a way that it might be shown to conform to the requirements of meaningful discourse as they conceived it. Here, however, education took a hand. Nearly all of the original group of logical positivists were educated in Austria and Germany where the idealist tradition was then still the dominant philosophy. Since Kant, the adherents of this tradition simply took it for granted that a radical bifurcation must be made between the logical and epistemological foundations of morality and those of empirical science. The positivists in effect took this bifurcation for granted, and so were not tempted to follow the lead of the American naturalists in trying to formulate a science of morality; because of their commitment to the ideal of the "unity of science," however, they could not accept the idealistic view of morals as a form of *Geisteswissenschaft*. If there is no empirical property of goodness or value, there is no such property at all; if moral discourse does not conform to the canons of the scientific method, then morality is simply not a form of knowledge (4). They concluded, therefore, that ethical concepts are "pseudo-concepts" and that ethical sentences express only "pseudo-propositions."

Their analysis of moral discourse must be viewed, however, from another aspect, for it is merely a corollary of an approach to the analysis of signs which regards ordinary language as an inadequate and logically imprecise vehicle of communication. The task of analysis, as the positivists conceived it, is not so much to determine the meanings of ordinary expressions, but to replace such expressions with a more exact or "ideal" language of science. Now as they are expressed in ordinary language, ethical sentences are grammatically indistinguishable from other sentences that express bona fide factual propositions. Because they are expressed in the indicative mood, as are ordinary factual statements, it appears at first look that the predicate terms of such sentences are used to assign a corresponding property to the things designated by their subject terms. Logically, however, ethical sentences are indistinguishable from imperatives such as "Shut the door" or "Keep off of the grass." It is indeed precisely this sort of misleading and confusing feature of ordinary language which, according to the positivists, renders it so poor a medium for clear thinking and exact statement; for this reason, so they contend, it must be replaced by a correct language which would contain no meaningless terms and would permit no pseudopropositions.[2]

Since, then, there is no way of specifying verifying conditions for ethical judgments, there is no way of showing any party to an ethical disagreement to be in error. From a logical point of view, therefore, ethical disagreement is entirely pointless. But in that case what can be the use of moral discourse? It may be nonsense; it is at any rate a very potent sort of nonsense in which empirically minded philosophers and scientists also indulge themselves unofficially when they are not at work. If value judgments are without meaning, this would appear to be the proof perfect that man is the irrational animal, since he ostracizes those whom he pronounces "immoral" and is frequently quite prepared to sacrifice even his life for the sake of a pseudoconcept. The solution to this paradox was provided by the distinction, first formulated by Ogden and Richards (9), between two radically different kinds of "meaning." One of them, which is characteristic of the language of science, is "cognitive meaning" or "descriptive meaning"; the other, which is exemplified in art, religion, and morality is "emotive meaning." The former is designative, and the statements involving it may be true or false; the latter is nondesignative and the sentences involving it are merely expressive and incitive.[3]

Problems of Emotive Theories of Ethics

Unfortunately, this distinction has created almost as many problems as it at first appeared to solve. In the first place, what in the world *is* emotive meaning, and how is it possible? Many critics, such as Max Black (2), have questioned whether there can be such a "mode" of meaning at all; others have doubted whether the emotive effects of language can be accounted for in the absence of any element of cognitive meaning; some have argued that it is merely a by-product of cognitive or descriptive meaning. But even if we waive these difficulties, there are other equally serious problems involved in the use of the notion of "emotive meaning" as a tool for analysis. If, for example, morality, poetry, and religion are all lumped together as "emotive," how is it possible to

---

[2] This view was perhaps most clearly developed by Ayer (1).

[3] This approach was carried to its greatest achievement in the work of Stevenson (12).

distinguish among them? And yet anyone who is actively concerned with these forms of discourse cannot believe that they have the same kind of effect or are employed in the service of the same kind of end. In a word, is not the word "emotive" simply another more pretentious, pseudotechnical way of saying "unscientific" which therefore tells us nothing positive whatever about the forms of words to which it is applied?

If there were space, other, even graver objections to the concept of emotive meaning might be raised. Nevertheless, it must be insisted that even this crude, vastly oversimplified classification of the meanings of signs was a great step forward. Just because it was so crude and so vague, it has been a goad to further research and to subtler, more complex theories of language. And once and for all, it helped to destroy the stultifying and pernicious illusion that language is or should be merely an instrument of scientific thought. Under it, the question-begging rule "Hunt the referent!" gradually gave way to a more flexible and more realistic approach to the variable functions of symbols.

The Plural Uses of Ordinary Language

More recently, under the impact of the teaching and later writings of Ludwig Wittgenstein (14), there has arisen within analytical philosophy a new movement[4] which, among other things, has helped to make good the defects and limitations inherent in the positivistic approach to the analysis of language. The proponents of this movement begin with the premise that ordinary language is multifunctional. They are concerned to determine, by careful study of particular forms of words, just what the various positive roles and uses of ordinary language may be. Their assumption is that when properly used, ordinary expressions are never meaningless and that the normal use of words in ordinary language is never without point. The task for analysis is not to replace ordinary language, but to determine its uses, and through this to illuminate the wider practices of which such uses are a part. This school therefore radically rejects the contention of Bertrand Russell that ordinary language is a crude repository of outworn metaphysics which cannot be trusted for the clear artic-

[4] This school is perhaps most clearly represented by the ethical writings of Toulmin (13).

ulation and communication of ideas. Like any language, ordinary language is a tool; and when correctly employed it is a sufficiently precise and flexible tool for the ordinary conduct of human affairs. In practice it is not misleading. It is only when philosophers ignore the contexts of its normal uses and applications that it proves misleading. Thus, for example, it is only when we ask what goodness or obligation is, in and by itself, that we lose our logical bearings and are tempted to adopt wrong-headed models for the analysis of ethical terms. Viewed in context, moral discourse is not a crude, prescientific form of speech which must be reconstituted so as to render it more amenable to the requirements of a "moral science." Such a science is not even a possibility, and any such reconstruction, were it to prevail, would in effect mean the supercession of the institution of morality altogether. But neither is the language of morals a merely expressive language for the venting and inciting of private feeling or emotion. Were it to become such, in consequence of insensitive philosophical tampering, the general social consequences would be incalculable. All models for the analysis and interpretation of moral discourse provide at best only partially relevant analogies which are inevitably misleading and invariably subvert the aims of understanding when taken more seriously as bases for "logical reconstruction."

The Language of Conduct: Organization of Social Behavior

The philosophers who hold the view in question accept the thesis that the language of conduct is a practical, dynamic mode of speech whose essential role is the organization and control of behavior rather than the description or prediction of matters of fact. So far they agree with the emotivists. Otherwise, however, the two approaches have little in common; for the new approach takes seriously, as the emotive theory does not, the fundamental distinction between moral judgments, which profess a certain objectivity and impersonality, and first-personal expressions of taste or interest, which neither have nor claim to have any "authority" over the judgments or conduct of others. It takes seriously, also, the normal assumption that moral reasoning is not just a way of "irrigating" someone's attitudes (although it may be this also), but an impersonal, rule-governed mode of justification to which the concept of validity may be relevantly applied. And in general the new approach regards moral discourse from an institutional viewpoint as a complex, if informal, machinery of regularized social adjustment and adaptation. Its adherents accept the imputation that there is a point in speaking of arguments as irrational and of decisions as arbitrary; and it takes seriously the prevailing assumption that in speaking of a supporting reason to a moral conclusion as a "good" or "bad" reason, we are expressing something more than our own first-personal approval or disapproval of it. The task of the moral philosopher is not to try to show what practical reasoning would be or ought to be if it were to conform to certain rules of inference which the formal logician or methodologist may prefer to regard as "valid." Rather is it to elucidate the patterns of deliberation and justification which, as they stand, determine what we mean in speaking of a process of moral argumentation as "invalid" or "irrational."

The Language of Conduct: Rule-Governed and Impersonal

The new approach, in brief, takes seriously common-sense appearances in the light of which the characterizations of moral discourse and of ethical terms presented both by the descriptivists and by the emotivists are bound to seem paradoxical. Morality could not become a science without a radical reconstitution of the very uses of such terms as "good" and "ought"; but such a reconstitution would no longer enable us to say (or do) "the ethical thing." It would be better, because less misleading, if the descriptivists really wish to transform the language of morals into a descriptive, scientific form of speech, simply to say with Nietzsche that we should go beyond "good" and "evil" altogether. Such a view is certainly worth considering, but it should not be allowed to masquerade paradoxically as a theory of morals. On the other hand, the terms of moral discourse are not such "open-textured" expressions of emotion as the emotivists contend. Governing the use of ethical terms, in the various distinctive contexts in which they occur, are rules of application that prescribe the manner in which ordinary substantive prescriptions and commendations are to be made. Such rules, however vague or flexible, still set limits to the sorts of judgment we are prepared to acknowledge as "moral." Each time we make or refuse such an acknowledgment we are not simply "venting" our own passing sentiments or wishes; rather are we in such a case invoking an impersonal linguistic ritual which serves to keep practical deliberation and disagreement within certain socially acceptable bounds.

The point is, then, not that we do not express our own attitudes in using the language of morals; on the contrary, if as we have suggested, the language of morals is an effective social device for the regulation of human relations, it would be exceedingly odd if moral judgments did not reflect certain basic social attitudes of the speaker. But moral judgments reflect our attitudes, as social animals, precisely because the latter have themselves been largely formed by habituation to the rules which govern the application of ethical terms. To parody Marx, it is not so much the individual conscience that determines the application of ethical terms, as it is the standard application of the terms which determines the conscience of the individual moral judge or agent. In short, it is through the constant employment of the language of morals that the individual is perforce obliged continually to re-enact certain impersonal social roles which willy-nilly render him, or at any rate his judgment, a "voice" or "conscience" of the social group. And when, for whatever reason, the individual misuses or misapplies the terms of moral discourse, he is automatically subject to the same forms of verbal rebuke which, in other domains, are directed against those who will not "talk sense" or "listen to reason."

These suggestions cannot be further explored here. It is hoped that enough has perhaps been said to indicate the increasing sensitivity and maturity of recent philosophical analyses of morals. What I have tried to show, among other things, is that the errors to which philosophical analysis are subject tend to be, like those that occur within science itself, self-correcting, and that out of the successive misconceptions and exaggerations which we have had occasion to observe there has gradually emerged a more and more adequate grasp of an exceedingly complex symbolic process. The end, certainly, is not yet; but enough is already understood concerning the language of conduct to be of use in the education of ordinary men. What remains to be shown is the relevance of these findings to general human enlightenment and to the conduct of life.

IV. The Practical Relevance of Analytic Ethics

As I believe, there are two important respects in which this analytical study of morals may be relevant to the practical concerns of men. One of these pertains to the findings themselves, the other to the method of analysis employed in reaching these findings.

The Language of Conduct and the Life of the Community

Now if, as we have maintained, the language of morals is a dynamic language which at the same time is subject to relatively definite rules of application in various contexts, there follows at once a corollary which is pertinent to the present purpose. That is to say, the patterns of moral discourse, including the prevailing forms of commendation, prescription, and justification, provide a kind of mirror of the prevailing patterns of interpersonal relation and hence of the underlying way of life of the community. To the extent, also, that the individual himself is not deviant, the analysis of moral discourse will also provide a sort of map of his character as a social being. Any ambiguities, vaguenesses, or inconsistencies in the one will at the same time reflect confusions, indecisions, and tensions in the other. Where, for example, incompatible analyses arise from an inability to accept common instances and counterinstances in trying to determine the range of application of ethical terms, this will at once suggest not a failure of analysis on the part of someone or other, but rather a lack of homogeneity in the moral attitudes of the social group. And where, conversely, analysis is not stalled because of such disagreements, there is indicated the presence of a common system of moral habits. Again, a great deal of interest in defining and redefining ethical terms will tend to reflect a lack of clarity or consistency in interpersonal relations or else an inadequacy of communal moral standards and practices to the satisfaction of underlying human wants or drives.

All this being so, it would appear evident that anyone who seeks to know himself as a moral being will perforce be obliged to reflect with some care upon the nature of moral discourse. And if, as most of us profess to believe, a grasp of the communal way of life is essential to intelligent participation in the guidance and control of human affairs, then the study of the language of conduct must be a matter of general human concern.

Correcting Popular Misconceptions

In the second place, it is only through analysis of moral discourse that one gradually becomes aware of its limits. Such understanding is all the more important precisely because, unlike mathematical logic or the theory of induction, moral theory, in one crude form or another, is already part of the public domain. As such it is constantly being used illicitly, in one way or another, to bolster or lend prestige to various substantive prohibitions or demands. As any teacher of ethics soon discovers, a great part of the difficulty of instruction arises from the fact that his pupils are usually already possessed of theories — or prejudices — of their own which they have acquired in the home or school or church. I mean by this not merely the obvious fact that most persons, by the time they have entered college, have well-established moral habits and attitudes but rather that they have fairly well-defined views concerning the meanings of ethical terms and the nature of moral judgment. To one student, so-called Protagorean relativism seems virtually self-evident; to another, brought up perhaps in a parochial school, the view that moral "truths" are laws of nature or divine commandments needs little argument; to still another, morality itself is a form of prejudice to be replaced by hygiene and social engineering. In short, there abound in the popular consciousness a great many preanalytic theories of morals, nearly all of which, unfortunately, involve profound misconceptions both as to the character of moral judgment and as to the possibilities of moral justification. And these, unhappily, deeply interpenetrate the whole moral consciousness of those afflicted with them. In what follows, I wish briefly to indicate how the findings of recent analysis may serve to correct some of these misconceptions, and so to clarify the deliberative practices of the layman.

If, for example, one clearly grasps the essentially practical or regulative role of value judgments generally and of the forms of reasoning intended to support them, one comes finally to understand, as one can in no other way, why it is that increased knowledge of matters of fact does not and cannot compel common agreement at the ideological or moral level. In this way one may be fortified against a peculiarly prevalent and virulent sort of disillusionment either with morals or with science or with both which afflicts those who have been led to suppose that there is a necessary connection between knowledge and virtue. If one also understands the fact that our moral judgments and hence our moral practice are fashioned in the light of socially conditioned patterns of commendation and prescription, one is far less likely to misconstrue or to object in the wrong way to the moral faults or failures of "insight" of those who systematically disagree with us. And one will see thereby that the remedy for such faults and failures is not to be looked for in statements of principle or in appeals to "right reason" which beg the very point at issue. "Self-evidence" is nearly always a sign not of god-given truth, but of thorough habituation. By learning this lesson properly through the study of the logic of moral justification and persuasion, one is thereby enabled to comprehend a matter of the greatest importance for intelligent cultural relations, namely, that the moral principles of one's own people, however beneficent, are not due to profounder insight into the metaphysical structure of the cosmos, but rather, for the most part, to a more fortunate cultural tradition. Conversely one may see that what we conceive to be moral obtuseness or bigotry is due, as a rule, not so much to stupidity or ignorance as to a less benignant human environment. In this way, also, one may gain a sense of the precariousness of any moral order and of the preciousness of those social and cultural circumstances in which alone a "reasonable" ethical system can grow and flourish.

With all this comes a gradual awareness of why it is that the basic problems of community and world order can never be resolved by direct religious or political propaganda, but only by a process of slow re-education. Such understanding is doubtless sobering, but it may protect the individual and the society against the self-destroying disillusionment which attends the inevitable failures of short-term moral crusades. At the same time it might help to save us from the now fashionable varieties of irrationalism which ascribe men's spiritual limitations to original sin and which make a fetish of human weakness or depravity without shedding any light whatever upon its causes or on the means of its removal.

The Ultimacy of Conscience

Possibly the greatest practical insight which the study of moral philosophy can impart is understanding of the fact, which old Kant long ago expressed in another form, that there is no way of "deriving" moral principles from anything beyond the consciences of men, and hence that there is no way whatever of guaranteeing the validity of any moral code by trying to "ground" it in science, or the nature of the universe — or in the will of God. Or, better because less misleading, one may see that any such "grounding" is, in practice, merely another symbolic device for articulating and regulating human attitudes which can be used effectively only among those who have already been practically conditioned to respond to it. The masks of conscience are many; the important thing is to understand them for what they are. Maturity comes when we finally realize that however we may disguise the fact by the symbols by means of which we conduct our communal affairs, everything in this domain is finally "up to us." Then we see that ours is the only responsibility, and that it is our own constitutional loyalty to principles of liberty, justice, and welfare that can alone provide a relevant practical ground to the rights and duties which, as we believe, should be the prerogatives of every man.

This is altogether a matter of understanding what one can and cannot do with the language of conduct. The great trouble with dogmatic theories of moral obligation which insist upon referring it to "natural law" or "divine commandment" is precisely that they prevent those who accept them from seeing why they find such doctrines attractive or "true," and, conversely, why others do not. By helping to remove such forms of parochial self-deception and hence of eventual disillusionment, ethical theory may make a very considerable contribution to the advancement of common practical understanding.

In the preceding remarks I have tried to suggest a few of the ways in which philosophical study of moral discourse may have a beneficial effect upon our grasp of one important aspect of human relations. Before concluding I wish to show also that the very methods employed by the analyst in trying to penetrate the thicket of human conduct are also useful and even necessary within the more concrete domain of substantive ethics itself. It should be remarked in passing, however, that I am not here attempting to blur the essential distinction between using the language of morals and talking about it. I am concerned, rather, with the applications of a method.

Clarifying Our Fundamental Goals in Life

Now it has been frequently maintained, and even today most philosophers would appear to hold, that the only practical relevance of reason in the conduct of life lies in its power to discover possible causes or means to ends upon which we have already decided. Since Aristotle many philosophers have argued that rational deliberation is and can be concerned only with the ways of achieving ends but not with the formation of the ends themselves. This, I take it, is the primary point of Hume's paradoxical remark that reason is and ought to be the slave of the passions. Such a view clearly implies that at bottom the formation of a decision is a nonrational or suprarational affair. (Those who have held it, incidentally, have not always seen that if this is so, it applies just as much at the level of means or proximate goals as at the level of so-called ends or ultimate goals.) Now undoubtedly there is an important grain of truth in such a view, although it is misleadingly expressed. This grain of truth is simply the logical point that a moral judgment, whether commendation, prescription, or imperative, cannot be logically derived from a theoretical or factual truth alone. Because it has been misleadingly formulated, however, the theory has given rise to the notion that all we have to do or can do in reaching a decision is to let nature take its course, to wait, that is to say, until the strongest of our conflicting interests happens to manifest itself. Despite its patent irrationalistic implications, such a view curiously involves an extremely intellectualistic conception of purposive behavior which is contradicted both by common sense and by contemporary psychological theory. For it evidently assumes that although we may not know in advance how to get it, we all do know at the outset what our ultimate goals are, and hence that we must accept these as "given" in any process of deliberation.

How inconsistently such a position is usually held is evident from even a cursory examination of Aristotle's own *Nichomachean Ethics;* for in that work Aristotle, instead of directing his main effort to determining the means to happiness, which he considers the universal end of human action, expends his energy in trying to ascertain what the true nature of happiness is. From a practical point of view — and Aristotle's aim in the *Ethics* was thoroughly practical — such an analysis would be entirely pointless were it the case that the goal or end to which all men aspire is unambiguous, well-formed, and fixed. The fact of the matter is that the work of most great ethical thinkers has been directed not to questions of means but rather to the still more difficult task of clarifying the primary aims of the good life. And their own disagreements, uncertainties, and confusions are themselves sufficient evidence that whatever else may be true of them, our fundamental ways of life are neither clearly understood nor universally aspired to. Professor Lewis puts the point succinctly when he says that "At least half of the world's avoidable troubles are created by those who do not know what they want and pursue what would not satisfy them if they had it." A similar thesis is implicit in the findings of contemporary psychoanalytic and psychiatric theory. If Freud and his successors are even half-right, most human action is governed by hidden motives that are imbedded in substitute symbols whose practical import we come to understand only with the greatest difficulty. Beyond this, however, the lives of even "normal" human beings are largely controlled by words and symbols whose meanings are ambiguous and ill defined. It is for this reason that the task of clarifying such golden words as "liberty," "justice," "democracy," "person," and "love" is so essential to the well-being of any people whose way of life is expressed in terms of them. For if they are unclear or confused or inconsistent, then the way of life is so also.

It is no part of my intention, as my allusion to psychoanalysis might seem to indicate, that philosophical analysis can provide an adequate therapy for mankind's ethical neuroses. What I do contend is that the clarification of ideals and the clarification of the terms by means of which they are articulated is a single process, and that in a humble way, every attempt to determine what sort of life one really wants to live involves essentially the same painful process of analyzing and clarifying the meanings and uses of words to which the analytical philosopher devotes himself professionally. The difference between them is not so much a difference in method as a difference in the thoroughness and sensitivity with which it is applied.

The point I am trying to make here cannot be adequately developed in the available space. It must suffice to close with a few random observations that may serve to illustrate my theme. Consider, for example, how frequently the hesitancy and confusion of our practice is correlated with a lack of understanding of the meaning of ideals to which we think we have committed ourselves. Consider how often practical disagreements not only between individuals but also between whole societies are due to failures of common understanding of ambiguities in the terms by means of which conflicting aims are expressed, and how baffled we frequently are as to the causes of such disagreements. Consider also how often practical misunderstanding and conflict arise from the fact that the same terms are unwittingly used by both parties to express different or opposing aims, or, perhaps more tragically, from the fact that different terms are unknowingly used to express what are or would be common aspirations if only the terms themselves were better understood. Communists and liberals alike constantly talk about something they call "democracy." Both appear to regard it as the consummation devoutly to be wished, differing apparently only with respect to the means to be employed. Yet how profoundly unlikely such a characterization is. Or, again and on another plane, such different moralists as Epicurus, Marcus Aurelius, Jesus, Kant, Hobbes, and J. S. Mill expressed their respective conceptions of the good life in terms which at least superficially express different and in some cases opposing moral attitudes. How can the man of pleasure, the stoic, the man of God and love, the incarnate rationalist, the incarnate egoist, and the utilitarian all be supposed to aspire to the same ultimate human condition? I do not say they can; but I do contend that the only way such a question could be answered is through the same sort of analysis which, on another level and in another context, is employed in trying to determine the meanings of "ought" or "good" and the logic of moral justification.

My contention is, then, that both the methods and the results of contemporary analytical ethics are indispensable adjuncts of enlightened moral practice, and that their study is therefore a useful or even a necessary part of any truly humane or liberal education. What this also means, if I am right, is that the analytical philosopher has not at all abandoned philosophy's ancient search for wisdom, but on the contrary is contributing his own important share to the world's all too skimpy fund of practical understanding. He makes his contribution partly by providing us with sharper tools and a clearer notion of the search itself, and partly in a more direct way by freeing us from ancient myths and fetishes which have created endless confusion and needless disagreement about matters that are not necessary parts of the tragedy of human existence. If in no other way, he would have done his share toward the advancement of human enlightenment and freedom by showing us how and on what terms morality can be a part of action. And his only but mortal enemy is the obscurantist and the mystagogue.

References

1. Ayer, A. J. *Language, Truth and Logic.* London: V. Gollancz Ltd., 1936.
2. Black, Max. *Language and Philosophy.* Ithaca, N.Y.: Cornell University Press, 1949. Chapter 9.
3. Broad, C. D. *Five Types of Ethical Theory.* New York: Harcourt, Brace, 1930.
4. Carnap, Rudolf. *Philosophy and Logical Syntax.* London: Kegan Paul, Trench, Trubner, 1935.
5. Dewey, John. *The Logical Conditions of a Scientific Treatment of Morality.* Chicago: University of Chicago Press, 1903.
6. Dewey, John. *Theory of Valuation.* Chicago: University of Chicago Press, 1939.
7. Dewey, John, and Tufts, J. H. *Ethics.* (Rev. ed.) New York: Henry Holt, 1932.
8. Moore, G. E. *Principia Ethica.* Cambridge: Cambridge University Press, 1929.
9. Ogden, C. K., and Richards, I. A. *The Meaning of Meaning.* New York: Harcourt, Brace, 1938.
10. Perry, R. B. *The General Theory of Value.* New York: Longmans Green, 1926.
11. Ross, W. D. *The Right and the Good.* Oxford: Clarendon Press, 1930.

12. Stevenson, Charles. *Ethics and Language.* New Haven, Conn.: Yale University Press, 1944.
13. Toulmin, S. E. *An Examination of the Place of Reason in Ethics.* Cambridge: Cambridge University Press, 1950.
14. Wittgenstein, Ludwig. *Philosophical Investigations.* Oxford: Basil Blackwell, 1953.

THE MORAL SENSE
AND CONTRIBUTORY VALUES

C. I. LEWIS

. . . To act, to live, in human terms, is necessarily to be subject to imperatives, to recognize norms. That is, to be subject to an imperative means simply the finding of a constraint of action in some concern for that which is not immediate, is not a present enjoyment or a present suffering. To repudiate normative significances and imperatives in general would be to dissolve away all seriousness of action and intent, leaving only an undirected floating down the stream of time, and as a consequence to dissolve all significance of thought and discourse into universal blah. Those who would be serious and circumspect and cogent in what they think, and yet tell us that there are no valid norms or binding imperatives, are hopelessly confused and inconsistent with their own attitude of assertion.

There is no need to look under the table for some source of such validities in general, and then exclaim because we do not find one. The final and universal imperative, "Be consistent, in valuation and in thought and action" ("Be concerned about yourself in future and on the whole") is one which is categorical. It requires no reason, being itself the expression of that which is the root of all reason, that in the absence of which there could be no reason of any sort or for anything.

In ethics, it is the Cyrenaic who, in words, repudiates this categorical imperative. He repudiates concern for any future: tomorrow is another day. Of course, he contradicts himself — not formally but pragmatically. There would be no logical inconsistency in his hortation, "Have no concern for the future," if it should be found engraved by lightning on a rock. But for us to take seriously one who puts it forward, or for anyone to take himself seriously in accepting it, would imply exactly such concern

Reprinted, by permission, from *An Analysis of Knowledge and Valuation* (La Salle, Ill.: Open Court, 1946), pp. 481-488, 503-510.

as this injunction advises that we repudiate. The content of the injunction is incompatible with giving heed to this — or any other — injunction. If, *per impossibile,* there could be an otherwise human being who was born a perfect Cyrenaic in native disposition, we could not persuade him to mend his ways by any conceivable argument. One who lived *in accord with* this Cyrenaic principle, but *not from* principle, would commit no inconsistency; and no consideration we could put forward would bother him. By native bent he would be impervious to all bother. But he would not preach Cyrenaicism — or anything else. He would represent a continuing mode of being, not an attitude or point of view. That is, the validity of this categorical imperative to recognize genuine imperatives of thought and action does not rest upon logical argument finally. Presuming that the one to whom the argument is addressed will respond to considerations of consistency and inconsistency presumes the validity of precisely what is argued for. The basis of this imperative is a datum of human nature. If a creature should be impervious to any concern for the future, and hence for consistency in his thinking and acting, then there could be no *in*consistency in any of his momentary attitudes; and we should not address arguments or hortations to him any more than to a fish or a phonograph record.

We do not in this book attempt discussion of those problems of mine and thine which are the peculiar questions of ethics. But in passing, we may observe that the fundamental dictum of justice, "No rule of action is right except one which is right in all instances, and therefore right for everyone," is likewise not a principle acceptance of which either requires to be or could be inculcated by argument where natively the recognition of it should be absent. Logically considered, it is a tautology: it merely expresses a formal character of the correct or justified, implicit recognition of which is contained in acknowledgment of the distinction between right and wrong. Given this moral sense, recognition of the principle is mere self-clarification; and where the moral sense should be lacking, argument for this or any other principle of action would be pointless. This moral sense may be presumed in humans; and creatures who lack it can only be lured by some kind of bait or driven by some kind of goad.

We must not pause upon such further and peculiarly ethical

problems raised by consideration of this nature of human life, and of its goods and bads, as predicated upon action and imbued with concern. There are certain implications only which are directly pertinent to our problem of values and the validity of evaluations. In particular, there are three such which are simple and obvious. First, if in one sense the determination of values must be eventually in terms of the value-qualities of direct experience, still in another sense no immediately experienced good or bad is final, but rather is further to be evaluated by its relation to the temporal whole of a good life. Second, a life good on the whole, which is our continuing and rational concern, is something whose goodness or badness is at no moment immediately disclosed, but can be contemplated only by some imaginative or synthetic envisagement of its on-the-whole quality. There is no good or bad of it which does not come by way of some goodness or badness found in living; but the manner of this synthesis — the manner in which a life is constituted good or bad by the goodness or badness of its constituent parts — is a question which does not answer itself. And the correct answer to it will disclose the final criterion of all values in experience. And third, since a life imbued with concern must be preponderantly active, the more characteristic and pervasive goods of it will hardly be those of passive enjoyment or those which are merely contemplative and, like the aesthetic, require some suspension of the active attitude. Both the more typical ingredient values which contribute to a good life, and the manner of their synthesis in constituting its overarching goodness, must be expected to reflect the characteristics findable in goods of action.

That the good life represents the *summum bonum* is, as we have said, not to be argued. It is the universal and rational human end, the end we aim at so far as we approve of our aims and of ourselves in aiming and do not recognize some perversity or foolishness or weakness of will in our motivations and our doings. That fact is a datum of the human attitude to life. It is not a datum of the sort commonly called psychological: we recognize in ourselves the perennial liability to the weaknesses mentioned, by which we are solicited to depart from this ideal of ourselves which still we cannot set aside. It is that norm which can be repudiated only by repudiating all norms and the distinction of valid from invalid in general, by reducing all that we can purpose or accept with the sense of rightness or correctness or validity to the status of the nonsignificant — to mere "psychological data."

Humans are subject to concern and to imperatives because future possibilities present themselves to us but do not present themselves with the poignancy of what is immediate and now. The lower animals — at least as we commonly think of them — are subject to no imperatives because in part nature looks out for their future by equipping them with instinctive and irresistible impulses adapting their behavior to what is to come; and for the rest, they have no inkling of this future and are at the mercy of it. A godlike creature also would be subject to no imperatives because, being "wholly rational," he would be as readily moved by consideration of the future and absent as by the present, and hence suffer no tendency to wayward sacrifice of a possible good life to immediate desire. Man, being higher than the animals but a little lower than the angels, is permanently liable to a kind of schizophrenia, and can neither be wholeheartedly impulsive nor wholeheartedly rational. The sense of the future moves him, but not sufficiently to make him automatically responsive. He has to "move himself" in order to come into accord with the dictates of the reasonable. Hence the sense of the imperative.[1]

By this imperative of rationality, the future, so it be certain, should weigh with us as much as the present, and possible good-

[1] However these facts of human nature should be expressed, they are more evident and certain than any scientific psychological account of human motivations is likely to be. The moralists have always been hard put to it to provide for a possible motivation by reason without making the "free moral agent" superfluous by portraying this motivation as impulsive, like that of desire and instinctive drive. And the psychologists may also have trouble over the point — if they do not ignore it — because, like the rest of us, they are prone to interpret causation in general in terms of an animistic metaphor, according to which natural causes *compel* their effects, and psychological laws compel psychological events to comply with them, as the police power of the state compels our conformity to enacted legislation. Plainly, nothing but a creature with a will can be compelled, since compulsion is doing what is *against* one's will. And *ipso facto* no cause or law compels us when we do what we choose or decide. Hence the denial of "self-determination" on account of universal motivation by psychological causes would be the absurdity of first setting up this animistic metaphor and then turning it against that kind of fact which alone gives it any content.

Assimilation of motivations *by reason* to self-determination merely reports a patent fact of experience, however that fact should be scientifically formulated.

ness in the whole of life must continually outweigh consideration for goodness in any part of it. But by itself this would never dictate any critique of present possibilities of satisfaction by reference to the future if the experience of each moment were insulated from that of every other and had no cause-effect relations with what lies beyond its own immediacy. If no present experience could be prejudicial to any future one or have any influence upon the whole of life, then there could be no criticism of a present enjoyment implied in our concern for the future it could not affect. Our reasonable desire always to maximize the present satisfaction and our continuing concern to achieve the same in future and in general would never be at odds with one another. The familiar fact that concern for the future requires a critical eye to present satisfactions turns upon the obvious consideration that an experience may be unqualifiedly good within its own boundaries but a regrettable constituent in life on account of causal relationships of it affecting the future; and what is, by itself and as experienced, disvaluable, may still be a desirable ingredient of life by reason of its influence upon further experience and hence by the contribution it may make to a life good on the whole. Any experience may have such instrumental value or disvalue, which is not an intrinsic quality realized within it but is found in the further experience to which it leads. And since experiences in general have both such intrinsic value and such instrumental value, the *final* assessment of the value of any experience must include reference to both.

There is nothing in this which is contradictory to the fact that intrinsic values — the value of that which is valuable for its own sake — are values found directly in experience, and that such intrinsic value of any given content of experience is a datum of the experience itself. The simple and obvious fact which calls for recognition is only this: that while the experiences of which life is made up have each its absolute and not-to-be-cancelled goodness or badness when and as realized, the value of *having* that experience has reference *also* to the instrumental effect of it upon the future. Value as immediately found is subject to no critique. But the *aim to realize it,* and the value of *having* that particular experience, are still subject to rational criticism by reference to the value which it may contribute instrumentally to any whole of experience in which it is included. Such instrumental value of having an experience is something over and above what it contributes merely by being an included moment of experienced good or ill.

Wholes of experience take precedence to distinguishable and momentary experiences included in them — that, again, merely expresses the rational imperative itself — and the value of experience as momentarily found is subordinate to the value which having that experience may contribute to the whole. The final and ruling assessment of value in an experience must answer to the continuing rational purpose directed to the comprehensive and consummatory end of a life found good on the whole.

3. This value characterizing a whole life is also intrinsic: there can be no goodness or badness of it except a value or disvalue to be realized in the living of it. But if it should appear that this value is the mere summation of the values immediately found in the ingredient experiences which make it up, then one reason why that conclusion does not in fact follow is just this reason that the relations of good or bad experiences in constituting a good or bad life are not that of a series of temporally juxtaposed and externally related moments but are that of ingredients which affect and qualify one another, the relation of components in a temporal *Gestalt*.

One experience may have such instrumental or contributory relation to another in any one of three senses. First, the two experiences may be causally related, not in themselves and directly, but indirectly only, through the objective states of affairs they signify. For example, the laborer may drudge for his weekly wages for the sake of the satisfactions to be got by spending them. But, let us say, he works as a matter of habit and because he knows he must: the experience of working is not alleviated by any quality of explicit anticipation, and the later spending is no more and no less a satisfaction to him than if he had received the money as a gift or found it in the street. Here the two experiences, of working and of spending, are causally related through the money earned, but the value-quality of neither is in any notable degree or manner affected by the other. In such a case we may say that the earlier experience is instrumental to the later one, but we shall not say that it is contributory to it.

The case might be different, however: the small boy may work long and hard for the price of a circus ticket, but his labor will be infused throughout with the value-quality of vivid anticipation; and his later satisfaction at the circus may also be enhanced by honest pride in having earned his own enjoyment. Here the one experience qualifies the other not only causally and instrumentally but also directly and in the manner of ingredients in a temporal *Gestalt.* Or to choose another example, the shy man may, by submitting himself to experiences which at first are disconcerting, acquire the more satisfactory social adjustment he desires. And the similar relationship characterizes learning in general as affecting later experience involving what is learned. Learning of any sort is an *experience* — or if there are senses of the word for which that would be false, then we should wish to exclude them. And the point is here that it is these experiences themselves, and not merely the objective causes or physical effects of them, which are essential to the value-character of what is later realized.

In these last two examples, we may still distinguish two slightly different relations of experiences involved, or speak of their relationship in two different ways. We may consider only the relation of an earlier to a later experience, whose value-quality is affected directly and not merely indirectly and causally; or we may speak of the relation of these ingredients to a whole passage of experience which includes both, and in which this qualification of the value-quality of one by the other may be mutual. We shall use the word "contributory" for either of these two relationships; that is, we shall say that an earlier experience such as learning contributes to a later experience which is thereby rendered more satisfactory, and we shall also say that an ingredient experience contributes to a temporal whole of experience the value-quality of which it affects throughout by being thus included. This slightly ambiguous usage of "contribute" and "contributory value" is the better justified by the fact that the one of these two relationships hardly occurs without the other.

However, it is the second of these — the relation of an experience to a whole in which it is included, and in which the distinguishable constituent experiences intimately and mutually qualify one another, with respect to their value-quality — which we would here stress. Working and achieving, for example, is a different total experience than achieving without working, and it is not a foregone conclusion that the effortless attainment of desire will be on the whole more satisfying. And either of these two may be a total experience which is differently valuable than that of getting something wished for and then having to pay the piper. It is in such wise that the value of an experiential whole may be affected not only by the values immediately found in its separate and included moments but by the relation of these moments of experience to one another. It may be that a life which begins badly but ends well is better than one which begins well but ends badly, even though the ingredient experiences which make it up should be as nearly comparable as could well be imagined and should differ only by what is involved in the different temporal order of them. It is by this kind of fact that the value realized in any whole of experience will reflect the character of it as a temporal *Gestalt*. . . .

But this — it may be thought — imposes peculiar difficulties upon all attempts at just appraisal of values, difficulties inherent in the attempt to determine such contributory value, and difficulties incident to the determination of goodness or badness in any projected or contemplated life taken as a whole. This may well be a fact. Finally just appraisals may be the most difficult thing in the world — and the most important. But if so, we should do ill to espouse a theory in which such genuine difficulties appear to be obviated by a specious simplicity of conception.

As a fact, however, such difficulties recognized in final value-judgment are only in small part affected by the difference of the conception here put forward from any other which would be plausible. Because any theory which recognizes as valid the ideal of a life which will be the best possible in the living of it must also recognize that ideal as the touchstone of all final evaluations. For a view such as Bentham's, for example, which sets the criteria of final evaluation — including reference to "purity" and "fecundity" as well as certainty or uncertainty — in the maximum balance of particular experienced goods over particular ills, it would be similarly essential to correctness in any final appraisal of particulars that the whole effect of them in any contemplated life must somehow be brought before us.

The major portion of the problem of such judgment of things

and experiences as finally contributive of good or ill to life is, of course, the general problem of accurate and adequate empirical knowledge. What will be the full consequences of this thing in question? What possibilities of living are open to us in the light of what is already determined or to be presumed as fact? How will this thing fit in with such antecedent facts so as to increase or to subtract from the possibilities of satisfactory living? There is no manner of approach which will provide a rule of thumb for meeting such questions or obviate the difficulties of them. And it is a commonplace that they constitute a principal problem for any-one who attempts to plan a good life for himself or has the temerity to advise another.

The one point on which the view here advanced might be thought to impose a difficulty which is peculiar and might not be encountered in some other is that this conception supposes that assessment of value in any contemplated life is antecedent to and not derivative from the assessment of the particular goods and ills contributory to it. It denies that the goodness or badness of life is constituted by an aggregate of particular satisfactions and dissatisfactions, irrespective of sequence and relations of these in this organic whole, and maintains that no calculus or other such rule will obviate the requirement that the value attaching to such a whole must be determined by some attempted synthetic envis-agement of it. But the precise difference here would be only that a Benthamite, while admitting the necessity of reference to the comprehensive whole of experience in order to determine with finality the value of any constituent in it, would still maintain that this final assessment can be carried out in piecemeal fashion by arithmetical procedures, as one can discover with accuracy and adequacy the whole length of a thing too big to "take in at one time" through recorded tally marks representing meter-lengths passed over. Such operations we should believe to have no appli-cation to the value-character of wholes of experience, on account of the organic character of the relation of constituents within any experiential whole in which they are included.

9. The value of any experiential whole is simply the value which would be found in it as a whole of experience. But assessment of it will obviously lack that certainty which attaches to immediate findings of value or disvalue in momentary experience. The sense

in which value is "found" in a whole life in the living of it obviously is not the same as that in which a contemplated landscape is found pleasing or barking one's shins is found painful. Our apprehension of what runs beyond the specious present requires some synthesis, and by reason of this requirement becomes a matter involving judgment and liable to error.

There are three ways in which such synthetic apprehensions of experiential wholes are subject to mistake. First, there may be mistaken judgment of their actual content so far as this falls outside the immediately presented. We cannot forecast with accuracy just what episodes will be included in the further unfolding of our project or the vocation to which we commit ourselves. And not only false anticipations of the part which is future, but also erroneous recollections of the past, are in some measure possible. This, of course, is merely that sort of error to which all empirical knowledge is liable, and with respect to it there is no problem which is peculiar to synthetic value-assessments. Second, one may be substantially correct in one's anticipations or recollections of experience in other respects and yet be mistaken about the value-quality of what is anticipated or remembered. The child may be disappointed in his ecstatic expectation of tomorrow, not because of any notable error as to the events which will take place but because those events, when he participates in them, may fail to measure up to his anticipations of satisfaction. This again is not a type of error affecting value-judgments only. One may make similar mistakes with regard to other qualities ingredient in an experience which is otherwise correctly anticipated — with respect to the taste of the meal one has ordered, for example, or the expected feeling of motion in one's first ride in an airplane.

But third, there is a kind of possible error to which assessment of the value in an experiential whole is especially liable — not specifically because it is *value*-quality which is in question, but because it is a difficulty affecting determination of any quality of a whole which runs beyond what can be apprehended at one moment, and is a quality of that whole which is affected by the character of it as a *Gestalt.* Because of the magnitude of such a whole, some manner of synthetic apprehension of it is required. And because the character of it which we wish to apprehend is affected by the manner of its internal organization, the kind of synthesis which is called for cannot be accomplished by treatment of it as an aggregate. If we borrow an old word and say that what is essential in such cases is a synthetic intuition, it is to be hoped that entanglement with various problems associated with "intuition" can still be avoided. Our familiarity with the type of experience in question should be taken as suggesting the intended meaning of that term here, rather than this mode of experience by the word. And if it be objected that there is no such thing as synthetic intuition, then let us reply by reference to such envisagement as that by which we hear a symphony, or discover that a journey is comfortable or uncomfortable, or decide that a lengthy undertaking goes smoothly and is a rewarding experience or proves difficult and tedious. The two facts which need to be emphasized are first, that to deny the possibility — the necessity even — of this kind of synthetic envisagement would be to fall into absurdity; but second, that to fail to recognize the kind of error to which this mode of apprehension is peculiarly liable, by reason of inadequacy in the attempted viewing together of what cannot literally be presented in one experience, would be a strange and inexcusible oversight.

Such attempted synthesis can be facilitated or prejudiced by antecedent judgment of details which must be included — as we do better in our hearing of a piece of music if first we have adequately grasped and have retained judgment of its component parts, or as we may better comprehend a picture as a whole when we have first reviewed the major features of its composition. And if such antecedent judgments fail to be correct, then this incorrectness of them will prejudice the accuracy of the synthetic envisagement of the whole in question. But even when comprehension of the parts and details is as adequate and accurate as may be, there is still possibility of mistake through possible inadequacy in the attempted synthesis itself: that fact is so patent that it hardly needs to be emphasized. Moreover, the errors to which such synthetic apprehensions are liable are not such as can be easily avoided by the critique of logic or any other epistemic canon beyond such as is involved in the general principle of consistency in judgment and in those cautions to be found in the general wisdom of experience. Evidence of this kind of error may on occasion be elicited from examination of objective facts of various kinds, particularly so far as the synthetic comprehension presumes or implies, and is supported by, judgments of included detail. Still, both the conviction of such error and any amendment of it are likely to be finally possible only through another and even more comprehensive synthetic envisagement.

10. For all these reasons, the value-assessment of experiential wholes can neither be directly certain nor capable of any decisive and final verification. What is to be assessed is a whole of experience *as experienced,* and there is no moment in which this whole can be presented in the actuality of it. It involves a reference to something which is past and remembered or something future and imagined, or both; or it concerns something possible and hypothetical, in part or altogether. The young man planning his life may wrongly assess what he contemplates because his expectancies fail to square with possible continuations of the present or because he fails to envisage correctly the value-qualities which middle age will find in what he plans and the episodes he attempts to envisage. And the old man reviewing his youth may forget past ills or fail to retain the poignancy of them, or he may color what he remembers with a nostalgia for the irrecoverable, and thus ascribe to his life on the whole a value which in some part is illusory. Whatever runs beyond the specious present but involves attempted valuation of experience as such is liable to errors of this kind in the attempted synthesis of apprehension.[5]

Thus although value-assessment of experiential wholes must depend on that kind of envisagement we would suggest by "syn-

[5] Apprehension of the directly given and present is itself synthetic. We do not attempt to deal with this problem and with the paradoxes involved in conceiving of the present as a stretch of time. The notion of the specious present is forced upon the psychologist in recognition of the obviously fictitious character of the temporality of experience as a mathematical continuum of unextended instants. The "least" experience is stretch of time. But any definite bounds of "the present" can be set only by some criterion which is arbitrary and alien to the character of experience as presented. Whatever such criterion be chosen, there is one paradox which is inescapable: if, e.g., the specious present be such a period as that within which we can count the strokes of the bell which has already rung, then in setting such bounds we leave outside the present the immediate impression of these countable strokes as preceded by others no longer countable. We could never become aware that the present lapses into the past if we should not be directly aware of a something which has now lapsed.

thetic intuition," and this does not have the character of discursive judgment, nevertheless in crediting what is thus synthetically envisaged, discursive judgments of the past and future are relied upon and correctness of them is implied. By the same token, value-assessments so arrived at are capable of confirmation in indefinite degree, in the general manner in which the historically reportable and the predictable can be corroborated or disconfirmed. In this, they share the character of nonterminating empirical judgments generally. Here, as with respect to objective matters of fact, there can be no final assurance beyond the possibility of doubt, and no procedure is open to us which will obviate the possibility of error. But our credence can be justified, and what we believe is always capable of becoming better assured by positive result of further tests of what is implied in it.

If by reason of the difficulties of it, we should seek to avoid such value-assessment of experiential wholes, then we shall find that quite impossible, since it is indispensable to any attempted rational direction of life and of our action. And if we should be minded to seek some simpler mode of arriving at such final value-assessment, then we shall find that there is none which could be adequate and genuinely will apply.

11. However, it would be untrue to life and to the facts of our experience and our actual value-assessments if we should suppose that in every evaluation of anything as contributory to a possible good life, there is or should be such attempted envisagement of that life on the whole and a prediction of the specific manner and occasions in which this contributory value may be realized. There are occasions when just such an attempt is called for; and these are the occasions of our most serious and important decisions. But for the same reasons which make probability only the best we shall attain, this kind of final value-assessment is the less frequently called for in practice. For the most part we are justified in simplifying our problem in one or both of two ways. First, we may break it up into parts. Just as the architect — who likewise recognizes that everything in his plan must be subordinated to the whole and evaluated by relation to it — still does not attempt to devise or judge every detail directly in that relationship, but instead by proximate relation to some lesser and included whole such as this room or this facade, so too we break down our con-

templated good life into major components and judge of minor constituents by their contributory effect on these — a good job, a good home, or a good vacation, a satisfactory conclusion of the task in hand. Or second, recognizing the multiple difficulties of accurate prevision and an adequate synthetic grasp, we make a kind of probability judgment of what will be contributed by the thing or action or passage of experience which comes in question, in view of the various possibilities and probabilites represented by the alternatives with respect to which we must decide. If it is a question whether we shall attend the theater this evening, we raise the point perhaps whether tomorrow we may be overtired and work will not go well. But for the rest we rely upon the general probability that such recreation will contribute to life; and even if this occasion should prove an exception to that, we need not later recant our judgment as unjustified. There are many realizable goods which, as experience in general assures us, are unlikely to do other than contribute to life — as there are many bad experiences which are unlikely to do other than detract. Having a good dinner may safely be relied on to make life a little better; and one does not readily think of circumstances under which an earache would really be desirable. To be sure, a good meal could wreck a life — one remembers the story about a mess of pottage; and perhaps an earache may one day prove essential to living happily ever afterward. But such chances are too small to be practical considerations.

Thus most judgments of contributory value in particular experiences are made provisionally and do not seek to go beyond the probabilities concerning the alternatives that life may present. Yet it all the while remains true that the criterion by reference to which value in experience would be finally determined must be this criterion of contribution to a life found good in the living of it.

But if, in view of the magnitude of any problem affected by relation to the whole of life and of the limitations of our discernment with respect to it, we should be minded to take an easier way, or to take the defeatist attitude, either in practice or in theory, then we are obliged to remember that it is as inescapable as it is difficult. The moral concern for the whole of life sets that end to which all particular aims must be subordinated, and constitutes the rational imperative.

REALMS OF VALUE

PAUL W. TAYLOR

B. Nine Ways of Classifying Values

1. What it means to classify values according to the points of view to which they belong has been examined. . . . The realms of value that emerge from such classification are universes of normative discourse corresponding to different points of view. In all civilized cultures there are eight points of view (or realms of value) that may be designated as "basic." We call them basic because of two factors. First, they *pervade* the culture, in the sense that the conduct of any given individual in the culture is always subject to a value system belonging to at least one of them and is usually subject to value systems belonging to more than one of them. Second, they are the *dominant* points of view in a culture, in the sense that they set the values of the major social institutions and activities which carry on the civilization of the culture. These major social institutions and activities are the moral code, the arts, the pure and applied sciences, the religion or religions, the economic, political, and legal systems, the customs and traditions, and the educational institutions. The eight basic points of view corresponding to these institutions and activities are the moral, the aesthetic, the intellectual, the religious, the economic, the political, the legal, and the point of view of etiquette or custom. There is no single point of view corresponding to the educational institutions of a society, since education is a process which may take place within *any* point of view. Thus there is moral education, aesthetic education, intellectual education, religious education, and so on.

Value systems belonging to the eight basic points of view are embodied in the organizations and institutions of a society. Thus the purpose of a social organization may be to fulfill *standards* which belong to one or another of them. Or else it may be governed by *rules* which belong to one or another of these points of view, and to carry on the organization's activities is to follow these

Reprinted, by permission, from *Normative Discourse* (Englewood Cliffs, N.J.: Prentice-Hall, 1961), pp. 299-303, 329-333.

(practice-defining) rules. A church as an organized social institution, for example, exists to further goals defined by religious values, and to practice a religion is to act in accordance with the rules of religious conduct (worship, ritual, prayer). Accordingly it is appropriate to judge a church from the religious point of view. In a similar manner it is appropriate to judge the activities of an art museum from the aesthetic point of view, the activities of a college or university from the intellectual point of view, and the activities of a political party from the political point of view. In all of these cases, however, it is also appropriate to judge the organizations from both the moral and the legal points of view, since their purposes are to achieve certain goals or to pursue certain ends *without* violating the moral code of the society and *without* breaking the society's laws.

In addition to the eight basic points of view or realms of value, every culture includes many nonbasic points of view or realms of value. Each of these corresponds to a particular *group interest* in the culture. One may speak of the military point of view, for example, as the universe of normative discourse or realm of value which is appropriate for judging the activities and policies of an army. The value system belonging to the military point of view contains as its supreme norm the standard of winning a war or defending a society against attack. An army as a social institution exists for these specific and clearly defined purposes and can legitimately be judged according to its ability to accomplish them. Similar considerations hold for all other social organizations with specific and clearly defined purposes, such as a professional baseball team, a hospital, a city's fire department, a local organization to preserve racial segregation (e.g., a White Citizens' Council in a Southern state), or a national organization to abolish racial segregation (e.g., the National Association for the Advancement of Colored People). In all such cases, it is appropriate to judge the organization in terms of its *group interest,* that is, in terms of the purposes of the group as a whole (as distinct from the *self-interest* of each member of the group). It is also appropriate to judge the organization in terms of whatever basic points of view its purposes belong to. Thus an army may be judged not exclusively from the military point of view, but also from the moral, political, economic, and legal points of view. In fact all the organizations just mentioned may legitimately be judged from the legal point of view, since they seek to achieve their purposes without breaking the society's laws. The same cannot be said concerning all social organizations, however. The organization of a juvenile street gang, for example, may have purposes that run counter to the law, and there are some organizations, such as gambling syndicates and "dope rings," whose purposes are explicitly illegal.

To say that it is not legitimate to judge the activities of a juvenile street gang or of organized crime from the legal point of view is to speak as a member of the group concerned. When we place ourselves outside the group and speak as a member of the society at large, then the legal point of view becomes relevant. We are then judging the group interest as a whole according to more basic standards or rules (i.e., according to standards or rules belonging to a more basic point of view). This brings out the fact that regarding any social organization, two types of evaluation are possible. One is an evaluation of the activities and policies of the organization within the framework of the group interest itself. Here we ask: How well do these activities and policies serve the purposes which define the goals of the group? How closely do they accord with the rules adopted by the group? The other type of evaluation is made outside the framework of the group interest. Here we ask: How good or bad, right or wrong are the activities and policies of the group according to standards and rules *not* included in the value systems adopted by the group? The distinction between these two types of evaluation is an instance of the distinction . . . between evaluating something within the framework of a given social practice and judging the social practice as a whole.

When we make value judgments of the second type (i.e., evaluating the activities and policies of an organization from a standpoint outside the organization), there is one point of view that is applicable to *all* organizations, namely, the moral point of view. Every culture embodies a moral code which is concerned with the welfare of the individuals in the culture; and since the activities and policies of every social organization affect, for better or worse, the welfare of at least some individuals in the culture, the culture's moral system is applicable. What is not so obvious is that the moral point of view is relevant to all social organizations even when we restrict ourselves to the first type of evaluation (i.e., judging the activities and policies of an organization within the framework of its group interest). For the activities and policies of any organization are at least in part *moral* activities and policies. They are moral in so far as the furthering of the organization's purposes affects the welfare of individuals who are members of the organization and who participate in its activities. It might at first be thought that the activities of a juvenile street gang or a White Citizens' Council can be judged from the outside according to the moral code of the society at large but cannot be so judged from the inside, since such organizations lack a moral code. But this is to confuse the moral *point of view* with particular moral *value systems*. Every organization has at least a rudimentary moral value system. (In the case of a juvenile gang or a White Citizens' Council, the moral system may be highly developed, with clearly defined rules and standards of right conduct, and with strict duties and obligations supported by strong sanctions.) It is true that a juvenile gang or a White Citizens' Council may have adopted a moral system which is in conflict with the moral system of the society at large. This would occur whenever acting in accordance with the moral rules of the group involves violating the moral rules of the society at large. To say that the moral point of view applies to all such organizations is to say that the rules of relevance which govern the *reasoning* of those who seek to justify value judgments, prescriptions, standards, and rules within the organization are the rules of relevance that define the moral point of view.

The eight basic points of view and the nonbasic points of view of different group interests are all to be distinguished from the point of view of *self-interest*. The basic points of view are those of society at large. The nonbasic points of view are those of subcultural groups or institutions. The latter are to be contrasted with the self-interest of each member of a group. An individual may participate in various groups and often he will adopt the group interests as his own. That is, he will take their points of view and try to live by their value systems. But he also has his self-interest to pursue and he may consider his group activities either wholly or in part from the point of view of prudence. This point of view is defined by those rules of reasoning according to which an appeal to one's self-interest is always relevant to the justification of a value judgment and any other appeal is always irrelevant. . . .

Whether a value is accepted rationally or irrationally has nothing to do with what kind of a value it is. Although different kinds of values are distinguished on the basis of points of view, and points of view are distinguished on the basis of rules of reasoning appropriate to them, one does not have to *follow* such rules of reasoning in order to *adopt* the values belonging to a point of view. One may adopt moral rules (of conduct), for example, and not be able to justify them according to the rules of reasoning that define the moral point of view. They are moral rules and not political, economic, or religious rules, because *if* they were to be justified by anyone, moral rules of reasoning would govern the argument. Similarly, an aesthetic standard is a standard whose adoption is justified from the aesthetic point of view, but this does not mean that everyone who adopts such a standard can in fact justify his adopting it. This is true also of intellectual values. It is perfectly possible to accept such values irrationally. This occurs whenever a person decides to believe an assertion or accept an argument on the basis of certain standards of truth and certain rules of inference, without being aware that he is using such standards and rules. He accepts them implicitly and is therefore unable to give good reasons for doing so. Indeed, it is quite rare for a person to examine his intellectual standards and rules in order to see whether they can be justified. Only the logician and the epistemologist carry out such an examination carefully and systematically, and it takes a high level of intellectual sophistication even to be aware of the problem. But standards of truth and rules of validity are used by everyone in everyday life. Most people are simply unaware of them and accept them uncritically. This is not to say that the standards and rules so accepted are false (unjustifiable). They may well be *objectively* rational. It is only to say that they are not *accepted* rationally, that is, that their mode of acceptance is irrational.

The distinction between objective and subjective rationality enables us to see more clearly what is involved in the classical ideal of "the examined life." It would appear that if there is such a thing as the most justified way of life and if we know what it is, the ideal is to have everyone in the world live that way of life. In order to bring about such an ideal as quickly as possible, it would seem that the best thing to do would be forcibly to control all societies in the world and indoctrinate everyone to accept automatically the values of the most justified way of life. In this manner, everyone's values would become objectively rational. Of course they would not be subjectively rational, but why should this bother us? If everyone is living what we know to be the good life, why deplore the fact that they have accepted that life irrationally? Indeed, if irrational acceptance can make people more deeply committed to their values than rational acceptance, there would seem to be every reason to *prevent* people from trying to justify their values rationally and so becoming critical and reflective about them.

Is this a legitimate conclusion to draw from the general theory of value presented in this book? I think not, for three reasons. In the first place, it rests on a mistaken conception of the nature of a rational choice among ways of life. In the second place, it does not take into account how conditions of a rational choice can be realized. In the third place, it overlooks the possibility that subjective rationality itself may be a part of the rationally chosen way of life. I shall consider each of these points in turn.

The concept of a rational choice among ways of life is the concept of an ideal. No one ever makes such a choice in practice. The concept merely gives meaning to the idea that one way of life is more justified than another; it does not tell us which way of life is the most justified. Indeed, if there were to be widespread disagreement among those who made a rational choice, no way of life could be claimed to be superior to all others. But even if we assume that one way of life would be preferred to all others under the ideal conditions of a rational choice, this still does not warrant our imposing by force any known way of life upon everyone. For no one knows, or ever will know, what that way of life is. If the conditions of a rational choice were approximated to a fair degree, we might be able to make claims with some degree of probability. But even these claims would have to remain open to future revision or rejection. The conditions of a rational choice are simply too ideal to allow us to have any confidence in decisions reached under conditions that we can now approximate in this world.

If this is the case, then our only reasonable hope is to be able gradually to increase the probability of our guess as to what the most justified way of life is. This process of a gradual approach to the truth requires that the conditions of a rational choice (freedom, enlightenment, and impartiality) be approximated more and more closely in the future. How can this be done? The answer lies in developing a kind of society in which everyone is not only permitted but is actually encouraged to make free, enlightened, and impartial choices. . . . Any attempt to impose one way of life upon everyone would automatically preclude the possibility of anyone's making such a choice. For a *free* choice demands absence of external constraint. *Enlightened* choice demands imaginative as well as intellectual knowledge of many different ways of life; this would be impossible if everyone were forced to live the same way of life. *Impartiality* demands that a person not choose between the way of life in which he was brought up and another way of life. It also demands that the person himself not be indoctrinated from childhood in one way of life, which is the very thing that would happen under the conditions in question. The point is that no one really knows which values are objectively rational and the only way to find out is by having an "open" society throughout the world, which tolerates and even encourages great diversity in ways of life and the freedom to choose among them.

There is a third reason why the critical examination of one's own life is compatible with the general theory of value presented in this book. There is the possibility that subjective rationality may itself be an integral and basic aspect of a rationally chosen way of life. It is not *logically* necessary that a free, enlightened, and impartial choice be the choice of a way of life which includes freedom, enlightenment, and impartiality. Nevertheless, the possibility that this would be the case must be left open. If it were to be the case, those values that were objectively rational would have to be subjectively rational as well. That is, they would constitute a way of life which required that people be able to give good reasons for their value judgments, prescriptions, standards, and rules. Such good reasons ultimately would involve the appeal to a rationally chosen way of life (though not everyone would be expected to make such a choice himself). Thus critical and reflective acceptance of values would be a part of the objectively rational way of life. It might even be the case that such a rational mode of acceptance would be one of the fundamental principles of a rationally chosen way of life. In living this way of life *it would be more important that people be able to give good reasons for their values than that they should accept a particular set of values*. Indeed, diversity and even conflict among the values accepted by people would become an essential aspect of that way of life. Tolerance would have to accompany such diversity and conflict, however, if the conditions for rational acceptance of values were to be maintained.

The classical ideal of the examined life is not antithetical to the theory of value presented in this book. Critical reflection upon the values of one's own society is absolutely necessary if a person is to seek a way of life that is rationally chosen. Even if it were the case that the way of life of his own society happened to be the way of life which would be preferred by everyone under conditions of a rational choice, he would not be able to *know* this unless he questioned the justifiability of all the values of his society. Only then would he know whether his society's value judgments and prescriptions could be verified, whether his society's standards and rules could be validated, and whether the value systems embodied in the structure and functioning of his society could be vindicated. To have everyone in a society make such a critical examination of his own values would require a whole educational process directed toward the rational acceptance of values as its basic goal. This is, indeed, what a liberal education means. Liberal education may be viewed in this light as a complex method for seeking the most justified way of life. In seeking the objectively rational as its end it must develop subjective rationality as its means. The educated man would be the one who steadily and impartially investigates the rational basis of his own and others' values, in order to discover those values (if there be any) which can be shown to be more justified than all others.

It may be the case that if we could know with certainty what the most justified way of life was, it would turn out to be a way of life which excludes the development of subjective rationality. But this is an idle question. We actually never can know with certainty which way of life is most justified. There is therefore every reason to develop and further the highest degree of subjective rationality we are capable of. Only in this way can we hope to attain a reasonable guess about the ideal way of life. Developing the capacity for subjective rationality, whether in everyone or in oneself alone, is an "open" commitment. The Socratic quest is a lifetime's endeavor for each individual, and each individual's pursuit of the quest is merely part of a task for humanity which has no end. The quest is a search for wisdom, and the final goal, which can never be reached, is knowledge of the good.

THE ROLE OF VALUE THEORY IN EDUCATION

J. DONALD BUTLER

B. Education and Axiology

Now, let us turn directly to educational concerns which involve value theory. I would like to observe that there is an essential and very close relation between education and axiology. There are four aspects of this close connection which I now see very clearly.

1. The first of these refers back to my second presupposition: the necessity for human subjects to participate in the realization of values in order for them to achieve them and enjoy them. If it is true, as I maintain, that whatever the ontology of a value is, persons or societies must be actively engaged in its actualization or they cannot possess it and enjoy it for themselves, then value realization is an educative process and necessarily involves people in a growth and development which is educational at its heart. It might be said that this is an educational dimension which is indigenous to axiology as such.

2. The second aspect of the close relation between education and axiology I should like to mention involves a characterization of the school as a unique institution in society. The uniqueness of the educational institution of society looked at in the light of value theory is that it is more especially a value-realizing institution than is any other institution with the exception of religion.

I have not been able to explore this adequately, as of course its validation involves a whole philosophy of social institutions. Whatever else the institutions of society do, they do seek to realize value. Business seeks economic value for its investors and aims, with varying degrees of honesty, to offer its patrons some other value the return from which is this same economic value. Government at its best seeks to maintain and further achieve values of social order, general welfare, and the common good, although this is always corrupted by the intention to gain other values which are not so generally enjoyed.

Reprinted, by permission, from *Educational Theory*, IV, no. 1 (January, 1954): 73-77, 86.

But my impression is that there is in almost all other institutions a kind of factualism in addition to value seeking, which is foreign to education. With reference to the individual pupil, education begins with him as he is at any given stage in his growth and nurture and seeks to convey him into a stage of development and value achievement which is not now actual. Socially, education begins with its society or culture as it is at a given point in history. It may make itself a completely subservient tool of that society or culture and thereby conceive its intention as conforming the new generation and so conserving the values, good or bad, which are actual in that culture. It may, however, and we hope it more commonly will, conceive of its function as reconstructive as well as conservative. In this event there enters a strong futuristic and axiological element into the educational task. The school not only conserves, it certainly does not destroy, what is good in the culture, but its vision reaches quite beyond this objective to conveying the society into a new orbit of value possession, in which that which is desired but is not now actual fact becomes more than an ideal or an objective, namely, a present realized possession of the culture.

3. A third aspect of the connection between axiology and education is the necessary relationship between educational objectives and value theory. Any objectives which can be conceived for any phase of life are an expression, consciously or unconsciously, of value judgments. And when objectives are proposed for education, whether general or specific, whether by teachers or administrators for individual classes or schools, or by national bodies such as the Educational Policies Commission, some answers to value problems are implicit in these objectives.

The significant imperative which this relation forces upon us is that if our aims and objectives are to be adequate, they require that we be thoroughgoing in our value thinking. This is one of the strategic points at which more adequate attention should be drawn to the role of value theory in education. Except for educational philosophers, it seems to me that virtually no one connected with education is aware of the connection between value theory and the formulation of objectives. Furthermore, there is not the needed comprehension of value problems necessary to the formulation of a value theory. Needless to say, none possesses a value theory unless the most popular superficial talk about values can be called such. And because of this vacuum in value thinking, there is not an adequate context for the formulation of educational objectives. Regardless of the value judgments which may be made of the essence of given educational objectives, those objectives cannot be adequately conceived unless they are formulated in the light of a value theory which is embraced with full cognizance of the problems involved, and which the theory is designed to answer. This, in turn, will involve equally responsible thinking in metaphysics and epistemology.

This underscores, as can be done at several comparable points, the importance of adequate background in philosophy of education as an essential requirement for all who become connected with the schools in any professional way. It also suggests the wisdom of encouraging lay discussions of the purposes and functions of our schools with the help of as expert guidance as can be secured. Such discussions should relate specifically educational concerns to as broad generalities as possible, in the hope that at the grass roots people may come to wise and discerning value judgments within the context of which to carry forward the educational functions of the community.

4. A fourth consideration concerning the relation of axiology and education is the significance for children and youth of their value problems and decisions.

The point as which the really vital learnings can take place is the point at which decisions have to be made between alternatives. While it is granted that there is a maturation dimension according to which the psychological appropriateness of decisions must be determined (younger children having more decisions made for them and being shielded from strenuous decisions where great hazard is a possibility, with an increasing reluctance on the part of adults to intervene as a child progresses from preadolescence through early and middle adolescence to adulthood), yet it must be recognized that the making of value judgments and decisions is central to education. Parents and teachers ought to be cautious in making decisions for their children or shielding them from difficult decisions; they should turn the occasions for such judgments and decisions to educational ends.

Value problems are the first reflective steps of maturing youth. They provide the first occasion for reflective decisions; therefore, value concerns in education are of unique importance with all children, but especially with adolescents because in their struggles and tensions are the early occasions for genuinely reflective decision.

Of course it may be unlikely that every child can become a philosopher who builds for himself a theory of value, relates this value theory to a metaphysics, and validates both by a theory of knowledge. But every child must come eventually to live his own life with some measure of responsibility. The closer he can approach a theory of value within which his value judgments can make some real sense, the more adequate and responsible he can be in facing the demands of life. It is for this purpose that his value experiences can be made educational. A given value problem and the decisions which resolve it do not comprise the whole story of value experience. Value problems constitute, it seems to me, the first significant reflective steps of maturation. No doubt they are preceded in childhood and somewhat in preadolescence by problems of causality, the kind of inquisitive concern which is expressed in questions regarding how the world came to be and where babies come from. But real, responsible reflection begins with value problems.

C. Schools Should Be Permissive Regarding Value Decisions

All of these considerations regarding the relation of axiology and education seem to me to point in the direction of an educational institution which is predominantly permissive in relation to the value decisions of growing children and youth. The schools should freely provide opportunity for value consideration, decision, and realization; they should not withhold consideration, predetermine or force value decisions, and then expect value realization to go on within this predisposed framework.

Of course, actually there are many vested interests pressing in upon the schools which are uneasy about open discussion and objective analysis of the particular province which they are concerned to have protected from such consideration. The present witch-hunt phenomenon is an instance of political and economic vested interests seeking to prevent freedom of discussion which might encourage or give birth to opposing loyalties. Another area in which free discussion is commonly prevented by such pressures is in the area of religious or antireligious loyalties. On the one hand some religious interests prefer schools in which there is a kind of rationalistic control of the doctrine which is taught. Though diametrically opposed, a secular way of life, virtually equivalent to a religion in order of devotion, is nevertheless very similar to religious thought control in the desire to see that a scientific world-view is taught. By way of carrying the example further it seems to me that the solution is in neither of these alternatives and that neither alternative gives discerning attention to the value issues involved.

While of course there are many decisions about the education of their children which must be made by parents, by elected authorities, by administrators, and by teachers, there are also many decisions which must be made by pupils which are an essential part of education and apart from which genuinely educative activity cannot go on. I am often surprised at the number and extent of decisions it is commonly assumed that parents, teachers, administrators, and school officials must make. Many of these decisions, it seems to me, are going to be remade by the pupils in spite of the decisions that have already been made for them. And, I believe that most decisions which call for review by the pupils are rightly pupil decisions in the first instance anyway. The value concerns of growing children and youth call for such indigenous decisions by them, and with respect for these our schools should be more permissive than dominant.

1. There are certain very general values which the adult community, as expressed in the direction of school life, must prize. The first of these is that it will prize itself. It will prize its own community life as a vital matrix into which new generations are born and in which they grow and are nurtured. It will prize its heritage not so much as a fixed fund which is transmitted from generation to generation, but as a living stream of which the present generation is a living cross-section and the present living expression. The adult community as expressed in its direction of school life will prize and respect the child. It will respect the

child by not thinking of him as one who is to be conformed only to what is the present adult culture. It will rather respect the child as a measured but distinct object of hope for the future. It will also respect the child as a person, as a soul with a destiny, a destiny which may reach beyond the human culture and the human orbit. And it will be concerned not to place any ceiling over this destiny restricting it to temporal boundaries. The adult community will also value its subgroupings. While it should move by majority decisions, majorities should not be so dominant and so devoid of understanding as not to leave place for the healthy dissent and nonconformity of minorities.

2. While one could get lost completely among the trees if he were to attempt to consider the specific value areas in which pupil decisions are made, yet some endeavor should be made to indicate what some of these are, at least by representation. One of the most common areas of value experience where youth finds it necessary to make decisions is the realm of ethics. As children become preadolescents and especially as they grow into adolescence and adulthood, they are confronted with many problems of right and wrong. This is one important area in which maturation and certainly education calls for thoughtful judgment. Social questions concerning war and peace, race, and class distinction also press in upon youth, especially in this time of tension and quiet revolution. With boys, the certainty of early military service increases the urgency by making it very personal and immediate. Varying somewhat with individual presuppositions, home and community backgrounds, religious, political, and economic problems evoke some serious thinking and call for some measure of judgment. Such problems are important in themselves, but they are also important because they can open out into even more fundamental metaphysical and epistemological concerns. However, they are not likely to serve such a worthy end if they are intercepted prematurely by a dominating or oversolicitous sponsorship. The truly educative concern will meet such occasions for serious thought with an attitude which permits genuine deciding by children and youth; it will not offer the shortcut of ready-made answers, nor will it shield efficiently from the real hazards of genuine decision-making.

3. In addition to decisions which have just been described respecting the evaluation of specific values, there are other decisions having to do with the whole of value experience which should be regarded as areas in which decisions have to be made in the process of maturing. These are judgments concerning the foundations of and nature of value. It seems to me that any education would be superficial which did not make some provision for judgment concerning such fundamental considerations, however fully it makes provision for specific value judgments. These general value concerns mentioned now in the light of the pupil's learning experience relate to the basic presupposition with which this paper began, and also constitute a final conclusion. My argument regarding the place of these presuppositions in education is that instead of education being authoritarian with these or other presuppositions made explicit as the rational basis of the education provided, or instead of the schools being authoritarian by opposing such principles or precluding study of them and judgment concerning them, education should rather be an open-ended process providing occasion for decision about such basic loyalties as these.

a. Values either are or are not rooted ultimately in God. Now, what I am saying is that instead of our teaching that they are or instead of our teaching the antithesis of this presupposition, our education should be so constructed that every pupil is at least given an opportunity to make a decision about this very belief.

b. Similarly, being related to God is either the foundation of all value realization by an individual or a society, or else it is irrelevant. My argument is that instead of begging the question on this presupposition, education should be so constructed that there is the occasion for decision concerning this important concern.

c. And finally, either man is able of himself to relate himself to God or such other matrix out of which it is believed that values arise, or else he needs to be related by a power or a Person beyond himself. Again my contention is that education should not answer this question for the pupil but instead provide the occasions in which the learner will come to make his own decision, a decision which he will necessarily make for himself eventually when and if it is really made.

DOES ETHICS MAKE A DIFFERENCE?

KINGSLEY PRICE

I

We are all familiar with a widespread view as to the relation philosophers bear to practical men. It is the view that common sense affords no reliable guidance to practice, and that the ordinary man needs a philosopher to tell him what ought to exist and what he ought to do to make it real. It can be derived, not quite properly, from Plato's doctrine concerning the role of the philosopher king; and it probably stems, in part, from that ancient source.

This familiar view is sometimes found in the thought of those who consider education. Educational activities, they say, may be directed toward the development of persons and societies of many different sorts. The philosopher can show the educator toward which of these sorts of persons and societies he should direct his energies. The teacher and the student cannot guide themselves. Their path must be marked out for them by the ethical philosopher. We have all run across this view in concrete form when, coping with some practical problem, teachers or administrators or members of the student council have asked us how a certain solution for it appears "from the philosopher's point of view."

There is another view of the relation between ethical philosophy and the practice of education. The goals toward which educational activity is directed, it runs, may be shown to be worth all the more trouble by educationists themselves. All men, however ordinary or nonphilosophical, are altogether competent to find out values for themselves. Ethical philosophy offers no guide for the choice of nonphilosophers; ethics, rather, is itself little more than a summary of what all men know by instinct — or at any rate, in total independence of subtle and dark reflection. Sufficient unto the task is the common sense thereof; and the man involved in education makes his own choices rightly — settles upon his objectives both remote and near — without appeal to those who per-

Reprinted, by permission, from *Philosophy of Education 1966,* Proceedings of the Twenty-second Annual Meeting, Philosophy of Education Society, 1966, pp. 70-74.

form some different function. Something of this attitude must have informed Quintilian's distrust of philosophers and, however polite his respect for books of philosophy, the sturdy independence of mind of many a teacher and administrator of the modern day.

These antithetical attitudes toward the relation between philosophers and educators appear, as well, on the level of theory. Some hold that ethics as a theory determines the values involved in education as a theory. Ethics consists in statements that value terms like "good" and "ought" refer to or presuppose certain traits; and it informs us what kinds of individual character, of society, and of individual and social conduct possess these traits. The theory of education contains statements that certain kinds of persons and societies are good, and that teachers and students, as well as others involved in the enterprise of education, ought to endeavor to realize them. It easily appears, therefore, that the theory of education is, at least in part, the result of an application of the principles of ethics to educational phenomena — that it is, along with politics and other social sciences, a chapter in ethical philosophy. Thus, we find one recent author[1] arguing that the resolution of educational problems — and presumably the statements of that resolution — requires that they be reduced to more fundamental issues in philosophy, including ethics, and another[2] holding that the choice of procedures and goals in education depends upon criteria that can be found only in ethics.

Not all contemporary authors agree that the theory of education is subject to ethics. Seeming to take their cue from William James, some[3] hold that philosophy is only a method — the method of obdurate, serious, and careful thought about any subject whatever — and that, itself owning nothing substantial, the theory of education can borrow nothing substantial from it although it shares philosophy (the method of serious thought) with all other genuine theories. Education as a theory, they hold, presents solu-

[1] Harry S. Broudy, *Building a Philosophy of Education* (Englewood Cliffs, N.J.: Prentice-Hall, 1954), pp. 17-26. But in this passage, he also suggests a slightly different view.

[2] Phillip H. Phenix, *Philosophy of Education* (New York: Henry Holt, 1958), pp. 16, 285.

[3] Foster McMurray, "Preface to an Autonomous Discipline of Education," *Educational Theory*, V no. 3 (July, 1955); G. Max Wingo, *The Philosophy of American Education* (Boston: D. C. Heath, 1965), p. 14.

tions for educational problems that are wholly its own; it is, with respect to ethics and philosophy in general, an autonomous discipline.

II

Is the theory of education thus autonomous? If it is, then it carries within itself the guarantee of the values and procedures it recommends. Ethics makes no difference to it. If it is not, then ethics must show it the distinction between direction and drift — between procedures and goals appropriate to educational activity, and those that are not. In that case, ethics makes a great part of the difference between education and aimless instruction or something worse.

In order to settle the question whether ethics makes a difference, I shall describe the theory of education and consider its relation to ethics. The theory with which I am concerned does not exist; there is no theory of education now established. I shall describe, rather, the very general structure of the theory that educational research may be approaching, and ask whether a theory that exhibits this pattern is, in any way, dependent upon ethical philosophy.[4]

The theory of education, if it existed, would embody a perfected understanding of the processes through which a culture is transmitted and enhanced from one person or generation to another; it would embody a perfected understanding of educational phenomena. It would need to contain statements of three different kinds, and these statements would be related in certain ways. I shall describe the statements of each kind and the relations they bear to one another.

In the first group, there are statements of the conditions in which the various subjects education transmits and fosters are taught and learned effectively. "If the student practices on dry land first, he will learn to swim more quickly"; "if its similarities and dissimilarities to his own culture are made evident to him, the student will master the history of a culture that is past"; "if he

---

[4] For a fuller discussion of the theory of education, see Kingsley Price, "Discipline in Teaching; in Its Study and in Its Theory," in John Walton and James L. Kuethe (eds.), *The Discipline of Education* (Madison: University of Wisconsin Press, 1963).

does some experiments himself, the student will assimilate experimental science"; "if correct responses are rewarded and growing tendencies toward wrong ones punished, the student will learn the former faster" — these typify statements of the first kind; they are teaching statements.

In the second group, we find rules for teaching. "To teach the student to swim, let him practice outside the water first"; "to establish an understanding of any past culture, point out its similarities to and differences from the student's own"; "to foster an understanding of experimental science, let the student perform experiments"; "to further learning of any subject, reward successes and punish failures when they become numerous" — these typify the rules employed in teaching.

Teaching statements are acceptable only if they are based upon empirical or scientific methods. The statements about how people learn to swim, to understand history, to master the sciences, and to learn anything whatever cannot claim our allegiance unless careful observation shows them to be true or probable. The data organized and described by these empirical procedures — the activities observed — are those of teaching in its various forms. And in this part of the theory of education, there is no facet of method or of data that suggests ethical philosophy.

Statements of the second group — teaching rules — are derived from those of the first group in a way that is obvious. We simply invert the order of the components and change the mood to the imperative. We transform the sentence "If the student practices on dry land first, he learns to swim quickly" into the rule, "to bring about quick mastery of swimming, let the student practice on dry land first." The method for arriving at these rules consists in this transformation of teaching statements. The statements of the second group are useful rules for teaching if those of the first group from which they are derived are true or probable. Their utility consists, simply, not in their bringing about anything that is morally virtuous, nor in their being in any way morally obligatory. It consists, rather, in their bringing about a situation prefigured by the truth or probability of the statements from which they are derived. And in this second part of the theory of education, we find again no suggestion of ethical philosophy.

In the third division of the theory, we find statements of moral value. "Democracy ought to exist"; "people ought to be intelligent and kindly"; "knowledge should be furthered for its own sake and for its practical uses"; "teachers and students ought to follow the rules that produce mastery of subjects and further those more remote objectives" — these typify the moral statements that constitute the third part of the theory of education.

The relation of these moral statements to those of the first and second groups is fairly clear. They determine what statements are teaching statements, and what rules, teaching rules. There are many statements and rules that might be but are not incorporated in the theory of education. "Rewarding mistakes in arithmetic produces arithmetical incompetence" and "authoritarian discipline of the young produces authoritarian character" may both be true. And we can derive from them the rules: "to produce incompetence in arithmetic, reward mistakes," and "to foster authoritarian character, discipline the young in an authoritarian manner." But if we adopt the fostering of intelligence as a goal of education, we shall not admit the statement and the rule for bad arithmeticians into the first and second parts of our theory. And if the third part of the theory asserts the value of democracy, the first and second must exclude the statement and the rule for authoritarian character. The scientific basis and the teaching rules erected upon it must subserve the moral values the theory of education adopts; and this is another way of saying that the moral values incorporated in that theory determine the content of its rules and those parts of scientific knowledge it includes.

What is the source from which our theory draws its moral statements? It cannot draw them from the social sciences. History, cultural anthropology, social psychology, sociology, etc. may formulate beliefs as to what is good and bad, right and wrong that pervade classes, nations, or even the entire race; but their formulations can never be moral statements. They can never be more than descriptions of what some or all men believe. They cannot tell us, for example, that Judas ought not to have betrayed his master, nor that all men ought to love one another. At best, they can tell us that these statements enjoy a widespread credence. But the theory of education must include statements as to what is good and what ought to be done, not statements as to what men believe in these respects.

Can our theory find its moral statements in common sense? In this domain are all those judgments in whose making the reflective procedures of science, philosophy, theology, etc. play no significant role. Many form a part of tradition, and are passed down from one generation to another as part of the spirit of the group, of the nation, or of the age. Some of these are moral judgments. By tradition, many hold that women ought to remain at home, that burial rites should be observed, that filial piety is a duty. And these customary moral judgments may be perfectly genuine although they are accepted without question from the past. Others are more spontaneous and out of keeping with tradition. They characterize the prophet and the seer, the innovator and the genuine revolutionary. The gospel of universal love; liberty, equality, fraternity; the classless society — these ideas express moral judgments to some degree discontinuous with the traditions in which they arose. In their original forms, they were advanced with spontaneous urgency and without reflection. We all make judgments like them though not on so grand a scale, and these spontaneous moral judgments dwell in the domain of common sense along with those of custom.

It is in common sense that the third part of the theory of education finds its material. Its data are the everyday moral judgments of common men, compacted out of custom and out of spontaneity. It might be supposed that the method our theory follows is one of simple introspection. The theorist of education simply looks into his own mind and finds the statements that people the third region of his domain. If this were true, the occupants of that region could owe no allegiance to ethical philosophy. For they cannot find their parentage in ethics since it exists in common sense, and they stem from the latter through a method — that of simple introspection — which, being the instrument of many theories, cannot, by one of them, be borrowed from another. If the method and the data that yield the third part of our theory are in this way logically independent of ethics, the entire theory is autonomous because, as we have seen, the first two parts owe no allegiance to it.

Our question, then, resolves itself into the question whether the method for securing the value statements in the theory of education is one of simple introspection of the moral judgments of common sense. The answer is that it must be such a method, but that it must be a good deal more besides. The moral judgments of common sense are not, all of them, mutually coherent. Indeed, the more intently we regard them, the more striking their incoherence becomes; so that the more carefully we introspect them, the more obvious the need for something in addition to simple introspection appears, in order that the third division of the theory of education should be established. "Where a man must choose between himself and others, he ought to prefer his own interests"; "all men should act benevolently"; "each man should count for one and only one"; "intelligent, well-informed votes ought to count for more than those that are dull and ill-informed"; "universal peace ought to reign"; "some wars ought to be fought" — all these judgments find a home in the customary morality of common sense; but some of them are obviously incompatible with others. Moreover, the spontaneous moral judgments of prophets and seers and ordinary men uniformly break with tradition. We cannot constitute the third division of the theory of education by the method of simple introspection. It would lead us to incorporate in that theory values that are fundamentally opposed; and this opposition in the third division would generate incompatible teaching rules and incompatible teaching statements. It would endow the theory of education with a pervasive contradiction.

The moral statements that occupy the third division of the theory must be consistent with one another, and the method by which they are drawn from common sense must assure us that they are so. We accomplish that result in several ways. Sometimes, our allegiance to conflicting judgments may be retained by attaching modifiers to one or both of them. Thus, we continue to judge that all men ought to keep their promises, and that no one should deliberately harm others, by modifying the former with the phrase, "except where the injury of keeping the promise exceeds the benefit of breaking it." In the same way, we retain our allegiance to democracy and to the principle of equal justice by limiting the scope of majority rule by the rights of minorities. In other cases, we totally reject one of the judgments as at least some have done with the judgment of vengeance — the judgment of an eye for an eye, a tooth for a tooth, a life for a life.

Moreover, the statements in the third division must be valid.

The moral judgments of common sense are, by definition, held without reflection; and there is no guarantee that careful thought about any one of them will not show it to be invalid, mistaken, or unacceptable. But if our third division should include such a statement, the theory as a whole would contain a fundamental flaw. It would contain a teaching statement and a teaching rule that lead to the production of something morally opprobrious, for it would harbor a moral value that would require such a statement and such a rule.

But the method of simple introspection cannot certify the validity of any moral judgment in common sense. Each presents itself as valid to introspection, but their mutual incoherence shows that some other method must be employed to establish the acceptability of any. A few of these may be self-evident — incapable of rejection or modification. But this trait is revealed not to simple introspection, but by clarity to prolonged reflection and impartial doubt as the work of Butler and of Sidgwick suggests, or as that of Kant suggests, by some absurdity in their denials. Others may be derived as conclusions in arguments, stemming from premises that are self-evident. That men ought to love one another may be self-evident, and that they ought to establish democracy may be a conclusion in a moral argument. The statements in the third division of our theory must be consistent and valid; and while the method of simple introspection enables us to find them in common sense, they must survive comparison, modification, dialectical examination, and rational argument before they can be admitted.

Simple introspection cannot deal with a third difficulty. The moral judgments of tradition and of spontaneity receive expression in the use of moral value terms. Similar terms occur in common sense judgments that are not moral, and the difference is quite unclear to the uncritical mind. Judgments of expediency, of technique, and of morality all may be expressed by use of the words "good" and "ought." Consequently, one might mistakenly exalt a principle of expediency or technique into one of morality — might suppose, for example, that the principle, "in order to advance his own interests, one ought to make use of others whenever possible," is an overriding moral principle. In order to decide what statements should occupy our third division, the value terms that common sense employs must be analyzed with a view to finding out what traits moral predicates attribute to conduct and to things, or presuppose that they possess, or at any rate, what use they serve in moral, as opposed to other kinds of judgment. The analysis of value terms is no part of simple introspection; and since the value statements of the third part of the theory of education must be consistent, valid, and clear, the method employed to put them there must be rational and analytic, as well as simply introspective.

In its first and second divisions, the theory of education is altogether independent of ethics. With respect to the last, however, it is not. The methods that must be used to determine what moral judgments shall occupy this domain are those of ethical philosophy. Since our theory is, in this way, indebted for its method to ethics, it is not autonomous.

This heteronomy of the theory of education is not what one might think. It does not mean that ethics provides for that theory any moral judgment of its own devising. For the common-sense moral judgments the theory of education includes — selected, sorted, validated, and systematized though they be — are not the creatures of ethics. Ethical philosophy, like theory of education, must take them from the great reservoir of common sense where custom and spontaneity have deposited them. . . . Ethics, too, cannot invent new moral judgment; it must receive them from outside itself. The dependence of the theory of education on ethics is that of a theory that lacks one method which another employs, and requires what that method can produce when it works upon a body of data common to both.

Nor is this heteronomy anything more than theoretical. The person who works at the theory of education might also work at ethics. He might, himself, rationalize the common-sense moral judgments that education needs. Ethical philosophy makes a difference to education — the difference of a method that may be adequate to support the values it incorporates; but this theoretical dependence does not mean that the one profession depends upon the other. Educationists need not receive their values from philosophers. They always have the alternative of being philosophers themselves.

EDUCATIONAL VALUE STATEMENTS

CLIVE BECK

I

C. L. Stevenson, in "The Scientist's Role and the Aims of Education," has recently recommended that scientists join in the activity of making educational value statements, and that educationists have their value attitudes "straightened out under the guidance of beliefs that are well verified."[1] The argument underlying his recommendation is that since scientific knowledge is in some way relevant to questions of value in education, this knowledge must be utilized, otherwise some rather absurd educational judgments will be made, perhaps with disastrous results. As he puts it, if the scientist "won't risk making value judgments, then I'd like to ask who *is* going to make them. There's always the possibility that those who aren't reluctant to make them will turn out to be . . . complete asses."[2]

Now while this argument, and Stevenson's conclusion, seem to be unexceptionable, there are two difficulties which might be raised with respect to his discussion. The first is this: Stevenson does not provide enough information about the nature of the relevance which scientific knowledge has for educational value questions. We are not told what kinds of scientific knowledge must be sought, or by what principles conclusions are to be drawn on the basis of this knowledge. And without this information, it is difficult to see what, if anything, is being recommended. To what kinds of educational question should, say, the physicist apply himself? And what scientific knowledge should, say, the infant school teacher seek to obtain? It seems to me that Stevenson does not, even in principle, provide an answer to questions of this type.

A second difficulty in this: On Stevenson's general theory of value, there is really no sense in which one value attitude is any

Reprinted, by permission, from *The Monist*, LII, no. 1 (January, 1968): 70-86.

[1] In Israel Scheffler (ed.), *Philosophy and Education* (Boston: Allyn and Bacon, 1958), p. 50. Hereinafter cited as "The Scientist's Role."

[2] *Ibid.*, p. 44.

more legitimate than another. We might *say* that one was more legitimate, but in doing so we would be simply expressing an emotion, issuing an imperative, and performing an act of persuasion. Legitimacy in attitudes, like goodness in acts, is not an objective property or state of affairs that one can make true or false statements about. The problem, then, is that of assigning a status to Stevenson's recommendation that educationists have their attitudes "straightened out" under the guidance of well-verified beliefs. For, on the one hand, Stevenson gives the impression that straightness in attitudes is an objective property (and it is upon his giving this impression that the plausibility of his argument depends); but, on the other hand, he maintains the contradictory view that value properties cannot be objective. Of course, in a sense, Stevenson is justified in allowing this inconsistency; for if value statements are only persuasive, emotive, and imperatival utterances (as they are, on his view), one means of persuasion is (objectively) as permissible as any other. However, the paradox is that if the reader understands and accepts the general theory of value which Stevenson is advancing, he will fail to be persuaded by the recommendation which is being made.

Now, these two difficulties are related. It might be argued that, in order to achieve the aim of having his recommendation for educational inquiry adopted, all Stevenson need do is paint a vivid picture of the proposed program and its consequences, and thus awaken a response in the readers.[3] But this brings us back to the first difficulty: Stevenson does not give a clear specification of the proposed program. And this is not just an unfortunate omission. For, on an emotivist-imperativalist theory of value, one simply cannot specify which facts are relevant to value questions, or which principles must be followed in arriving at value conclusions on the basis of scientific information. Scientific propo-

---

[3] This would be in accordance with standard emotivist-imperativalist theory. See, for example, P. H. Nowell-Smith, *Ethics* (Baltimore: Penguin Books, 1954), p. 319: "The most a moral philosopher can do is to paint a picture of various types of life in the manner of Plato and ask which type of life you really want to lead." See also R. M. Hare, *The Language of Morals* (Oxford: Oxford University Press, 1952), p. 69: ". . . if pressed to justify a decision completely, we have to give a complete specification of the way of life of which it is a part."

sitions cannot even back up evaluations, despite Stevenson's claim to the contrary,[4] and hence there is no possibility whatever of arriving at criteria of relevance or principles of inference. This is why Stevenson must rely, for persuasive effect, upon giving the impression that some attitudes are objectively straighter than others; whereas, strictly speaking, his view must be that the utilization of scientific knowledge can never render value attitudes or beliefs objectively any more (or any less) correct or beneficial. On his general theory, no objective justification, in terms of "better" or "worse," can be given for the application of scientific knowledge to educational value questions.

Now, it seems clear that many scientific questions *are* relevant to educational value questions. And the great strength of Stevenson's discussion is that he gives some acknowledgment of this fact. However, nonobjectivists cannot have it both ways. It seems impossible to escape the conclusion that there are two major weaknesses in all nonobjectivist theories of educational value statements, of the kind advanced by Stevenson, R. M. Hare,[5] and D. J. O'Connor[6]: (i) they cannot, without inconsistency, explain the fact that it is important to base one's value inferences upon true premises; and (ii) they cannot furnish us with principles for determining the relevance of facts, or with principles for drawing conclusions on the basis of facts.

II

In view of these serious deficiencies in contemporary nonobjectivist accounts of educational value, one would be justified, it seems to me, in proposing some alternative accounts; and this is what I intend to do in the present paper. Of course, because of the continuing and radical disagreement among philosophers over the nature of value statements, it would be difficult to give any account of *educational* value statements which did not raise more controversial issues than could be dealt with in a single paper. However,

    [4] "The Scientist's Role," p. 50.
    [5] See "Adolescents into Adults," in T. H. B. Hollins (ed.), *Aims in Education* (Manchester: Manchester University Press, 1964), pp. 47-70.
    [6] See *An Introduction to the Philosophy of Education* (London: Routledge and Kegan Paul, 1957), Chapter 3.

one must begin somewhere. And I shall content myself with out-
lining a theory, giving some positive arguments in its support, and
showing how well it can be applied in educational contexts. In
what follows, I shall refer to the theory which I shall advance as
"EOT," this particular abbreviated form being chosen because of
the empiricist-objectivist nature of the theory.

A valuable object is always valuable *for*[7] a certain population
(or kind of population);[8] and the following is a set of logically
necessary and sufficient conditions of an object's being valuable
for a certain population: (a) it is satisfying, enjoyable, etc.
and/or leads to satisfaction, enjoyment, etc. and/or to the avoidance of dissatisfaction, pain, etc., all with respect to the population
in question; and (b) it is practicable for that population.

The list, "satisfying, enjoyable, etc.," is given here in order to
avoid the traditional charge that theories of the class to which
EOT belongs are preoccupied with pleasure, to the neglect of
other related states and experiences. The word "practicable" is
used, in a broad sense, to refer not only to the compatibility of an
object with other objects, within a framework of limited resources,
but also to the capacity of an object to promote other ends. The
inclusion of condition (b) within the conditions of an object's
being valuable has the consequence that EOT is not open to a
traditional objection to hedonism, namely, that an object may
bring satisfaction and yet not be good: on EOT such a state of
affairs is perfectly possible.

Since (a) and (b) are sufficient conditions of an object's being
valuable, and since the question of whether or not (a) and (b)
obtain is an empirical question, it follows that value statements
are empirical statements, assessable in terms of truth or falsity.
Further, a value statement is objective, in that it is nothing more
nor less than a statement that something is (objectively) the case.
It may be *made* subjectively — under the influence of some emotion or prejudice, and without due regard for the relevant facts —
but it is about some objective matter. In a sense, it is relative,

---

[7] "Valuable for" in the sense of "valuable for the lives of" rather than
"valuable in the opinion of."

[8] Correspondingly, good objects are good for a certain population, right
acts are right for a certain population, and so on. But in the interests of
brevity, we shall restrict our discussion to the valuable.

since it relates to the satisfactions, enjoyments, dissatisfactions, pains, and so on, of the population in question; but it is not relative to the beliefs or attitudes of the inquirer. To the inquirer, *qua* inquirer, it is objective.

EOT should not be confused with classical utilitarianism, according to which the criterion of value for a person P is the greatest happiness of the greatest number. On EOT, the value of an object for P depends upon the beatific properties and the practicability of the object *for* P. This does not exclude altruistic virtues or public duties: a person may perform an act precisely because it serves the well-being of another, and he may be justified in doing so. However, action for the good of others must be justifiable in terms of the agent's own well-being. Otherwise, it simply is not justifiable.

Now, unlike Stevenson's theory, EOT provides an explanation of why one must base one's value conclusions upon true premises and valid arguments. One must do so because value statements are factual statements, the truth of which depends upon their being made on the basis of true premises and valid arguments. Further, again unlike Stevenson's theory, EOT provides criteria of relevance and principles of inference. Those facts are relevant to a value question which show how and to what extent an object fulfills conditions (a) and (b) for the population concerned; and those objects are valuable which fulfill conditions (a) and (b) for the population concerned.

Apart from those advantages, there are other reasons for accepting the thesis that (a) and (b) are logically necessary and sufficient conditions of an object's being valuable. One reason for accepting (a) and (b) as logically *necessary* conditions of value is this: Valuable objects typically give rise to valuing behavior — attention, excitement, caring-for, and so on — on the part of the person(s) for whom they are valuable. And when they do not call forth such a response, the reason is either that the object is not recognized to be valuable, or that it is recognized to be valuable, but weakness of will, laziness, or the like prevents this recognition from being given full expression. Now, how is this typical response to valuable objects to be explained? It must be the case that valuable objects typically fulfill conditions (a) and (b). For if an object serves one's enjoyments, satisfactions, or pleasures (or the avoidance of dissatisfaction or pain), it is understandable if one pays attention to it and becomes excited about it; but otherwise, normally, it is not. And if an object is practicable (as well as serving one's satisfactions), it is understandable if one cares for it; but otherwise, normally, it is not. One may conclude, then, that valuable objects typically fulfill conditions (a) and (b); and this conclusion gives support to (though it does not establish) the view that (a) and (b) are logically necessary conditions of an object's being valuable.

Another reason for accepting this view is the following: It is commonly held, apparently with justification, that an object's being valuable for a person provides a reason for action for that person. This is held to be logically so: it is not just a contingent fact about value and reasons for action. But if a valuable object does not serve the satisfactions, enjoyments, or pleasures (or the avoidance of dissatisfaction or pain) of the person for whom it is valuable, or is not practicable for that person, how could its "value" ever provide a reason for action for that person? Why should a person do something which does not fulfill these conditions?[9] It would seem that if the reason-giving nature of value statements is to be explained, it must be acknowledged that valuable objects logically necessarily fulfill conditions (a) and (b).[10]

But are (a) and (b) logically *sufficient* conditions of an object's being valuable? It seems to me that they are. For, on the one hand, they form the basis for a concept of value which is coherent within itself, and which adequately explains the typical response to valuable objects and the reason-giving nature of value statements; and, on the other hand, there seem to be no other independent logically necessary conditions of an object's being valuable.

[9] A person may well have reason to promote the happiness of another, but only if doing so is essential to his own well-being. This is so even in moral situations, although in the case of moral actions one often does not have one's own well-being *in mind* while performing the action.

[10] For a variant of this argument, see G. E. M. Anscombe, *Intention* (Oxford: Basil Blackwell, 1958), paras. 35-41; and Philippa Foot, "Moral Beliefs," *Proceedings of the Aristotelian Society*, LIX: 83-104. Anscombe and Foot make wants, rather than satisfactions, dissatisfactions, etc. the ultimate criterion of value; but the general structure of their argument is the same.

It has sometimes been suggested that societal approval is a logically necessary condition of an object's being valuable; but surely an object (say, an educative experience) may be valuable for a certain person without that person, or anyone else, approving it or even being aware of its value. Again, it has been suggested that a divine ordinance is required in order to make certain types of object valuable; but it seems clear that the mere fact that "God ordained it" does not furnish one with a reason for action. There must be some other factor as well, such as that one takes delight in obeying God, or that God punishes the disobedient. But this brings us again to conditions (a) and (b). It would seem that if conditions (a) and (b) are not fulfilled, an object cannot be valuable, no matter what other conditions obtain; but if they are fulfilled, then logically necessarily the object is valuable, even if none of the other proposed conditions obtains.

III

We must now embark upon a systematic though necessarily brief survey of the advantages afforded by EOT in the field of education. This study will serve not only to demonstrate the merits of EOT as a theory of *educational* value statements but also to extend the account of EOT given so far. To begin with, and as a sequel to the discussion of Section I, we shall take up the problem of nonfact-stating utterances: emotive utterances, imperatives, persuasive utterances, and so on.

It is apparent that a large proportion of educational utterances which are of the form "X is good" or "Y ought to be done" are not, when taken as a whole, fact-stating. For example, emotive utterances, commands, instructions, persuasive utterances, decision utterances (that is, utterances which incorporate a decision as an integral element), warnings, exhortations, and recommendations often occur in educational contexts in value statement form. But clearly, an expression of emotion or a command does not state that something is the case, and cannot be assessed in terms of truth or falsity. It would be absurd to respond to the exclamation "Bother!" with "Yes, that's true," or to greet the instruction "Draw this vase" with "No, that's false." And similar remarks may be made about all the other nonfact-stating utterances men-

tioned. Are we to conclude, then, that value statements which
are incorporated in utterances of the kind in question are nonfact-stating and incapable of being assessed in terms of truth or
falsity?

If we have an objectivist theory, such as EOT, this is not necessary. In every case, a distinction may be drawn between the value
statement incorporated and the total nonfact-stating utterance in
which it is incorporated; and the value statement so distinguished
may be described as "factual" and assessed in terms of truth or
falsity. Suppose that the utterance is, "It is not good to cover
such a wide range of topics in a history course," coming as an
emotive and imperatival utterance of a school principal to a history master whom he dislikes. Considered as an expression of irri-
tation and as a command, the utterance is not factual or assessable
in terms of truth or falsity. But the factual claim which is incorporated in the total utterance can be singled out and verified or
falsified on the basis of empirical evidence. Is it *really* bad for the
classes in question (whose well-being the teacher is concerned to
promote) to be covering a wide range of topics rather than study-
ing a few topics intensively? Which approach will serve best to
deepen their historical awareness and increase their grasp of historical concepts? Which approach will enable them to gain the
most benefit, in terms of ability to appreciate and grapple with the
world in which they live? In short, which approach will best serve
their happiness, in the long run and on the whole? These questions
can be asked and, in principle, answered, quite independently of
any assessment of the total nonfact-stating utterance in which the
value statement is incorporated. There is no need to see the expression of emotion and the imperative as elements within the
value statement, which render it nonfactual. Indeed, the converse
is the case: The value statement is an element within the emotive,
imperatival utterance, which serves to define and give support to
the utterance.

One advantage of EOT, then, is that it provides the basis for a
clear and convincing account of nonfact-stating educational utterances, of the kind in question. And, hence, it provides a procedure
for the assessment of such utterances: First, the value claim is
to be assessed, in terms of truth or falsity; then, on this basis and

in the light of other relevant facts (about the conventions involved, the precise nature of the speech situation, and so on), the appropriateness of the total utterance is to be determined.

IV

Another advantage of EOT is that it enables one to explain what might be called the "contextual relativity" of educational value statements. It has often been claimed that, in certain instances at least, one educator may legitimately deny a value proposition which another educator, equally legitimately, has asserted. For example, of a certain geography text, a primary school teacher may say, "That is not a good text," and a high school teacher, "That is a good text," and each be making a true statement. Such cases have been seen as providing a problem for objectivists and as casting doubt upon the worthwhileness of making educational value statements, except as a persuasive device.

On EOT, however, it is possible to explain such cases in terms of the principle that a valuable object is always valuable for a certain population. If both of the statements in the example are in fact true, it is likely that they may be filled out in some such way as this: "That is not a good text (for primary school classes such as ours); it is too theoretical in its approach, the vocabulary is too difficult, and it relies too much upon independent library research on the part of the pupil"; and, "That is a good text (for high school classes such as ours); it helps the students to gain a firm grasp of basic concepts, and it encourages them to make use of journals and reference material." Clearly, there is no contradiction here; for each teacher has a different population in mind and is not asserting anything which the other would be concerned to deny. Of course, if what was in question was the accuracy of the information given in the text, then the two statements would be contradictory; and one or the other of them would be false. Again, if what was at issue was the theory of geography underlying the book, the statements would be contradictory. But since the staters are concerned with the suitability of the text for different populations, and since what is seen as a weakness from the point of view of one population is seen as a strength from the point of view of the other, it is apparent that there are two different statements involved, and not the affirmation and denial of the *same* statement. Hence, the fact that both statements are justified need not force us to accept some form of value skepticism.[11]

V

A further advantage of EOT, similar in certain respects to the previous one, is that it enables one to cope, at the theoretical level, with differences in educational thought and practice from one nation or culture to another. Two problems have been associated with educational differences of this kind. One the one hand, it has been felt that these differences are so extensive that they cannot be explained merely in terms of natural prejudice and differences of opinion, and hence that one must resort to a nonobjectivist theory of value statements. On the other hand, and partly on the basis of the first conclusion, it has been queried whether one can carry out a valid assessment of the educational doctrines and practices of other nations and cultures.

On EOT, however, a great many differences in educational aims and practices can be explained in terms of differences (a) in what brings satisfaction, enjoyment, dissatisfaction, pain, and so on to different populations and (b) in what is practicable for different populations. Take, for example, the case where, because of cultural differences, the art courses given in the schools of two countries differ markedly in their content, the emphasis in each case reflecting local tastes and appreciations. On EOT, it may be quite legitimate for these school art courses to be worked out largely in the light of the artistic traditions of the respective countries in which the courses are given. For, in general, if a person does not learn to appreciate those (good) art forms with which

[11] The question might be raised: Why choose one population rather than another? The answer is that the population in question is determined by the original value claim. A value claim must have some population reference, if it is to be a claim at all; and the truth or falsity of the claim is to be determined in the light of this population reference. But what if some other stater chooses a different population? Then his claim is to be assessed relative to *that* population. But why favor one population rather than another? We are now in the realm of acting rather than stating; and the answer will depend upon the interests and responsibilities of the agent(s) concerned (see Section VI, below).

he is or can be in constant contact, he will miss out on a considerable amount of aesthetic satisfaction, and will to an extent be alienated, quite unnecessarily, from his fellow countrymen. Hence, the differences in educational thought and practice here need not reflect a vicious value relativism, but may be based soundly upon genuine differences in the appreciations and circumstances of the populations concerned.

Again, take the case of a relatively poor country, in which it is necessary for the state schools to make do with what other nations might describe as inadequate school buildings, insufficient staff, and too short a period of schooling for the less intelligent child. These limitations upon the educational system are unfortunate, but they cannot be helped, for the present at least; and statements made within this context about what is good educationally and what ought to be done must simply take these limitations into account. Now, it would be easy for a superficial observer of this situation to judge that the nation in question held education in very low esteem and did not see the necessity for "good" educational facilities. However, on EOT, there need not be any disagreement between nations here, but simply differences in practice arising quite understandably out of differences in what is practicable.

A great many national and cultural differences in education, then, may be explained (on EOT) in such terms and hence shown not to involve value disagreement at all.[12] Of course, genuine disagreement does occur over educational questions. But it seems possible that this may be explained in terms of bias and prejudice (to which value beliefs are peculiarly susceptible), in terms of ideological affiliation, and so on, apart from the normal factors making for differences between experts in any field of inquiry.

On EOT, then, it is possible to take cultural differences into account without placing educational value questions beyond the scope of rational assessment. Educational value is culturally relative in the sense that, if being brought up in a certain culture re-

[12] Morris Ginsberg, in his *On the Diversity of Morals* (London: Mercury paperback ed., 1962), Chapter VII, provides a much more detailed account of the way in which value differences may be explained without adopting a viciously relativistic position.

sults in a people's temperament and circumstances being different from those of a people which has a different culture, and if there is no reason for either group to change their temperament or circumstances, then what is educationally valuable for the one group will differ in certain respects from what is educationally valuable for the other. However, educational value is *not* culturally relative in the sense that it is relative to what is commonly believed or asserted to be valuable within a particular society (which is the more usual sense in which value is said to be "culturally relative"). Thus, the value beliefs and assertions of the members of a certain culture can be mistaken; and hence "culture criticism" is possible. But cultural differences are not to be ignored, for they are often such that what is valuable for the people of one culture is not valuable for the people of another.

VI

Yet another advantage of EOT is that it opens up the possibility of giving genuine reasons for action (a) to educationists and (b) to those being educated. For what better reason could one have for performing a certain action than that it serves one's happiness and is practicable? Thus, prescription, exhortation, and advice, both within the school and at various other points throughout the education system, may be placed upon a sound footing.

Of course, if an action *cannot* be defended in terms of what is satisfying, enjoyable, and so on and practicable for the agent himself, then reasons for performing it cannot be given, on EOT. But why induce people to perform actions which will not serve their happiness? This is surely not the aim of most educators. And while it is *precisely* the goal of *some* educators, in certain phases of their activity at least, such inducement must be rendered more difficult by an open rejection of the doctrine that an educational object may be good for a person and yet not serve his happiness.

It might be objected that, while EOT obviously provides a basis for exhorting the child and for advising the altruistic educator, it takes no account of the educator who is concerned only for his own well-being and that of his relatives and friends. How can he be shown that he ought to join in concerted educational enterprises, aimed at promoting the well-being of the child? Surely, EOTs will prove to be inadequate for this task.

However, it is clear that united educational activities would not break down if EOT was generally accepted. In the first place, in the great majority of cases, educationists are dependent upon the approval of some group or groups: for example, a voting population or an employing authority. If they do not, as far as possible, protect the interests entrusted to them, they are liable to be relieved of their positions, or at least denied promotion to higher positions. Accordingly, they *ought* to strive for the well-being of a much wider population than the one the well-being of which would normally be connected with their own happiness. Of course, to have the fear of incurring disapproval or of losing one's position as the sole reason for discharging one's responsibilities as an educator would normally be considered unworthy. But it serves as an important *supplementary* reason, at times, even for the most idealistic of educators.

Second, and more positively, educators normally desire to receive approbation for the quality of their work, whether from students, from fellow educators, from parents, or from a wider public. Accordingly, they have reason to carry out skillfully and thoroughly the task of legislation, administration, or instruction assigned to them.

Third, and still more positively, most educators, when they are placed in charge of a population whose well-being they are required to promote through education, soon come to have a desire for the well-being of some and perhaps all of the members of that population. They acquire a concern for the persons placed in their care and experience a genuine satisfaction at seeing their happiness promoted.

Fourth, educators normally come to acquire a professional and even an aesthetic interest in achieving the tasks assigned to them. Simply to see a piece of administration or a course of instruction taking a balanced and integrated form and serving its function comes to be a source of satisfaction in itself, especially when it is the result of one's own efforts.

And finally, there is the moral consideration that if one is in a position in which one has the opportunity to promote the well-being of others, one ought to take that opportunity, provided that it is the case, as it would seem to be, that at least a certain degree of morality is important for a man's happiness in society.[13]

Thus, if an object really is educationally valuable, on EOT, both the educand and the educator may be given sound reasons for seeking it.

VII

One other advantage of EOT is that it provides a basis for integrated inquiry into means and ends in education. It is commonly recognized that there is a close connection between questions of means and questions of ends; but for adherents of nonobjectivist theories of value this has presented a difficulty: How can a systematic, empirical inquiry into educational method be carried on while the question of aims keeps obtruding? Some have "overcome" this problem by making a sharp distinction between the two. G. S. Maccia, for example, distinguishes between the scientifically based technology of education on the one hand, and the goals to be attained on the other. He says that "the goals to be attained are not scientifically examined. They are simply asserted, and science is used to determine ways of achieving them.[14] However, this solution is not a very satisfactory one, even on nonobjectivist assumptions, as is evidenced by Stevenson's "The Scientist's Role," discussed earlier. It does seem that scientific propositions are often relevant to questions of ends, and that the formulation of means normally involves making certain assumptions about what is good as an end.

Now, on EOT, there is no general problem here. Since value questions are empirical, there is no reason why inquiry into means

[13] For a detailed defense of the view that morality "pays," see Philippa Foot, *op. cit.*, Section II. It is necessary to distinguish between "a reason for acting" and "one's reason in acting." While it is true that a considerable amount of moral behavior requires one's not having one's own well-being *in mind* at the time of action, yet this does not preclude one's reflecting at other times upon the importance for oneself of being moral and developing moral virtues.

[14] G. S. Maccia, "Science and Science in Education," in G. F. Kneller (ed.), *Foundations of Education* (New York: John Wiley and Sons, 1963), p. 362.

and inquiry into ends should not be carried on together. Indeed, they must be carried on together, if either is to be successful. According to EOT, while it is certainly possible to draw a distinction within educational theory between propositions about what is good as a means and propositions about what is good as an end, this distinction is not sufficiently important to justify the large amount of attention often accorded to it by educational philosophers. On the one hand, all educational value statements, whether about means or about ends, raise "ultimate" value questions. Even the statement, "This X is a (instrumentally) good X," *pace* D. J. O'Connor,[15] means more than that the X is efficient; for what is being claimed is not merely that the X is efficient, but that, being efficient, it is good, since efficiency is a good thing, serving as it does our well-being. And, on the other hand, all value statements, whether about ends or about means, make an (implicit or explicit) claim about means: that certain means are practicable, or that practicable means either are available or could conceivably be made available. Thus, if in formulating educational means one disregarded the question of educational ends, one would be faced with an endless and largely pointless task of developing every means which might possibly be of value in education. Strictly speaking, one would not even know which means "might possibly have value in education"; for this raises "ultimate" value questions. And if in formulating educational ends, one disregarded the question of educational means, it would be impossible to progress beyond affirming the value of happiness, health, material possessions, and a few other general goods. Even this would not really provide one with educational goals at which to aim, for perhaps a high degree of happiness, say, is impossible in our contemporary world, and should not be sought after; or perhaps care for one's health is incompatible with the pursuit of the fullest happiness.

On EOT, then, it is possible to explain why it is the case, as it would seem to be, that questions of means and questions of ends are inseparable; further, it is possible to construct a general framework for integrated inquiry into means and ends in education.

[15] *Op. cit.,* p. 53.

VIII

The final advantage of EOT which I wish to consider is that it throws light upon the question of the nature of educational theory. It is generally acknowledged that a large proportion of the propositions which go to make up what has traditionally been called "educational theory" are value propositions: propositions about what is good or what ought to be done in education. However, this constitutes a problem for a nonobjectivist who wishes to give an account of the nature of educational theory and defend the view that there is such a body (or group of bodies) of theory. For if educational value propositions are merely expressions of emotion, imperatives, or persuasive utterances, they are simply not describable as "theory." For theory by its very nature is about some objective matter.

But on EOT there is no difficulty here, at least in general. All educational propositions, whether they are value propositions or not, are about some objective matter and may be included within educational theory, provided they are sufficiently precise and have been advanced with due attention to the relevant facts. And the term "educational theory" can be used with significance, having reference to a group of bodies of theory, the ultimate purpose of which is to indicate what aims should be pursued and what principles and methods used in the practice of education. Apart from propositions about how and to what end education should be carried on, educational theory will include those propositions which are the fruit of such inquiries as educational psychology, educational sociology, educational history, comparative education, and educational research.[16]

A query might be raised about the possibility, even on EOT, of rendering educational value statements sufficiently precise to justify the use of the word "theory" with respect to them. However, while it is true that a statement such as "Group discussion is a valuable educational tool," as it stands, is imprecise, the same may be said of a great many propositions in, say, social theory, when

---

[16] There is also a narrower sense of "educational theory" in which the term has reference only to those propositions which represent the final stages of the inquiry into how and to what end education should be carried on.

taken in isolation: consider, for example, the proposition, "In primitive societies the social structure is more rigid than in nonprimitive societies." What is a primitive society, a social structure, rigidity? But clearly the propositions of social theory may be made sufficiently precise to justify the use of the term "theory"; and the same is true of value propositions. One method is that of giving explicit definitions. But the much more usual method is that of making one's assertions within the context of a whole body of theory, including propositions about techniques, propositions about human nature, propositions about what has happened in the past and what is likely to happen in the future, propositions about the findings of research, and so on. In this way, the meaning of each proposition may be specified, implicitly, by other propositions within the body of theory.[17]

IX

It does seem, then, that EOT has considerable applicability within the field of education. And this fact, together with the fact that plausible positive arguments may be adduced in its support, give strength to the claim that EOT provides an adequate account of educational value statements. Of course, the foregoing discussion has not been sufficient to establish EOT; in particular, more attention needs to be given to the objections inherent in contemporary nonobjectivist theories of value, and to objections based upon the phenomenon of value disagreement. However, sufficient has been said to show that EOT is worthy of consideration as a theory of educational value statements.

[17] B. P. Komisar and J. E. McClellan, in "The Logic of Slogans," in B. O. Smith and R. H. Ennis (eds.), *Language and Concepts in Education* (Chicago: Rand McNally, 1961), give a useful account of the way in which educational propositions may form a self-interpreting "system." Their account of educational value statements, however, is rather different from the one offered in this paper.

EDUCATIONAL OBJECTIVES
AND THE CONDUCT OF SCHOOLING

INTRODUCTION

As things are there is disagreement about the things to be taught, whether we look to virtue or the best life. Neither is it clear whether education should be more concerned with intellectual or moral virtue. The existing practice is perplexing; no one knows on what principle we should proceed — should the useful in life, or should virtue, or should the higher knowledge be the aim of our training; all three opinions have been entertained. Again about the means there is no agreement; for different persons, starting with different ideas about the nature of virtue, naturally disagree about the practice of it. . . .[1]

After considering some two thousand years of controversy concerning the aims of education, John Dewey discussed the danger to education of "externally imposed ends" and remarked, "It is well to remind ourselves that education as such has no aims. Only persons, parents, teachers, etc., have aims, not an abstract process like education."[2] More recently, Richard S. Peters has posed the question "Must an Educator Have an Aim?"[3] and, without reference to Dewey's analysis, has concluded ". . . it is erroneously assumed that education must be justified by reference to an end which is extrinsic to it."

It seems clear, however, that both Dewey and Peters regard education (both as concept and as activity) as being highly value-laden or directed. Just because education should not be regarded as primarily an instrumentality for the attainment of some external aim or end, it does not follow that education is neutral with respect to values or without value direction. For example, one could learn what is false and evil, but such learning would surely be called miseducative rather than educative. Such a value orientation is built into the concept and into all activities that are called educational. This stands in contrast to "learning" which does not

---

[1] From the Jowett translation of Aristotle's *Politics* (Oxford: Clarendon Press, 1885), p. 245.

[2] *Democracy and Education* (New York: Macmillan, 1916), p. 125.

[3] In *Authority, Responsibility, and Education,* 2nd ed. (London: George Allen and Unwin, 1963).

seem to have such a built-in value orientation.[4] "Teaching,"
which is in the middle in more ways than one, is treated by many
as being neutral, but by others (e.g., Scheffler) it is given a pro-
grammatic definition that ties it to education.

If the concept "education" is always value-laden, then questions
of personal or cultural relativism arise. But is seems that neither
Dewey nor Peters would settle for a relativistic account of education's built-in value. Peters has written that "It would be a logical
contradiction to say that a man had been educated but that he
had in no way changed for the better, or that in educating his son
a man was attempting nothing worth-while."[5] But when taken in
context it seems very likely that Peters is concerned with much
more than the logic of a manner of speaking. For Peters, questions
of "the better" or of what is "worthwhile" are not to be settled on
the basis of unsupported opinion either personal or social. Dewey
once remarked, "That education is literally and all the time its
own reward means that no alleged study or discipline is educative
unless it is worth while in its own immediate having"; nevertheless,
he preferred as a test (or as the necessary and sufficient conditions) for education, not "worthwhileness" but the following definition: "It is that reconstruction or reorganization of experience
which adds to the meaning of experience, and which increases
ability to direct the course of subsequent experience."[6] Many
things may seem worthwhile in the having but their educative
power must be assessed in terms of effect in subsequent experience.
And for Dewey, effect is to be judged not by compatibility with
personal or social preference but by demonstrable increased
control.

No doubt an important difference in value theory between
Dewey and Peters becomes evident at this point in spite of their
mutual abhorrence of externally imposed aims for education.
Peters evidently believes that the "worthwhileness" of worthwhile
(or intrinsically valuable) activities is some sort of objective (perhaps inherent) property and that some things, say, poetry, have

[4] Although Frankena, perhaps inadvertently, says ". . . we do not call
the formation of undersirable dispositions education or *learning*" (from
the article included in this section — italics mine).
[5] *Ethics and Education* (Chicago: Scott, Foresman, 1967), p. 3.
[6] *Democracy and Education*, pp. 89-90.

more of this "built in" than others, say, push-pin. By contrast, Dewey views "intrinsic" or "worthwhile in the immediate having" as merely a mode of valuing, and a mode that stands in sharp contrast to "evaluating," i.e., the objective assessment of value. For Dewey, the educationally relevant question about poetry and push-pin is not which is more worthwhile in its own right, but what are the effects in subsequent experience of teaching one rather than the other. Which results in greater increased control?

The fact that Dewey and Peters, starting from significantly different philosophic positions, can, nevertheless, agree about the disvalue of externally imposed aims, the value of poetry, and many other issues concerning the matter and manner of education, raises interesting questions about the relation of philosophic and educational problems.

Dewey has said: "When we come to act in a tangible way we have to select or choose a particular act at a particular time, but any number of comprehensive ends may exist without competition, since they mean simply different ways of looking at the same scene ... the different views had when different mountains are ascended supplement one another; they do not set up incompatible, competing worlds."[7] Presumably, by "comprehensive ends" reference is intended to general aims of education based upon philosophic conceptions of the nature of man, the nature of the good life, etc. What Dewey is advocating is, of course, not eclecticism, but a principle of complementarity. Written in this same spirit is our first selection for this section, "Educational Values and Goals: Some Dispositions to Be Fostered," by William K. Frankena. Does the Frankena article shed any light upon the question of what ought to be the relationship between a person's "position" with respect to the fundamental questions of general philosophy and the educational policies and practices that he advocates or supports?

In the next selection, Professor Broudy notes that administrators of any institution should operate on "the principle of least principle." This is to say that with respect to valuational problems, administrators should (for the sake of institutional stability) try to resolve disputes at the rule, procedure, or policy level rather

[7] *Ibid.,* p. 128.

than permitting an escalation to the level of fundamental principles. For Broudy believes that "when the issue is reduced to stark 'yes' and 'no' saying to a fundamental principle, the only action possible is war and the destruction of at least one of the contending parties." Nevertheless, the administrator of educational institutions is in a unique position and is not permitted the same moral latitude afforded to other public servants. To be an educational administrator, therefore, "One needs administrative adroitness to prevent raising the moral issue at every turn, but there must also be the moral integrity to recognize a moral issue when there is one and to deal with it morally when no moral alternative can honestly be entertained."

Is it the case, however, that there must necessarily be such a sharp break or discontinuity between "moral principles" and the valuational norms that operate at the "rule, procedure, or policy level"? The conduct of education is pervaded by valuational questions, ranging from the comparative worth or value of various subject matters and teaching strategies to the appropriateness (in, say, our democratic society) of various ethical or moral principles as part of either the matter of education, the manner of education, or both. Is this whole range of value questions subject to inquiry and decision that is reasonable and rational, or are some of the questions (perhaps those involving moral principles) subject only to "stark 'yes' and 'no' saying"?

At this point the reader may wish to consider whether democracy can be expressed as a set of principles (formulated on an ethical rather than a metaphysical level) and whether such a democratic ethic provides an adequate "fundamental commitment" for American schooling operating in an open society in which every person is free to hold whatever metaphysical position seems to him to offer the best justification for the democratic ethic. Given such a commitment, are all lesser valuational problems encountered in the conduct of schooling subject, at least in principle, to orderly investigation and reasonable resolution? Or if the central purpose of schooling in our society is "to educate," and if "education" has certain values or at least "direction" built into it, then, perhaps, education itself will suffice for a "fundamental commitment" without direct reference even to democracy.

In this connection the reader may wish to review Dewey's brief discussion of "The Valuation of Studies,"[8] in which he brings his own theory of valuation to bear upon the question of what studies should be included in the curriculum. The discussion proceeds entirely "within" his concept of education. This is to say that no reference is made to any external objectives or standards (e.g., the nature of man, the good life, the values of democracy, or the like). Dewey believed that since his conception of education is identical with "the operation of living a life which is fruitful and inherently significant," it follows that the various studies and activities that make up the curriculum should not be viewed as subordinate means to this end but as ingredients of the process. He then reasoned, in effect, that while any topic which has an immediate appeal to students (i.e., which they value intrinsically or as "worthwhile") has a prima facie claim to be included in the curriculum, one should ask, in view of the shortness of time, if some other appealing topic has greater instrumental value. In any event, the ideal should be that whatever is studied should be presented in such a way that students develop an interest in it for its own sake, or failing this, that they see its instrumental value for something that is of real concern to them. And "apart from the needs of a particular situation in which choice has to be made, there is no such thing as degrees or order of value."

These remarks by John Dewey may seem quite inadequate for determining the scope and sequence of the curriculum unless one remembers that a vital part of the "particular situation in which choice has to be made" is, on the one hand, competent teachers and curriculum-makers who are themselves, hopefully, "living a life which is fruitful and inherently significant" and on the other, students already vibrant with interests and concerns that have momentum and direction. Dewey was not concerned with providing a formula for building a curriculum from zero, but rather with making suggestions as to how we may choose more wisely from the overwhelming array of materials that are suggested by tradition, by educational research, and by teaching experience.

Concerning the scheme of values that the teacher brings to curriculum-making and the many other tasks of teaching, the next selection, by J. F. Perry and Philip G. Smith, suggests a mode of

[8] *Ibid.,* pp. 279-285.

analysis (based on the work of Henry D. Aiken) that "may be useful in a consideration of the bewildering maze of valuational problems that run through the theory and practice of education." After noting that the same valuational terms perform different functions in different situations, it is suggested that valuational discourse takes place on four noticeably different levels with "different kinds of arguments, objections, and 'good reasons' appropriate or relevant at each level." The article then presents a brief discussion of some of the problems encountered at each level of valuational discourse in the context of education.

In the final selection Professor Clayton notes "the central and pervasive role of value judgments" not only in teaching but in the study of education. He sees a responsibility of philosophy of education to provide "disciplined guidance about the evaluation of value judgments and to recommend methods and procedures to reduce the arbitrary character of value claims." After differentiating the normative sense of "value" from descriptive and other uses, Professor Clayton discusses in some detail certain "middle-range" valuational problems that arise in the study and practice of education.

EDUCATIONAL VALUES AND GOALS:
SOME DISPOSITIONS TO BE FOSTERED

WILLIAM K. FRANKENA

I

There has been much impatience with what R. S. Peters calls "the endless talk about the aims of education," but this talk continues to go on, and we are invited to add to it on this happy occasion. Indeed, those who deny that education has ends or that educators must have aims seem always to end up talking about much the same thing in a slightly different idiom. At any rate, I am quite ready, at least on this occasion, to assume that there are values or goals which it is the business of education to promote, whether they are external, imposed, and far-off, or internal, autonomous, and nearby. I shall also assume that the values or goals which education is to promote consist of certain abilities, dispositions, habits, or traits. To have a single term for them I shall call them "dispositions," taking this word not in the narrower ordinary "sunny disposition" sense, but in the wider one common among philosophers.[1] So far as I am aware, there is really only one view that might reject the concept of dispositions in this sense, namely, existentialism,[2] and, as we shall see, even it seems to advocate our developing certain dispositions or, if you prefer, choosing certain postures.

Which dispositions is education to foster, then? Desirable ones, of course, since we do not call the formation of undesirable dispositions education or learning, but which ones are these? One answer is that the task of education is to foster the dispositions desired or regarded as desirable by the society doing (or paying for) the educating. This answer has a certain practical realism about it,

Reprinted, by permission, from *The Monist*, LII, no. 1 (January, 1968): 1-10.

[1] Dewey prefers the word "habit" but uses "disposition" also. See *Human Nature and Conduct* (New York: Henry Holt, 1922), end of Pt. I, Section I; *Democracy and Education* (New York: Macmillan paperback ed., 1966), p. 328.

[2] See O. F. Bollnow, *Existenzphilosophie und Pädagogik* (Stuttgart: W. Kohlhammer Verlag, 1962), pp. 14ff.

but it is hardly a philosophical one, since it equates the desirable with what is desired or thought to be desirable. A properly philosophical reply would say that the desirable dispositions are those required either for the moral life, the life of right action, or for the good life, a life of intrinsically worthwhile activities. I shall not try now, however, to present even an outline of the content of the good life, of the requirements of the moral life, or of the dispositions to be fostered in view of them. Instead, I shall take a somewhat different approach, also philosophical in a sense, which strikes me as interesting. I shall look at the three main movements in recent philosophy to see what dispositions they advocate our fostering. What interests me is that, different as they are, these three movements seem to offer us, not indeed the same, but *supplementary* lists of dispositions which we may combine, perhaps with certain corrections and additions.

In doing this I do not mean to aid and abet the tendency toward eclecticism already too far advanced in so-called philosophy of education, which I join Reginald Archambault and others in decrying.[3] I should hope and maintain that the promotion of the dispositions to be mentioned can be defended on a properly philosophical basis and must be eschewed if it cannot be. On the other hand, I think that it can be defended on more than one philosophical basis, and that we may agree on the following lists of dispositions even though we start from different philosophical premises. This is one reason why I am taking the approach I do. Each of us must have a philosophy of his own which serves as the basis of his thoughts on education, not just an eclectical synthesis of philosophical phrases and social science jargon, but, at least in the area of public education, formal or informal, we must manage some kind of agreement in our working conclusions about the dispositions to be promoted.

In what I shall say I can of course, only be rough and suggestive, rather than accurate or complete.

II

The three movements I refer to are (1) Deweyan experimental-

[3] R. Archambault (ed.), *Philosophical Analysis and Education* (London: Routledge and Kegan Paul, 1965), p. 3.

ism, instrumentalism, or pragmatism, (2) analytical philosophy, and (3) existentialism (*cum* phenomenology). These, apart from Thomism and Marxism, are the main currents in western philosophy today. Let us consider first Deweyanism, the philosophical movement most familiar to American educators. What is characteristic here, so far as education is concerned, is its emphasis on what Sidney Hook calls, "the centrality of method," the method of reflective thinking, scientific intelligence, or experimental inquiry. The concept of the method, with its five stages, is well known. It is thought of as *the* method of thinking, and the main task of education is regarded as that of fostering the habit of thinking in this way in all areas of thought and action. Get the power of thinking thus, Dewey virtually said, and all other things will be added unto you. What interests me now is the fact that this habit of thought is conceived of as involving a whole family of dispositions: curiosity, sensitivity to problems, observational perceptiveness, regard for empirical fact and verification, imaginative skill at thinking up hypotheses, persistence, flexibility, open-mindedness, acceptance of responsibility for consequences, and the like. Being associated with thinking, these dispositions have a strongly intellectual cast, though Deweyans reject the distinction between intellectual and moral dispositions and think of them as at least quasi-moral — and sometimes stress this practical aspect of them so much as to be charged with *anti*-intellectualism. They are dispositions whose matrix is the practice of empirical science. If we assume that this practice is one of the things human beings must be good at, then we may take this family of dispositions as among those to be fostered, even if we do not conceive of them exactly as Dewey did.

Analytical philosophy comes in various styles and must not be identified with either the logical positivism and therapeutic logico-analysis of yesteryear or the ordinary language philosophy of today. In one style or another it has become more or less dominant in British and American philosophy, and is beginning to be influential in the philosophy of education.[4] Now, analytical philosophers of all sorts have tended to adjure the actual making or propounding of ethical, normative, or value judgments, and to be

---

[4] See *ibid.*, pp. 6, 13.

chary about laying down aims or principles for education and about making educational recommendations. They tend to limit philosophy to conceptual and linguistic analysis and methodological clarification. This attitude has been relaxing lately, but, in any case, there is a set of dispositions which are held dear by all analytical philosophers, no matter how purist: clarity, consistency, rigor of thought, concern for semantic meaningfulness, methodological awareness, consciousness of assumptions, and so on. These dispositions have been nicely characterized as "logical values" or "values in speaking [and thinking]" by J. N. Findlay.[5] Typically, analytical philosophers think, with some justice, that these values have been neglected both in theory and practice by Deweyans and existentialists, as well as by speculative philosophers, Hegelian, Whiteheadian, etc. — and especially by nonanalytical philosophers of education. Whether they are right or wrong in this, it does seem clear that their values should be among our goals of education at all levels. The title of a recent book proclaims that clarity is not enough,[6] and perhaps it is not, but it is nevertheless something desirable, and even imperative, both in our thinking about education and in our thinking about other things.

Existentialism is characteristically opposed both to analytical philosophy (though there are now some attempts at a rapprochement between these two movements) and to pragmatic empiricism. It is suspicious, among other things, of the "objectivity" so much prized, in different ways, by these other two movements. The implications of existentialism for education have begun to get attention from O. F. Bollnow and others,[7] but this is not what concerns me now. What interests me is that existentialism presents us with a third family of dispositions to be fostered: authenticity, decision, commitment, autonomy, individuality, fidelity, responsibility, etc. These are definitely moral (or, at any rate, "practical") dispositions as compared with the more intellectual, logical, or scientific ones stressed by Deweyan and analytical philosophers; but they are moral or practical dispositions that relate to the

[5] See *Language, Mind and Value* (London, 1963), pp. 105-127.

[6] H. D. Lewis (ed.), *Clarity Is Not Enough* (London, 1963).

[7] See Bollnow, *op. cit.;* G. F. Kneller, *Existentialism and Education* (New York, 1958); Van Cleve Morris, *Existentialism in Education* (New York, 1965).

manner of life rather than to its *content* — not to *what* we do so much as to *how* we do it. To quote a recent writer: "Existential morality is notorious for its lack of content. But it does not cease for that reason to be morality. Everything is in the manner, as its sponsors would, and do, say."

As one of these sponsors does say:

> Value lies not so much in what we do as in how we exist and maintain ourselves in time . . . words like *authentic, genuine, real,* and *really* . . . express those more basic "existential values," as we may call them, which underlie all the valuable things that we do or say. Since they characterize our ways of existing in the world, they are universal in scope, and apply to every phase and region of our care. There is nothing that we say, or think, or do that may not be done either authentically . . . or unauthentically. . . . They are not "values" at all, in the traditional sense of this term, for they cannot be understood apart. . . . They are patterns of our lived existence in the world.[8]

I do not wish to suggest that an "existential" manner or posture is enough, and certainly not that we should be in a state of "anxiety" all the time, but it does seem plausible to maintain that there is a place in education for the development of such "existential" virtues along with others supplementing or even modifying them. There is at least *some* point in "the underground man's" remark in Dostoevsky's *Notes,* "perhaps, after all there is more 'life' in me than in you."

III

Thus we see that even though representatives of all three of our philosophical movements are typically reluctant to "talk about the aims of education," each movement itself enshrines or espouses certain dispositions that may well be included among the aims of education by those of us who do not mind such talk. The three philosophies are in general opposed to one another, and one cannot simply combine them, but the dispositions they value may be

---

[8] See respectively, C. Smith, *Contemporary French Philosophy* (London, 1964), p. 229; J. D. Wild, *Existence and the World of Freedom* (Englewood Cliffs, N.J.: Prentice-Hall, 1963), pp. 161-165. See also Whitehead's remarks on "style" in *Aims of Education* (New York: New American Library, Mentor Books, 1949), p. 24.

combined and included in our list of those to be cultivated in education, though perhaps not without some pulling and hauling. This is the main point I wish to make. I should like, however, to subjoin a few further points.

(1) Of course, we can espouse the Deweyan list of dispositions, even if we do not conceive them exactly as he does, only if we assume that empirical inquiry of a scientific kind is a good thing — sufficient, necessary, or at least helpful to the good or the moral life. This, however, is an assumption that would be denied only by certain extreme kinds of rationalism, irrationalism, and other-worldliness. In the same way, an adoption of the analytical philosopher's list of dispositions as among those to be cultivated involves assigning at least a considerable value to clarity, rigor, etc., an assignment which only an extreme irrationalist could refuse to make, though, of course, those who do make it will not all have the same conception of clarity or rigor. As for the existential virtues — it looks as if they can and must be accepted in some form by almost anyone who takes morality or religion seriously, that is, by anyone whose approach is not purely aesthetic, conventional, legalistic, or spectatorial.

(2) It seems to me that existentialism and its sisters and its cousins and its aunts do not put sufficient store on rationality, meaning by this roughly the set of dispositions prized by the Deweyans and the analytical philosophers taken together. Indeed, they tend to suspect and impugn it. Yet, even if we confine ourselves to the *how* of our approach to life and let the *what* take care of itself, it seems at least irrational to neglect the virtues of logic and science. To quote Israel Scheffler, "We are . . . faced by important challenges from within and without . . . whatever we do, we ought, I believe, to keep uppermost the ideal of rationality, and its emphasis on the critical, questioning, responsible, free mind."[9]

(3) Even so, the existentialists (and their sisters and their cousins and their aunts) are perhaps right in feeling that the values of rationality must at least be supplemented by those of

[9] "Concepts of Education: Some Philosophical Reflections on the Current Scene," E. Landy and P. A. Berry (eds.), in *Guidance in American Education* (Cambridge, Mass.: Harvard University Press, 1964), p. 26.

commitment and engagement, as S. T. Kimball and J. E. Mc-
Clellan have argued,[10] along with many others who think that our
western culture is in danger of being overcome by its "committed"
opponents. (In this perspective it is a bit ironical that our
"uncommitted" are precisely those who are most attracted by
existentialism.)

(4) Of course, if we try to combine rationality and commitment
— the first without the second being empty and the second without the first blind — we must find some teachable kind of union
of open-mindedness and belief, of objectivity and decision. This is
one of the crucial problems of our culture, as has often been
pointed out.

(5) In my opinion, none of the three families of dispositions
includes enough emphasis on sheer (not "mere") knowledge, the
intellectual virtue so esteemed by Aristotelians — not just knowing
how (which was given a big boost by Gilbert Ryle) but knowing
that, the kind of knowledge contained in the findings of history,
science, and other cognitive studies (including knowing *why*).
One reads, for example, that a college education must have as its
goals "intellectual initiative and mature self-reliance," a statement
which roughly synthesizes Dewey and existentialism, but there is
enough "formalism" in me to make me convinced that education
ought to promote not only certain "qualities of mind [and char-
acter]," but also certain "forms of knowledge," even if the knowledge must sometimes be second-hand and not acquired "by doing."[11] To parody Bertrand Russell, the good life, moral and
otherwise, is a life inspired by certain qualities of mind and character and guided by knowledge, actually possessed knowledge *that*
is important both for the guidance of action and for the content of
the good life. I therefore feel some agreement with Maritain when
he writes that contemporary education has too much substituted
"training-value for knowledge-value . . . mental gymnastics for
truth, and being in fine fettle, for wisdom."[12] As Jerome Bruner

---

[10] *Education and the New America* (New York: Random House, 1962).
[11] See P. H. Hirst in Archambault, *op cit.,* pp. 117f., for a discussion
of this point.
[12] *Education at the Crossroads* (New Haven, Conn.: Yale University
Press paperback ed., 1943), p. 55; cf. Aquinas' remark that "The first
thing that is required of an active man is that he know."

puts it: "Surely, knowledge of the natural world, knowledge of the human condition, knowledge of the nature and dynamics of society, knowledge of the past so that it may be used in experiencing the present and aspiring to the future — all of these . . . are essential to an educated man. To these may be added another: knowledge of the products of our artistic heritage. . . ."[13] John Stuart Mill was, no doubt, right in attacking education that is "all *cram*" and does not provide "exercises to form the thinking faculty itself," but he went too far in adding, ". . . the end of education is not to *teach*, but to fit the mind for learning from its own consciousness and observations. . . . Let all *cram* be ruthlessly discarded." For Mill himself goes on to insist that each person must be "made to feel that . . . in the line of his peculiar duty, and in the line of the duties common to all men, it is his business to *know*."[14] It seems to me to follow that there is place in education for some "teaching" and even some "cram." I grant it may be that, if we seek first to form the thinking faculty itself (i.e., certain qualities of mind), then all other things will eventually be added unto us, including knowledge. But must we wait until after school is over for them to be added? *Can* we?

A recent cartoon about education has a father saying to his child sitting in a high chair with his food before him, "Think. Assimilate. Evaluate. Grow." It seems to me that this is to the point as a spoof of a certain conception of education, since the word "Grow" does not add anything, and that a more sensible view would say, "Think. Assimilate. Evaluate. Know."

(6) There are, of course, certain other sorts of dispositions that must be added to the three families indicated above as goals of education. There are, first, moral dispositions relating to *what* we do and not merely to *how* we do it, e.g., benevolence and justice (i.e., knowing *what* to do and being disposed to do it), second, the dispositions involved in aesthetic appreciation, creation, and judgment (not just "knowledge of the products of our artistic heritage"), and third, the dispositions required by the democratic way of life, so far as these are not already covered.

[13] *On Knowing* (New York: Atheneum, 1965), p. 122.
[14] See his essay "On Genius" in K. Price, *Education and Philosophical Thought* (Boston: Allyn and Bacon, 1962), pp. 455f.

(7) In what I have said thus far, I have had *public* education primarily in mind. *Private* education, formal and informal, may add still another group of dispositions, namely, those involved in religious faith, hope, love, and worship. However, some care is needed, perhaps even some reconstruction, if one proposes to combine a Deweyan emphasis on scientific intelligence or an analytical philosopher's emphasis on clarity and rigor with anything like a traditional theistic faith. If one proposes to foster such a faith, one must at least give up trying to cultivate also a disposition to rely on logic and science *alone* as a basis of belief and action. If one wishes to insist on the necessity of the latter disposition, one must reconstruct the traditional conception of religion and God — as Dewey did in *A Common Faith*. Of course, if one means by religion merely some kind of basic commitment or other, or any kind of ultimate belief about the world whatsoever, or a vague "duty and reverence" (as Whitehead does),[15] or simply whatever an individual does with his solitude (Whitehead again), then all education is and must be religious (as Whitehead says), even an atheistic or militantly antireligious one. Then "the Galilean" has indeed conquered, but then he has also become very, very pale — so pale as to be indistinguishable from or to his opponents. For, even if one has a "religious" belief in this wide sense, one may still also believe that

> . . . beyond the extreme sea-wall, and
> between the remote sea-gates,
> Waste water washes, and tall ships founder,
> and deep death waits. . . .

as Swinburne did.[16] I say this because of what one finds in some discussions of the place of religion in public schools, where, from the premise that every ultimate belief is a religion, the conclusions are drawn, first, that religion both is and should be taught in public schools, and, second, that therefore theism (or Catholicism, Protestantism, and Judaism) may and should be taught there. As for private schools and colleges — whether they should in fact

---

[15] *Aims of Education,* p. 26.
[16] "Hymn to Proserpine." Or as B. Russell did in "A Free Man's Worship."

foster religious dispositions in a narrower theistic sense is too large a question to treat here; the answer, I suppose, assuming that there should be private schools and colleges at all, is that it depends on the purposes for which they exist.

CONFLICTS IN VALUES

HARRY S. BROUDY

In one way or another value conflicts at all levels, metaphysical, societal, personal, within value domains and among them, sooner or later come to roost on the shoulders of the school. And because the highest responsibility rests with the administrator, he must inevitably divide his activity between coping with value conflicts on an institutional basis and acting out his own role as a value witness. His training must inevitably provide for both dimensions or make the tragic mistake of neglecting to do so. Yet they require skills, knowledge, and attitudes of quite different orders. We are prone to take care of the coping, managing, manipulating dimension by instruction but to pay our respects to the dimension of self-cultivation and commitment by intermittent exhortation — in ritualistic paragraphs at the opening and closing of the lecture, book, or course. This in a way is understandable, for we know much more about making men efficient than about making them men.

It is easy to become cynical and witty about the way an administrator copes with conflict, especially if one is not an administrator. However, it is a mistake to believe that administrators can or even should always operate at the level of fundamental principle in coping with conflict. The primary function of the administrator is to keep his institution at its job, whereas at the level of controversy about ultimate principle all action stops.

If there is a guiding principle in dealing with conflicts in principle, it is: Don't let them occur. This gives us the rule: Deal with a conflict at the lowest level of principle that the situation and your conscience permits. We might call this the principle of least principle. I would like to generalize this to show why this is not necessarily the result of cynicism but rather a necessity of institutional life in an imperfect society.

We have to go back to the mechanisms by which we make a

Reprinted, by permission, from Ohm and Monaghan (eds.), *Educational Administration — Philosophy in Action* (Norman: University of Oklahoma Press, 1965), pp. 49–54.

distasteful but necessary function tolerable. Care of the sick, disposal of the dead, punishment of evil doers, for example, are distasteful but necessary functions in a society. One way of getting people to perform them willingly is to conventionalize the procedures, i.e., depersonalize them into standard procedures performed according to rules. If the rules can be derived from science, so much the better, because in doing so we have arrived at the professional stage of the function. To the professional sickness, death, filth, and corruption are problems to be understood, not ordeals to live through. They are not his troubles and wisely *he* turns to other professionals when the troubles are his own. There is probably no task so revolting that routine, method, theory, a degree, or at least a special uniform and title cannot render tolerable.

The devising of regular and sanctioned procedures for dealing with value conflicts is a standard function of an institution and especially of those administering it. I have heard a noted university president say that his goal was to have a policy, a rule, and a procedure to cover every possible contingency in the conduct of a university. Whether this is an administrative dream or nightmare, I do not know, but the import is clear. Given such a state, no issue of principle would ever have to be raised, and if ever mistakenly raised, could be resolved, i.e., be kept out of the newspapers, by procedural means.

The way in which this device is applied at times has its comic and tragic aspects. Example: Negroes march in protest against housing discrimination. Administrative response: Arrest the leaders for obstructing traffic. Example: A student cheats on an examination, is caught and reported to the administration. Response: Expel him from school because he has not paid his laboratory fees for the semester.

These are examples of what might be dubbed *procedural* irrelevance. Rather than face an issue on its obvious merits, one disposes of it by removing one or more of the parties to the dispute on charges that have nothing to do with the issue in question. Such procedural irrelevance is roughly the counterpart of the logical fallacy of irrelevant thesis.

Another solution might be called procedural interposition. Example: A faculty member protests that he has been dismissed unjustly. Response: File the protest with this and this committee and take X steps in such and such a sequence, if you wish to have your protest adjudicated. This postpones the need to face the value issue for a long time, and, if the petitioner is not a man of courage and persistence, forever.

Or one adopts a diversionary solution. Example: Two valuable members of the faculty cannot agree on departmental policy. Response: Give each his own department or promote one of them to an administrative post.

These gambits, not to speak of the numerous ploys in terms of force, compromise, oblivescence, obfuscation, persuasion, and fatigue, are all devices to avoid raising fundamental issues and especially the moral issue. In such radical problems as automation and federal aid to education, the controversy is kept as long as possible on the procedural griddle in the hope that some sort of acceptable action can be found that will obviate facing the conflict in principle. And this must not be dismissed as cynicism or cowardice, for societies, if not individuals, are well aware that when the issue is reduced to stark "yes" and "no" saying to a fundamental principle, the only action possible is war and the destruction of at least one of the contending parties.

It would be strange indeed if the massive enterprise of formal education did not behave as do other institutions, and if its administrators did not, as all administrators must, seek the knowledge and techniques whereby conflicts in value are managed. It would constitute a remarkable exception to the rule if these techniques for coping with conflict did not employ the principle of least principle in doing so.

And yet the administrator of the educational institution is not in quite the same position as the administrators of other social institutions. The business administrator can fall back on the principle that business is business, and the politician can fall back on the principle that good politics is what keeps the party in power. The educator, however, deals with nothing but values — human beings who are clusters and constellations of value potentials. Nothing human is really alien to the educational enterprise and there is, therefore, something incongruous about educational administrators evading fundamental value conflicts. A lapse in moral integrity that in a businessman or a politician or a lawyer is merely deplored in an educator becomes intolerable. The public will never quite permit the educational administrator the moral latitude that it affords some of its other servants. For to statesmen and soldiers men entrust their lives and fortunes, but to the schools they entrust their precarious hold on humanity itself.

Whether or not the public is right in this way of looking at the educator is not the point to be settled here, and some people in school "business" undoubtedly chafe under the honor so thrust upon them. The training of school administrators has to take account of a situation in which value conflicts have to be minimized but not swept under the rug. One needs administrative adroitness to prevent raising the moral issue at every turn, but there must also be the moral integrity to recognize a moral issue when there is one and to deal with it morally when no moral alternative can honestly be entertained.

At this point one gets the feeling that this is where Western civilization came in and that this has all been said before. For example, we seem to hear again that precursor of all that is really important both in philosophy and in the philosophy of education, Plato. Plato laid the groundwork for the training of administrators, especially educational administrators, because the instrument of political administration was to be education in both the formal and informal senses of that word. Now the guardians were trained, if you recall, both to know and to be, and to be what they knew. In other words, they not only knew about value and had glimpsed the absolute norms, but they themselves were the embodiments of these norms so far as human beings could embody them. The philosopher-king was expected to be wise as well as well bred and scholastically apt.

It is easy to dismiss the Platonic training of the guardians as a utopian counsel of perfection, but the Platonic teaching is more valuable for what it tells us about our problems than for the solutions it proposes. Lacking a rational social order, an administrator will always face a profound existential tension between his own value commitment and the management of the enterprise placed in his charge, a tension between sensitivity to principle and a flight from it. Without efficiency in coping with conflict, the enterprise will collapse dramatically; without a strong commitment to a value hierarchy, the enterprise dies more quietly and gradually but no less surely.

One can end this essay by uttering the truism that there is no easy solution and the equally obvious injunction to train our school administrators in both knowledge and virtue. Whether one could do this and still let them give the ordinary hostages to fortune in the form of fame and family is as doubtful now as it was in Plato's thought. Plato did not think that it was either safe or wise to force leaders to choose between private and public good. In this we are more utopian than Plato.

Given our times and conditions, about the closest we can come to schooling for a viable union of wisdom and efficiency is a combination of foundational knowledge for the former and science and technology for the latter.

Foundational knowledge, both as to fact and value is a large-scale map with both cognitive and evaluational dimensions. It is formed by really good and thorough general education plus the foundational study of educational problems. It supplies the concepts for building a hierarchy of value. While this does not make our administrator a connoisseur, it does acquaint him with the paths of connoisseurship in the several value domains; and while it does not of itself dictate his own life style, his own pattern of theme and variation, of dominance and subordination, it does expose him to the most distinctive patterns our history has so far turned up.

Whoever interprets his problems and those of the school on such a map does not thereby have a rule for solving them, but he does know in what domain the problems belong. He knows where reality ends and hypocrisy begins. Whoever has a well-developed interpretative map is not automatically happy or serene in his work, but he is not a yokel who perspires too freely and readily in every predicament. He knows when to raise the moral issue and when to divert people from raising it. He can sleep nights and look his colleagues in the eye. This, one might say, is the "good enough" stage in the development of an administrator.

However, the schoolman, like every other man, cannot forever escape the choice between saying "yes" or "no" to fundamental questions. Like all men, to be somebody he has to be a living witness of this commitment, whether he says "yes" or "no." Whether he persuades by argument or by charm, if he is to lead, he must act out a value schema that makes connection with aspirations and impulses that stir all men — some clearly, distinctly, and compellingly, some only vaguely and dimly, no more than a restless moment in a dream.

LEVELS OF VALUATIONAL DISCOURSE
IN EDUCATION

JAMES F. PERRY AND PHILIP G. SMITH

A useful proposal for structuring valuational discourse is found in
H. D. Aiken's "Levels of Moral Discourse."[1] According to Aiken,
we can distinguish four levels of discourse which he calls (1) "ex-
pressive-evocative," (2) "moral," (3) "ethical," and (4) "post-
ethical" or "human." These levels are to be distinguished primarily by the different functions performed by the same valuational
terms when used at each of the levels. Because of different functions there are different kinds of arguments, objections, and "good
reasons" appropriate or relevant at each level.

Without examining all of the meta-ethical questions involved in
the Aiken article, we shall suggest first, that his analysis can be
generalized to apply to any kind of valuational discourse (rather
than just moral discourse) and second, that such a generalized
analysis may be useful in a consideration of the bewildering maze
of valuational problems that run through the theory and practice
of education. While fully acknowledging our indebtedness to Professor Aiken we make no claim to having expressed *his* point of
view. Especially in connection with the fourth level we have
deliberately departed from what we take to be some of his presuppositions.

The Expressive-Evocative Level

Whether heatedly or dispassionately, and whether by using ges-
tures and facial expressions or by using words such as "good" and
"bad," most of us express our feelings countless times each day.
In the classroom we sometimes express our feelings by assigning

Reprinted, by permission, from *Philosophy of Education 1969,* Proceedings of the Twenty-fifth Annual Meeting, Philosophy of Education Society,
1969, pp. 105-112.
[1] H. D. Aiken, "Levels of Moral Discourse," *Ethics,* LXII, no. 4 (July,
1952); also in *Reason and Conduct* (New York: Alfred A. Knopf, 1962),
Chapter 4.

rewards and punishments or by offering or denying opportunities. When this sort of thing is done at what Aiken calls the expressive level, we do not expect to be called upon to defend our expressions with good reasons. An expression of a feeling merely indicates that the feeling is actual; it does not imply a claim about the value of the object or event toward which the feeling is directed.

This is not to say that we may not have reasons *for expressing* our feelings. In addition merely to venting our emotions, we sometimes express our feelings in order to influence someone's decisions or behavior, or in order to enable others to understand us and thus to enable them to predict our own future behavior. But unless there is something rather obviously unstable or problematic about the situation, we tend to use valuational language at this level in an unreflective manner. In most situations we do not have to stop and think about it in order to know how we feel, and to the extent that we tend to be open and frank and not given to dissembling, we tend to express our feelings without giving much thought to the effects of such use of valuational terms.

In the classroom this may present serious problems. Involved here is the practice of using expressive valuational language for the purpose of valuational structuring.[2] Teachers use valuational language to exhort, to express empathy, and to encourage empathy, and they promote "valuational sets" by the use of valuational terms more or less disguised as factual descriptions. Some of this practice is probably inevitable in any complex teaching situation and it may be that under certain circumstances it is an essential and desirable means toward important educational objectives. Our concern at this point is merely to note how the use of a generalized version of Aiken's analysis quickly enables one to spot this comparatively unstudied aspect of classroom teaching and to recognize that the pedagogical problems connected with this use of valuational language are not reducible to the problems of the logic of evaluations. The question "Was it pedagogically

[2] Philip G. Smith, "Verbal Operations in Classroom Instruction," Chapter IV in David W. Ecker, *Improving the Teaching of Art Appreciation* (U.S. Department of Health, Education, and Welfare, Cooperative Research Project #V-006, Ohio State University Research Foundation, November, 1966).

appropriate for the teacher to express a certain valuation in a certain way at a certain time?" is quite different from the question "Could the expressed valuation be defended as a value claim or proposition?" The second question is really an invitation to escalate the discourse to a higher level.

The Moral Level, or, the Level of Case Evaluations

Aiken points out that two kinds of considerations are acknowledged to be relevant at the moral level: factual means-ends claims, and moral rules or standards. If I claim that X is good, I am operating at the moral level if I point out that X is a means for achieving Y (where Y is conceded to be good) and/or if I point out that X is a kind of Z (where Z is conceded to be good). My claim can then be challenged by arguments or evidence to show that X is not a means for achieving Y, or that X is not a kind of Z, or that there are other overriding considerations.

In practice, as Aiken points out, valuational discourse at this level frequently contains ellipses and elisions. When only conclusions are stated they may appear to be merely first-level expressions of personal preference: "Caesar was a great general," "This is an 'A' paper." Differentiation between levels depends upon function, and function is related to intention, point, and context. For example, the statement "Caesar was a great general" made by an elementary school teacher may be seen, in context, to be nothing more than an attempt at valuational structuring (however questionable this may be from an instructional standpoint). The same statement made as an aside during a lecture by an accomplished historian of military affairs has a significantly different function. From the standpoint of intent, the distinction is a matter of whether or not the assertion is a conclusion from good reasons either stated or held in mind.

In the studies of teaching conducted by B. Othanel Smith, it was found that it is very common for teachers to call upon students to make what we have called "case evaluations." Professor Smith reports, "But all too often, when the student makes a decision in these cases, the teacher either accepts or rejects it without regard for the facts and criteria involved." From this, Professor Smith concludes that "this practice of disregarding facts and criteria is probably the chief defect of teaching in the domain of valuation."[3]

Certainly when what is at issue is a case evaluation, a lack of regard for the relevant facts and criteria is a mark of poor or confused teaching. But the Aiken analysis should enable us to see that "teaching in the domain of valuation" involves much more than case evaluations. And this is, perhaps, especially true in teaching in the arts, the topic to which Professor Smith was addressing his remarks. The domain of valuation includes effective and conative aspects that are not necessarily reducible to the cognitive operations involved in case evaluations, and case evaluations do not exhaust even the cognitive aspects of the domain of valuations.

Nevertheless, failure to make explicit the facts and criteria involved in case evaluations is a serious fault not only with respect to teaching in the domain of valuations but also with respect to the complex web of evaluations involved in the selecting, organizing, and presenting of any content of instruction and in evaluating and reporting student progress. Too many ellipses and elisions here give teaching the appearance of being either highly arbitrary or else based on some artful mystique to be learned only by an extended apprenticeship. This, in turn, is fatal to any program of teacher preparation that strives to lift teaching to the level of a professional practice.

It is almost axiomatic that education is permeated with values; less well understood is the corollary that the various tasks and procedures that constitute *teaching* are laced together into actual teaching methods or strategies by a series of evaluative decisions. It follows that the logic of teaching (in contrast to logical structures within the context of instruction) is the logic of evaluative judgments. Our analysis of levels of valuational discourse in education uncovered, at the expressive level, the need for psychological and other scientific study of the pedagogical effects of valuational language; we now suggest that it is an understanding of the case evaluation level that is at the heart of the logic of teaching.

---

[3] B. Othanel Smith, "The Logic of Teaching in the Arts," *Teachers College Record*, LXIII, no. 3 (1961).

The Ethical Level, or, Norm Evaluations

When valuational discourse proceeds at the case evaluation level, the soundness of the rules and standards used to justify value claims is taken for granted. When we question such rules or standards, asking whether they are based on good reasons, we shift the discourse to the ethical level in Aiken's analysis or, when the analysis is generalized, to the level of norm evaluations.

To the extent that any domain of valuation (e.g., moral, aesthetic, educational) is well structured with clear and widely accepted rules and standards, valuational discourse tends to remain on the first two levels. But there are occasions for further escalation of the discourse. Changing conditions or increased knowledge of consequences may bring to light a conflict between two or more rules, or it may be found that the consistent application of certain standards has results that were unintended. There may also be crossovers from one domain to another. For example, the application of some educational rule or standard that appears appropriate from a pedagogical point of view may become unacceptable when viewed from a moral point of view.

Regardless of the conditions or causes that animate valuational discourse, at the level of norm evaluation the essential characteristic is an impersonal criticism of standards or rules. They and/or their consequences are judged in the light of higher-order norms or principles. For example, at the second level of discourse the moral question is "What ought I to do in this situation?" but at the third level the ethical question is "What moral standards ought one to follow in a situation such as this?" In order to answer the moral question the appeal is to moral rules or standards; in order to answer the ethical question the appeal is to ethical criteria.

Principles in any valuational domain or "point of view"[4] may exist at various levels of generality but principles of the highest order always appear empty (i.e., abstract and not prescribing any particular concrete act) at the level of case evaluations. Consider, for example, the golden rule or Kant's maxim. This "emptiness"

---

[4] Paul W. Taylor, *Normative Discourse* (Englewood Cliffs, N.J.: Prentice-Hall, 1961).

is an essential characteristic, for such criteria function as a base for criticism of the more specific standards and rules. The function of principles of the highest order is to define a domain or point of view. This is to say that the highest-order ethical principles show what it means to be moral, or to take the moral point of view.

In the context of education, "objectives" perform a similar function and in the language of education, this term covers a very wide range of levels of generality. On the one hand we speak of the objectives of American schooling and on the other of the objectives of the instruction planned for tomorrow's eighth grade general science class. Nevertheless, it is "objectives" that provide a base for criticism of educational standards and rules. For example, the statement "This is an 'A' paper" may be viewed as a conclusion in a case evaluation when such a judgment was arrived at in the light of standards or rules established for the assignment. But the appropriateness of the assignment and its standards may be criticized in the light of the instructional objectives. These in turn may be criticized in terms of higher-order objectives until finally we arrive at a consideration of what are sometimes called the aims of education. At this level of generality what is needed, as John Dewey clearly recognized, is some "empty" principle that will define the domain or point of view — for example, the principle of "growth," or the definition of an educative experience as one that adds to the meaning of experience and increases control over the course of subsequent experience. To criticize this principle as, for example, Boyd Bode did,[5] because it does not specify what one ought to do in any particular case, is simply to misunderstand its point and function. A proper criticism of such a principle would more likely take the form (à la Peters)[6] of a conceptual mapping of "education" in relation to both subordinate concepts (e.g., "teaching" and "learning") and superordinate concepts (e.g., "man," "rationality," etc.) in order to explicate and assess the scope and thrust of the principle.

[5] Boyd H. Bode, *Progressive Education at the Crossroads* (New York: Newson, 1938).

[6] Richard S. Peters, *Ethics and Education* (Chicago: Scott, Foresman, 1967).

It follows that the moves involved at the level of norm evaluations ought to be mastered by those engaged in the justification of objectives or the development of prescriptive theories within the field of education. At the highest level of generality such prescriptive theories are usually known as normative philosophies of education.

The Postethical or Human Level, or,
The Level of Existential Commitment

Consider now the question "Why ought *I* to do what one ought to do?" That is, "Why ought I be moral?" Or, at the more generalized level, "Why should I be responsible about valuational decisions?" Or, in the context of education, "Why should I be educated?" When such a question is asked *within* the levels of discourse so far discussed, it is in a sense quite meaningless, for it says, in effect, "I now know what I ought to do but I still don't know whether or not I ought to do it!"

Nevertheless, as Aiken points out, the fact that we recognize that there are some occasions on which asking such questions is not meaningless suggests a fourth level of valuational discourse. According to Aiken, "There is a sense in which man transcends all his works and is 'free,' albeit at his peril, to junk any and all of them at any time. I am bound to the rules of morality so long as I am responsive to the demands of a 'rational' moral being. But nothing can give them authority over my conduct unless I, in virtue of my attitudes and wants, are moved by them."

Aiken asserts that, at the fourth level, once again "decision is king." But one might add that "reason may still be parliament," and decision at this level should not be confused with the more or less spontaneous expression of personal preference by valuational language at the first level. Consider the persuasive and evocative function of valuational terms: At the first level the appeal is to desires and attitudes that dance on the surface of personality; at the fourth level the call is to the very roots of man's humanness and rationality. At this level an appropriate response to the question "Why should I be reasonable?" might be, "Come, join with me in the life of striving to be reasonable and see if you don't find it good."

In the context of education it is the human level of valuational discourse that provides the arena for doing philosophy of education in the traditional grand manner — a literary account of a "life style" (in education and elsewhere), an attempt to "tell it like it is" when seen from the inside. In such an account valuational terms are invitations to empathetic understanding and identification — they are ways of saying "Come, join with me." They point toward the virtues of universal coherence — the absence of working "at cross purposes," the solving of all problems at once (without generating new, and possibly greater, problems). At this level it doesn't make much sense to ask for justification (in the form of a second- or third-level argument) of the key or intrinsic values. But it is also a confusion of levels to suppose that nothing more is involved in such systematic invitations to existential commitment than a sophisticated form of the emotive language used in the first level of valuational discourse.

Now, of course, it is possible to view the schools in a purely instrumental sense, as educational planners sometimes do, abdicating all responsibility for deep philosophic commitment. Final decision concerning the role of the school may be viewed as a political decision quite beyond the responsibility of professional educators who are properly concerned only with accomplishing the mission assigned to the schools by society or by the state. It may be that some who take this position are victims of a confusion of the fourth and first levels and, desiring to remain within the domain of "orderly objective decisions," see no way of entering the dialogue concerning commitments that seem to them doomed to be "subjective," "arbitrary," or "hopelessly relativistic." But we take it that in a free, democratic society, there is really no such escape from freedom. Unless responsibility is accepted for the personal, existential commitment appropriate at the fourth level of valuational discourse, the ideal of both moral autonomy and truly "liberal" education is shattered on the rocks of legalistic and heteronomous standards of value.

Concerning "teaching in the domain of valuations," until students have developed some of the habits involved in being reasonable, formal study of the logic and structure of evaluative judgments is not likely to result in much more than some form of "knowing that"— that is, a formal knowledge of the structure of such judgments. It is only after a person is already disposed (that is, feels obligated) to do what ever it is that *one ought to do* that a study of rules and standards becomes meaningful in a personal sense. And, unfortunately, it is only after the two are put together — that is, only after a person feels that he ought to be reasonable about oughts — that ethical or other forms of valuational education (in contrast to moral or other forms of training) are likely to be efficacious.

Finally, concerning the study of philosophy of education, since one does not empathize or identify with what is strange or alien, to an "outsider" a view from the inside is generally not very convincing. It appears, therefore, that until a student is already striving to order his understandings and commitments concerning education into a comprehensive view or philosophy, a systematic study of the attempts of others to do so is not likely to have much real point or bearing in his life.

Hopefully, this analysis of four levels of valuational discourse in education should prove helpful in understanding: (1) the various kinds of valuational problems encountered in the conduct of schooling; (2) some problems encountered in the teaching of valuations; (3) the importance of differentiating: the empirical study of the pedagogical effects of the use of valuational language, the study of the logic and structure of evaluative judgments as the key to the logic of teaching, the study of the logical structure of the content of instruction, and the study of philosophies of education as persuasive accounts of what it means to be committed to some systematic conception of education.

EDUCATION AND SOME MOVES
TOWARD A VALUE METHODOLOGY

A. STAFFORD CLAYTON

That teaching is pervaded by value choices and judgments has been clearly pointed out by John L. Childs: "Judgments about life values inescapably pervade and undergird the whole process of providing and guiding experience. More than many teachers realize, a scheme of values — a structure of things considered significant, worthful, and right — operates in their endless responses to the daily behavings of their pupils." Furthermore, these educational value judgments cut to the core of human concerns, and teachers inevitably encourage dispositions and habits about fundamental matters. Educational values "have to do with such elemental things as the rights, the responsibilities, the beliefs, the tastes, the appreciations, the faiths and the allegiances of human beings." The fullness of the teacher's involvement with values is part and parcel of his role as an agent of choice.

> In order to encourage, we must also discourage; in order to foster, we must also hinder; in order to emphasize the significant, we must identify the non-significant; and finally, in order to select and focus attention on certain subject-matters of life, we have to reject and ignore other subject-matters. Were our values different our selections and our rejections would also be different. The process of selecting and rejecting, of fostering and hindering, of distinguishing the lovely from the unlovely, and of discriminating the important from the unimportant is unending in education.[1]

It is readily apparent that contemporary conditions have not invalidated the thrust of these remarks. The growth of knowledge, the acceleration in the means of communicating it, and the centrality of educational concerns in the national effort have underscored rather than vitiated the significance of Professor Childs' words.

Reprinted, by permission, from *Educational Theory*, XIX, no. 2 (Spring, 1969): 198-210.

[1] John L. Childs, *Education and Morals* (New York: Appleton-Century-Crofts, 1950), pp. 19-20.

It should also be recognized that what Professor Childs said of acts of teaching also holds for the study of education. When one puts his mind to the consideration of educational problems, acts of valuing may be identified throughout one's endeavors. In designing the content of teacher education, in organizing it into programs of teacher education, and in appraising the outcomes, judgments about criteria are central. In systematic inquiry and research into educational problems, questions of selection, focus, and relevance are frequently decisive. A paraphrase of Professor Childs' words may be appropriate. More than many inquirers recognize, "a scheme of values — a structure of things considered significant, worthful, and right"— operates in the selection and design of what in education is studied. Since questions about selection, interpretation, explanation, and evaluation characterize the study of education, as well as acts of teaching, critical attention needs to be given to the norms upon which judgments are based.

The recognition of the central and pervasive role of value judgments in teaching and in the study of education does not, however, take us very far in the direction of what we need to know. To tell us that values pervade education is not to reveal in what way we ought to proceed with normative processes in educational study and discourse. We have yet to inquire into what constitutes competence in judgments of value. One of the distinctive tasks of philosophy of education is to provide disciplined guidance about the evaluation of value judgments and to recommend methods and procedures to reduce the arbitrary character of value claims.

Before mapping out some ways in which normative judgments may be more adequately controlled and evaluated, several clarifications are in order.

In the first place, we propose to talk about the normative in the full range of educational concerns. Our discourse is not limited to moral, aesthetic, religious, political, or other specified contexts. We are talking about the general role of value judgments in the widest range of human affairs.

Some hold, contrary to the view here taken, that only vague and imprecise moves can result from so general a concern with the normative. In their view, only specific detailed study of the fields of the ethical, the moral, the aesthetic, and the like can yield determinate recommendations of an adequate kind about normative judgments. Thus one must turn to specific moral, aesthetic, or political theorists to inquire with meaningful precision into valuative matters. As distinct from this view, it is here proposed as a heuristic notion that the study of value judgments may profitably center in a more general concern with the normative. This is particularly appropriate in the field of education. In the practice and in the study of education the normative appears not already refined into academic disciplines but in the matrix of complex human conditions and efforts. If we center exclusively upon the substantive contributions of the established divisions of academic thought, we may very well overlook the features of methodology which in education are most needed. Furthermore, what we want to look at cuts across academic fields and is common to value choice in different contexts.

Second, our attention to the normative will focus upon the intellectual moves that justify normative claims. We shall not be trying to settle the question "What are the right values to be used in teaching or in the study of education?" Rather we are asking, "What are we to do in judging values?" Additionally, we shall not be concerned with the sociology of norms, with the community as the locus of value consensus, or with the social dimensions of value inquiry, and our concern is clearly more restricted than a complete theory of valuation. It is limited to what might be called the informal logic of normative discourse. In this sense we might also talk of applied logic or logic as it is put to use in argument. We seek to be methodologically clear about the recommended moves one should make in dealing with "norms" when we use that term in the sense of criteria involving commitments.

Third, the concern with the moves that are made in normative discourse is not narrowly restricted to the value theory of a particular philosophic school or position. We are concerned with defensible moves in normative discourse, not a theory of values in the sense of argument about the status or source of values as ontological entities. For example, although we shall make use of Dewey's distinction between prizing and appraising, this does not entail the espousal of some particular interpretation of a pragmatic theory of value. We want to map out what educators should attend to in their general management of value claims rather than discuss the absolutist-relativist positions in value theory and the like.

Although these stipulations concerning the present treatment of the normative may merit more extensive discussion, it may be sufficient to have indicated the general sense of their meaning in order to clear the ground for the moves we are about to indicate.

We begin by distinguishing three general senses of "value" and shall call these the mathematical, the descriptive, and the normative uses of the term. We make this distinction in order to see that when we speak of teaching and the study of education as pervaded and undergirded by value judgments, we need to distinguish the normative or prescriptive sense of "value" from other uses.

The mathematical sense of "value" will not detain us long for this use does not entail any sense of *ought* or *should* but simply ascribes a function to some variable in an equation. "As the value of A increases, B decreases" exemplifies a nonprescriptive sense of "value." This use is also exemplified in the logician's talk of the truth-value of propositions.

By the descriptive use of "value" we mean those statements which assert a value-fact. To say that someone values something or that something has value asserts a fact of prizing or pricing. Something is as a matter of fact prized or deplored. Something has a price that one is willing to pay for it; it may be an economic matter, expressed in terms of a medium of exchange, or a matter of relative importance with reference to time and energy that one is willing to expend for it. This use is not different from a report of any other fact.

In the purely descriptive sense of "value" we talk about what we like or what we want, but we are not concerned with the appraisal of the criteria used to rate what is regarded as valuable. The value is simply had; its character as valuable is immediately present. The scrutiny of the criteria by which it is appraised as valuable is not at stake. There may be questions as to whether people really prize what they seem to. There may be investigation as to how many people make the same prizing. Inquiry into the factors which lead to certain prizings may be undertaken. When we center narrowly upon the description of valuables or upon exposing the causes that lead to prizings, we have not penetrated to appraisive questions about the criteria involved in moral choice.

In teaching and in the study of education much of this descriptive sense of valuing occurs. Teachers expound on the values of a group of people or of a thing valued. Values in the sense of existing social norms are taught to the child. There is even much talk about "the value-centered humanities" which have only this sense of a concern with value-facts in literature and works of art. In the social studies one may be told that teaching concerns not only the acquiring of facts about political-civil life but also the acquiring of the values that are expressed in it. In these and other instances of the kind, when the school is said to teach values, it is to teach prizings. The educational task is seen as one concerned with the replication of assessments; questions concerning the criteria premised in the assessments are submerged.

If the act of prizing is all that is meant by "making value judgments," then the root job of considering the weighing and appraising of normative judgments is unsensed and minimized. All we can do is to study values as though they were facts. In this use one does not probe the reasoned grounds for value commitment. Furthermore, the common equating of value with desire, with subjective feelings, leads to notions that value matters are arbitrary opinions. When values are simply prizings, all that we can do about them is to exhort and extol; we feel secure in "selling" our values to others. There is no discipline for the adjudication of conflicts between values. The source of these consequences is found in the fallacy of the reduction of values to the status of facts.

If we are to understand more fully the observation that teaching is pervasively and fundamentally colored by choices concerning life values, we shall want to distinguish between prizing and appraising, between discussions about prizings and arguments justifying normative judgments. In contrast with assertions that something is valued, a normative claim asserts a valuation with reference to nonarbitrary norms. Something is valuable by virtue of its characteristics that fulfill some requirements posted by a standard. We know not only that something is prized but that the grounds for the prizing are specified by criteria that tell us exactly what is worthy of being prized. In the normative sense of "value" attention focuses upon the appraisal and justification of the norm and this sense conveys the prescriptive sense of "ought."

We should be clear that this prescriptive sense of "normative" is distinguished from other uses which may be encountered in educational discourse. The judgment expressing *should* or *ought* is distinguished from a statistical sense of "normative" deriving from "the norm of a distribution" or the norm as the group of subjects upon which a test has been standardized. To say "We are interested in the accumulation of normative data that are predictive of learning disabilities" is to use the term "normative" with reference to data which adequately sample a population and are distributed about some measure of central tendency. If the words "should" or "ought" are used with reference to this context, they have the force of prediction, not prescription. "Normative data" are data which tell us what we should expect from normal cases.

The maintenance of this distinction is important if we are to avoid reading off "average" as "desirable." Average, normal, or typical performance of any kind makes no moral claim, nor are deviations from the statistical norm abnormal in a pejorative sense. The central tendency of a distribution has nothing to recommend morally; the typical is frequently not the morally preferable. If the tyranny of the norm is to be avoided, we must avoid this variety of deriving an "ought" from an "is."

Normative valuing, distinguished from prizing and from statistical normalizing, involves an assessment of worth. If it is not arbitrary, it involves a judgment open to others in which one thing or quality is graded or ranked with reference to a criterion. In grading one judges an instance with reference to a general standard identifying what is graded and how well the instance fulfills the criterion. Ranking is a matter of judging whether something is better or worse than, or equivalent with, another thing with reference to a criterion identifying what is relevent to and what counts in the ranking.

If our rankings and gradings are to be nonarbitrary, i.e., justified by some ordered and scrutinized process, normative judgments need to be looked at in two dimensions. One asks whether the thing or quality declared to be valuable has, with reference to the criterion, the characteristics assigned to it. We inquire into whether the valuable has the good-making or the bad-making characteristics indicated by the norm. The other is whether the norm is an appropriate one. We inquire into the justification of the norm. A fully normative judgment makes a two-fold claim. One is that whatever is ranked or graded fulfills or fails to fulfill the norms. The other is that the norms are valid ones to apply to what is being considered.

It will be helpful to illustrate with reference to a common task in teaching. Consider the teacher evaluating the discursive writing of his students, in short, grading papers. If his grading is non-arbitrary, he has certain norms in mind. Grammatical errors should be avoided; the paper should take account of certain facts; sentences should be clearly worded; paragraphs should have internal coherence; reasoning should be cogent; the paper should have something significant to say. The teacher assesses the good-making and the bad-making characteristics of the paper as they are posted by the norms. His responsibility is to determine not only that the paper has the characteristics but also that the norms being used are appropriate ones.

In a similar way we could see more clearly what is involved in a wide variety of tasks in the study of education if we took care to identify the two-fold responsibility in normative judgment. The teacher in his role as curriculum designer not only contrives whatever enters the school experience by ranking or grading alternative possibilities, but he justifies these moves with reference to norms that specify what is to be entered as valuable. The items of the content of the curriculum become valuable, as distinct from "are prized" or "are usually there," to the extent that the norms guiding his selection are clearly reasoned.

In research concerning the characteristics of good teachers, the criteria establishing "good teachers" in some sufficiently operational sense are essential to determining whether teachers have these characteristics. Inquiry which is not sensitive to what counts as worth-making in delineating criteria will not be helpful in telling us something that we can count on concerning the characteristics of good teachers.

The educator as participant in the forming and implementing of educational policy is similarly responsible for defensible norms as well as for actions in their behalf. In instances where questions of academic freedom arise, he grades or ranks the behaviors of agents in the situation with respect to norms concerning due process, the freedom of thought and of inquiry, the educational responsibility of authorized autonomy, and the like. Without clear and good reasons about the norms and spirited use of them, the situation is likely to degenerate to manipulation of power by groups guided only by their own prizings.

The point is that critical reasoning about the justification of the norm is an indispensable aspect of the educator's concern with values. Declarations of valuables without adequate defense of the norm by which the valuable is established fail to offer their credentials.

But we can go further than this in sorting out the moves that characterize adequacy in normative judgment. Educators make many kinds of judgments which involve values but in which the norm is not directly inquired into or justified. These judgments are not simply prizings because they are reasoned about with reference to criteria. But the criteria themselves are assumed to be valid rather than being made at that point the focus of study. In these instances we say something like this: We have sufficient reasons to take it for granted that these norms are appropriate. They are assigned a prima facie validity. Good reasons would have to be offered for an exception to them. This does not mean that the question of their appropriateness and adequacy may not be raised; rather they are judged to be sufficiently warranted to proceed with their use in finding good-making characteristics.

In grading papers the teacher judges that a paragraph does not have internal consistency. He judges that the norm is sufficiently clear and appropriate to determine whether the student's writing has good-making qualities. The teacher does not have to stop and entertain an argument about the relation of one sentence to another and the introduction of unrelated considerations that obscure the integrity of paragraphs. He uses the norm in making a characterizing judgment. On another occasion he will, if he is a good teacher, explain the norm in a host of ways so that its use in a variety of characterizing judgments may be shared.

In making characterizing judgments one is selecting and interpreting particular instances as falling within those of an agreed upon worth-making category. The category itself is not under scrutiny. It becomes so only if the characterizing judgment is challenged. The judgment is normative in the sense that it is a norm-using, but not a norm-defending, judgment. Characterizing judgments are made with reference to norms and involve appraisal of valuables but since appraisal of the norm itself is not undertaken, they fall short of fully appraisive normative judgments.

In the characterizing judgment the norm is used as a criterion to determine whether the particular event or instance falls within the class of those things marked off by the criterion. The judgment is public in the sense that the criterion is shared and open to inspection. Such a judgment, since it is persuasive, differs from the immediacy of the act of prizing. It expresses a commonly agreed upon way of assessing an incident; on prima facie grounds knowledgeable people assume that the criterion is valid and effective.

The characterizing judgment merits more attention in making judgments than it is commonly given. In selecting and interpreting what is taught it is used time and again where a fully appraisive judgment is not demanded. Its use is analogous to that of an adjustive habit in that continuity in plan and action is not interrupted. Yet, like a flexible habit, it may be guided by cognitive processes and is open to reconstruction as conditions vary. It economizes by reserving the moral thrust of the fully persuasive "ought" for instances meriting that deeper justification. It enables us to distinguish between situations where the full moral stance of the "ought" is not needed in order to get on with the processes of education.

Consider the norm that rejects plagiarism. Its most frequent use is on prima facie grounds: "You ought to say it in your own words rather than crib another's." The teacher can then get on with the job of promoting original expression. The more fully moral "ought," typically called for in the conflict between conflicting moral claims, involves looking into the competing worth-making features of norms. In such situations one is dealing not with a predictive "ought" but with an obligatory "ought." The full significance of the moral "ought" involves a critically conscious appeal to obligative norms used to persuade agents in a shared act of their common concern for others by means of arguments that justify norms. Here the teacher guides, leads, and demonstrates in a full capacity as moral agent.

Yet the characterizing judgment needs to be monitored — reserving the stronger term "discipline" for the more fully appraisive judgment — so that characterizing value judgments may be adequately public. Here we can call attention to the need to characterize the valuable clearly so that what merits consideration is identified. The categories serving to place the valuable in some domain receiving attention need to be sufficiently clear so that they can serve prima facie requirements. Characterizing judgments are rule-governed in that, for example, exceptional conditions need to be entered and weighed by a process that is open to inspection. Since characterizing judgments occur within some matrix of purpose, sufficient clarity of purpose is called for in order to determine what abets and what hinders or denies the end in view. We are not here trying to exhaust the consideration of what monitors the characterizing value judgment. Rather, it is suggested that in marking it off as an area of concern we open the door to fuller consideration of conditions promoting clarity and effectiveness in judgments serving this function.

At this point we pause to recapitulate. We have argued that making value judgments is not one undifferentiated act. It is analyzable. We can distinguish the sense of "ought" in characterizing judgments where the norm or standard is taken for granted. When evidences concerning the valuable are obtained, the judgment concerns the extent to which they fulfill the requirements of the standard. The good-making and bad-making characteristics of the valuable are judged with reference to the prima facie norm. The norm itself is not justified; its worth-making characteristics are accepted; they are not inquired into. On the other hand, in the fully appraisive, typically moral judgment, to which we now turn, the responsibility is not only to weigh the good- and bad-making features of the valuable but also to defend the norm itself. By what processes shall the worth-making aspects of the norm be justified? We shall be concerned with questions about relevance in norm-making, questions about priority or precedence of norms, and questions about the validation of norms.

Questions of Relevance in Norm-Making

The worth-making characteristics of norms, if norms are to be justified, are not just vaguely related in some wholesale way to a process of appraising. There is a difference between saying that two things are related and saying that something is relevant to something else. Relevance is a specific kind of relationship, one in which bearing or pertinence is shown. To speak of questions of relevance in norm-making is to speak of so stating the norm that it reveals as clearly as possible what counts as worth-making. What is included and what is excluded as contributing to the fulfillment of the norm are to be made public. If we are to judge the appropriateness of the norm for the instance in which something is evaluated, we need to know that what counts as worth-making is relevant to the case at hand and that the reasons urged in support of the norm are good ones, i.e., are relevant to it.

Consider again the teacher who is evaluating the student's essay. Some of the norms are taken for granted. The paper should show correct grammatical form. The standards are supplied in the rules: avoid comma faults, incomplete sentences, split infinitives, and the like. However, other norms are also involved. The essay should have something to say; it should be organized; it should have a certain completeness so that it stands on its own. It should have a cogency of reasoning. It should make its case in view of readers who may hold different points of view. The point is that if the teacher is fulfilling his normative responsibilities, the evaluation of the paper involves clarity about the relevance of the worth-making characteristics of the norm. Presumably, if the teaching is good, the student can build into his essay that which is called for by the relevant norms. He becomes self-critical through considered use of the relevant criteria in his writing.

Questions of relevance in norm-building are not exhausted by making clear what counts as worth-making. That which counts can be shown to bear at certain key points in the appraisive judgment. The relevance can be pin-pointed. In the student's writing at certain places cogency of argument may be more relevant than suggestion through the use of metaphor or analogy. At other places the reverse may be the case. The teacher can point out what counts in his ranking or grading of the paper by specifying the pertinent worth-making features looked for in a good paper.

Requirements of relevance not only demand precision about what counts as worth-making. They also express a concern that the maximum of considerations has not been overlooked. In evaluating the student's paper richness of detail, smoothness of style, and the like may be relevant. Whether they are not depends upon the purposes centered upon in the instruction.

Furthermore, considerations of relevance are supported by reasoned argument. Reasons are offered in support of the relevancy of the worth-making characteristics of the norm. The defense of the norm is not arbitrary. The evaluator can offer reasons which support or deny the relevance of the norm to the particular aspect of the student's writing.

Additionally, the function of rules in regard to considerations of relevance ranges beyond their use in making characterizing judgments. In the case of the latter, as we have seen, existing rules provide a framework for identifying good- or bad-making characteristics. Rules of usage are taken for granted; the teacher's function is to teach communication through observance of the rules. The teacher interprets the rules, is concerned with their balanced application. In this sense he is explaining the rule to the learner, but he is not making new rules or justifying them to his colleagues.

In making judgments about the relevance of worth-making characteristics of norms, we could say that rules of relevance should be followed. However, it is not clear that rules of relevance are commonly known in the sense pertaining to rules of usage. Relevance is a matter, as we have suggested, of pin-pointing the particular bearings or pertinence of worth-making features of norms to conditions of situations. This indicates rule-making as well as rule-obeying, and rule-making should be argued rather than imposed by decree.

Furthermore, attention to rule-making in judgments of relevance involves care about another distinction in the class of things called rules. Some rules are primarily definitional; they state the way words are used in the communication of meaning or in a common endeavor. Adverbs modify verbs, adjectives, or other adverbs; in chess pawns move only one block forward save for the initial move which may be two. Such rules specify how the game is to be played. Other rules, however, are not analytic with respect to the game; they are contingent as to the strategy of achieving the ends in view of the game. They are "if . . . then" rules to be interpreted with respect to the conditions one is in and the consequences that typically follow in situations of a similar kind. While definitional rules are central in characterizing judgments, strategic rules are more focal in matters of relevance. When one claims that an aspect of a norm is relevant, he is not merely appealing to a known rule; he is offering an argument that conditions and consequences call for attention to the bearing of something that has been overlooked.

The significance of this attention to rule-making as well as to rule-obeying is that justification of the norm does not consist simply in rationalizing a received norm. It involves building the norm — clearly not *de novo,* for norm-building may be communicated and shared — by giving the norm such attention that its worth-making characteristics are vitalized and highlighted in the situation one faces. Such attention enables the norm-using agent to scrutinize and assess the norm rather than accept it as complete and final, already present and waiting to be replicated upon demand. In arguments about the relevance of the worth-making features of the norm one contributes to the norm those features which give it compelling, yet nonarbitrary, impact on the quality of our judgments.

Questions of Priority in Appraisive Judgments

If one has determined the relevance of the worth-making characteristics of norms, he then faces the question of which of two or more of these characteristics takes precedence over the others. Of two competing, relevant, worth-making features, which has priority?

Here the logic of norm-making suggests that the judgment focuses on the reasons advanced for the relevance of the worth-making considerations. One judges the cogency of the reasons and the consequences in the situation at hand of arranging the various criteria in some order of priority. Although not every worth-making feature competes with or excludes others, yet in normative judgments not everything can be had at once. Some aspects of norm fulfillment may reasonably be assigned precedence, relative to and conditional upon others.

Consider again the teacher's need for normative clarity in assessing students' papers. The teacher may reason that the norm of having something to say takes priority over avoiding split infinitives. He may reason that the worth-making characteristics of innovative thinking weigh more heavily than cogency of argument. If the student's paper is to be critically appraised in this fashion, not only must the paper have the property, but the teacher must be able to reason critically about the weight to be assigned to the various criteria used in his teaching. The normatively sensitive teacher knows what he is looking for in his students' papers because he has clarified the relative priorities of his worth-making standards. Perhaps the teacher says to himself something like this: "It is more important that my students have something original to say than that they say it perfectly. Although they should avoid gross grammatical errors, it is a higher good that they express their own ideas. Thus they will be encouraged to think creatively and avoid simply cribbing the ideas and expressions of others." Judgments of priorities in the worth-making features of norms pervade the many different things that are done in teaching, and since being clear about the centrality of a purpose frequently involves removing some other purpose from the center of attention, ordering the worth-making features of norms promotes constancy and clarity in pursuit of purposes.

Care in these matters is indicated by the teacher who notes that he ought not to push Johnny beyond a certain point in the mastery of a particular learning for fear of alienating his later learnings about the matter. The teacher assigns priority to what he judges to be of higher worth. The teacher says in effect, "The continued concern of the student with something that challenges him surpasses the worth of pushing through to complete mastery at this time." The teacher arranges his priorities with good reasons for assigning priorities in his standards. Of course at another time the teacher may reassign priorities differently, judging that more complete mastery takes precedence over the student's sense of present achievement.

It should be clear that I am not talking about a general hierarchial system of values. Questions of priority of the worth-making components of norms are judgments made in the context of situations. Though some priorities are held to endure, they do so by virtue of a recurrent appraisal of their worth in concrete situations.

It should also be clear that this does not mean a general softness and looseness about the teacher's sense of values. It recommends against the rootless assigning of good-making characteristics of what is valued in favor of reasoned argument about competing worth-making features of norms. Reasons, rather than clichés, should be appealed to in this process.

Questions about the Validation of Norms

Questions of relevance and of priority in the worth-making features of norms do not exhaust the logical moves in the justification of norms. There remain questions about what we appeal to in the criticism and appraisal of norms. Granted that we support worth-making characteristics with relevant reasons, that we have not overlooked relevant considerations, and that these good reasons help in justifying priorities among worth-making characteristics, we still need to know that the selected standards are the right ones, that they ought to be used. Moves of this kind concern the validation of norms. In general, we validate norms by appealing to higher ones.

With reference to the grading of papers again, the teacher says: "Having something significant to say is a relevant norm. Further, it outweighs the rigid observance of rules of grammar." The teacher validates this having something significant to say by appeal to the higher norm that he ought to encourage the student to think creatively for himself. It is a higher norm in the sense that it subsumes the worth-making standard of "having something significant to say."

What do we mean by saying that a higher norm subsumes a lower one? Part of what we mean is that the higher norm has prima facie appropriateness as a universal. The case for an exception to it has to be made. There are sufficient reasons and evidences to warrant the desirability of creative thinking on the part of the student. If there were to be an exception to this norm or qualification of it, one would have to argue the point by using good reasons.

One could, however, push the question of the validation of the norm a step further. He could ask what validates the norm expressing the desirability of creative thinking. Here the justification might take either of at least two forms. One might argue that he deduced this norm from a still more general normative principle or set of normative generalizations. By continuing this process one could, in principle, arrive at that norm which is not validated on prima facie grounds or on grounds of its relations with the other norms but which is self-evidently good for all men at all times everywhere. The final norm is in this sense absolute. Some philosophers hold that only as one pushes the justification of norms back to the absolute has one any solid basis for his middle-range norms.

The other avenue of justification of more ultimate norms takes the form of the appraisal of consequences. One looks to the consequences in social practice of the more general normative principle. One may push the justification of norms back to an ultimate principle — say, the principle of moral equality — but in this view the justification of the most ultimate normative principle is not exempt from the total consequences that it produces in the way of life of a people.

The issue beween these two avenues of justification of ultimate norms continues to be basic in modern philosophy. Without further elaboration of it, it seems fruitful to mark off moves of this kind from other moves in the justification of norms. Here one is not only reasoning about questions of relevance, priority, and subsumptive relations in norm-making. He is reasoning about the status and security of ultimate norms. Such reasoning involves a position or point of view on philosophic issues in value theory.

Without seeking anything approaching a full dissection of this matter, it might be said that there are several alternatives at this point. One could push the justification in the direction of search for an uncompromising absolutism of ultimate norms. Or one could search for the security of norms in the mutually supporting pattern of values found to be expressions of the qualities of a good life — a kind of relational absolutism — which may transcend the value pattern of a given society. A third avenue might be suggested by speaking of the vindication of norms. This might take the form of arguing that our highest values are confirmable as reasonable and just, defended against denial or disbelief, on the grounds of their producing consequences that bear maximum goods for the human situation as it is perceived. Although philosophers of education may properly pursue the grounds of commitment at various levels of ultimacy, the concern of this paper has a focus in the middle range of normative moves on the assumption that teachers and students of education can profitably explore mid-range problems in the justification of norms without settling some of philosophy's larger questions.

Let us put the matter again in terms of the teacher's evaluation of the student's paper. The teacher validates the norm of "having something significant to say" by giving good reasons for bringing it under a universal about encouraging creative thinking. He reasons about exceptions to this presumptive norm. What aspects of creativity take precedence over rules of good grammar and rhetoric? He further justifies the norm of promoting creative thinking by reasoning about it in relation to other universal norms such as the moral principle of equality of treatment. He may pursue a course searching for final values, unequivocal for all men everywhere, or his reasoning may pursue a more relational and contextual basis for the security of ultimate value. At a minimum, the teacher sees whether his norms are mutually supporting, whether they add up to a consistent pattern of direction in grading papers and in other teaching acts. He may go further to vindicate his total framework of values as reasonable and just in the context of the human situation. In short, in the validation of norms it is fruitful to pay attention to what I have called the middle-range moves in the justification of norms.

We now review the major distinctions and moves involved in making value judgments and in the general field of normative discourse.

Following Dewey's distinction between primary values and evaluated values, we marked off primary value judgments in the sense that when something is said to have value, the value is simply had. Reasons or justifications, to the extent that they are present, are descriptive; questions about standards have narrative or factual import. It is only as one moves into considerations about evaluated values that considerations of the normative in a qualitative sense arise.

We then noted that a normative judgment involves a two-fold claim: on the one hand, something evaluated has good-making or bad-making characteristics or may be neutral with reference to a standard, and, on the other hand, the standard is specified by delineating its worth-making features.

We then distinguished characterizing from appraising aspects of normative judgments. In characterizing value judgments norms are commonly agreed upon or taken for granted. In appraisive value judgments they are to be justified. Rules are involved in both characterizing and appraisive judgments, but the more fully normative judgment involves rule-making. In the logic of appraisive judgment, since norms are to be justified, questions about relevance, priority, and validation of norms are focal.

Philosophers of education are concerned not only with the making and recommending of value judgements; everyone does that. They are not alone in pushing valuables. They do rise to the occasion of justifying the norms whereby valuables acquire their value. They do this not only by clarifying rules of normative discourse, but they also go beyond the rules by justifying them and scrutinizing the appraisive judgments involved in rule-making. In the final analysis this pushes them back to questions of the ultimate security of values, but questions of relevance, precedence, and vindication of norms indicate a middle-range set of concerns of such focal importance in educational thought and talk that philosophers would be well advised to devote more attention to them.

MORAL EDUCATION

INTRODUCTION

There is a strong temptation to begin any collection of readings on moral education with Plato's *Protagoras*. But aside from the fact that this work is already well known and widely available, the central question "Can virtue be taught?" no longer seems to be the most fruitful way of introducing the topic of moral education. Perhaps, following Aristotle, most philosophers of education today would concede that virtue comes neither by nature nor against nature but that whatever individuals acquire by way of virtue or its opposite comes through learning. If we view teaching as the deliberate attempt to guide learning, then there is a strong presupposition that whatever can be learned *could* be taught. And the central question becomes "What should be the manner and the matter of moral education?"

In any event, our first selection is a classic of a different type, age, and culture — an excerpt from *The Adventures of Huckleberry Finn*. Many thoughtful young people today are considering moral questions and issues with a seriousness that puts to shame the facile moralizing of some of their elders. In talking with these young people one quickly senses that they, like Huckleberry Finn, have somehow managed to learn more and better than they have been taught. But in addition to the fact that a precarious society can hardly afford to count on such more or less serendipitous learning, one also senses that the very urgency of their quest for answers poses another danger. Those persons who insistently *demand* definitive answers are, unfortunately, very likely to find them. But a moral simplicticacity is the traditional price the devil exacts from all who insist upon having the comfort of certainty.

If, however, we are to take seriously the idea of moral education, it would seem that we do need a definitive answer to the question of how to mark off the moral from the nonmoral. Professor Soltis tackles this problem in his article "Men, Machines, and Morality" and concludes that "unless some specific ethic is assumed, there seems to be no way to tell a moral rule or value from a nonmoral rule or value." From the standpoint of philosophy of education this appears to lead to the conclusion that "any argument or program for moral education is empty unless it does assume some particular ethic and then if it does, the fruitful point of contact for either acceptance or rejection is with regard to the assessment of the particular ethic involved and not with the general notion of moral education itself." Therefore, "the real heart of the issue is in hidden particular ethical systems."

After this article the reader may wish to consider whether in a free society the public schools have a right to engage in moral education if this must involve "hidden particular ethical systems." But, perhaps, the conclusions of Professor Soltis can be softened and rendered less inhibitory by the following considerations.

(1) In order to undertake an educational program in any subject matter area (whether morality, literature, social studies, or physics) is it necessary to know precisely the boundaries or is it sufficient to start with merely some of the characteristics of the heartland? (2) If our usual attempts to mark off the moral from the nonmoral (e.g., "corrigible human acts which have a significant impact upon the character or well-being of any person") always involve some ethical assumption, is it the case that such assumption constitutes a particular ethical system? (3) Are the minimal ethical assumptions necessary to launch the concept "moral" discordant or consonant with the value load found in the concept "education"?

In the next selection, Professor Scheffler points out that moral education (as distinct from certain kinds of training) requires that "To teach *Y* that one ought to be honest is thus not merely to try to get *Y* to be honest; it is also to try to get *Y* to be honest out of conviction." But, unfortunately, it may be the case that "a serious attempt to accomplish the second may delay and even impede the achievement of the first."

This brings one to a consideration of the roles of reason and habit in moral education which is the subject of the article by Professor Peters. It is suggested that necessary habits of behavior can be developed in such a way that they do not rule out the development of a rational code. Professor Peters believes that "Habits need not be exercised out of force of habit" and that, from the point of view of moral education, it makes a very great difference at what age and in what manner habits are formed.

But this, of course, is a matter for empirical research and "a matter about which psychologists and practical teachers will have much more to say than philosophers."

Following this line of thought leads to the next selection which is from the work of Piaget, who, incidentally, is not so boundary-conscious concerning the proper domains of philosophy and of empirical studies. Believing that among social relations two extreme types can be distinguished (relations of constraint and relations of cooperation), Piaget reasons that there is a parallelism existing between moral and intellectual development and that while relations of constraint "contribute to a first type of logical and moral control," relations of cooperation are necessary to bring about the development of intellectual and moral autonomy.

Piaget then considers what educational methods seem most compatible with what he has learned from his research and concludes that many traditional methods seem "to be contrary to the most obvious requirements of intellectual and moral development." He finds much more reasonable the methods advocated by Dewey, Sanderson, and Cousinet. Nevertheless, what is really needed is the development of scientifically controlled *educational* research, for "pedagogy is very far from being a mere application of psychological knowledge."

Having pursued this more empirical line into the problems of moral education, there is the danger of concluding that to the extent that research into the *causes of actions* is successful, it destroys the whole ideal of moral responsibility and autonomy. In order to correct this possible error, we turn again to Professor Peters for discussion of the relevance to morality of the theories of Freud and Marx. Professor Peters argues, "Terms like 'rationalization' and 'ideology,' which cast aspersions on beliefs, are verbal parasites. They only flourish because common experience has provided hosts in the form of rational beliefs and genuine principles." He concludes, "The burden of the message of both Marx and Freud was that a man who understands the causes of social evils and personal predicaments is in a position to do something about them. Understanding paves the way for action as well as for sympathy."

At this point the question of the relation of fact and value cannot be avoided. Is the teaching and learning of values substantially the same as or substantially different from the teaching and learning of facts? In addressing this question Professor Sleeper provides us with a useful review of the naturalistic fallacy, and drawing upon the work of Ryle, Wisdom, Strawson, and Ramsey, concludes, "It is the facts themselves, in the end, that will determine which of all possible worlds is indeed 'the best.' So the teaching and learning of values is not a categorically different process from the teaching and learning of facts."

Finally, there is another dangerous misunderstanding that may arise from speaking of the development of "moral autonomy" as the goal of moral education. The word "autonomy" may suggest a personal relativism that would seem to run counter to the categorical character of moral obligation. Perhaps the expression "moral autonomy" should be construed to mean not only "self-governing in moral matters" but also "being moral in one's self-governing." After all, most of us would probably agree that it is only in connection with acts that are corrigible and, in that sense, only to the extent that we could be self-governing, that truly moral issues arise.

Nevertheless, there is still the problem of providing an education that, to use Taylor's terms, teaches the obligation to make moral decisions that are "objectively" justified and, on the other hand, teaches the acceptance of what is ultimately a personal responsibility for accepting, rejecting, or reconstructing rules and standards in particular cases.

In our concluding selection, by Professor Thomas D. Perry, it is suggested, in effect, that our problem is not the finding of "moral truth" as the justification for our judgments, but rather it is to make judgments in accordance with a "morally reasonable" procedure. The universal or categorical aspect remains not in relation to the content of the judgment but because the *procedure* is "binding on everyone." Professor Perry then provides us with a review of some of the problems involved in arriving at objectively sound moral judgments and explains (in enough detail to be suggestive to educators) what seems to be involved in a morally reasonable judgmental procedure.

YOU CAN'T PRAY A LIE

MARK TWAIN

Once I said to myself it would be a thousand times better for Jim to be a slave at home where his family was, as long as he'd *got* to be a slave, and so I'd better write a letter to Tom Sawyer and tell him to tell Miss Watson where he was. But I soon give up that notion for two things: she'd be mad and disgusted at his rascality and ungratefulness for leaving her, and so she'd sell him straight down the river again; and if she didn't, everybody naturally despises an ungrateful nigger, and they'd make Jim feel it all the time, and so he'd feel ornery and disgraced. And then think of *me!* It would get all around that Huck Finn helped a nigger to get his freedom; and if I was ever to see anybody from that town again I'd be ready to get down and lick his boots for shame. That's just the way: a person does a low-down thing, and then he don't want to take no consequences of it. Thinks as long as he can hide, it ain't no disgrace. That was my fix exactly. The more I studied about this the more my conscience went to grinding me, and the more wicked and low-down and ornery I got to feeling. And at last, when it hit me all of a sudden that here was the plain hand of Providence slapping me in the face and letting me know my wickedness was being watched all the time from up there in heaven, whilst I was stealing a poor old woman's nigger that hadn't ever done me no harm, and now was showing me there's One that's always on the lookout, and ain't a-going to allow no such miserable doings to go only just so fur and no further, I most dropped in my tracks I was so scared. Well, I tried the best I could to kinder soften it up somehow for myself by saying I was brung up wicked, and so I warn't so much to blame; but something inside of me kept saying, "There was the Sunday-school, you could 'a' gone to it; and if you'd 'a' done it they'd 'a' learnt you there that people that acts as I'd been acting about that nigger goes to everlasting fire."

It made me shiver. And I about made up my mind to pray, and

Reprinted, by permission, from *The Adventures of Huckleberry Finn* (New York: Rinehart, 1948), pp. 212-214.

see if I couldn't try to quit being the kind of a boy I was and be better. So I kneeled down. But the words wouldn't come. Why wouldn't they? It warn't no use to try and hide it from Him. Nor from *me,* neither. I knowed very well why they wouldn't come. It was because my heart warn't right; it was because I warn't square; it was because I was playing double. I was letting *on* to give up sin, but away inside of me I was holding on to the biggest one of all. I was trying to make my mouth *say* I would do the right thing and the clean thing, and go and write to that nigger's owner and tell where he was; but deep down in me I knowed it was a lie, and He knowed it. You can't pray a lie — I found that out.

So I was full of trouble, full as I could be; and didn't know what to do. At last I had an idea; and I says, I'll go and write the letter — and *then* see if I can pray. Why, it was astonishing, the way I felt as light as a feather right straight off, and my troubles all gone. So I got a piece of paper and a pencil, all glad and excited, and set down and wrote:

> Miss Watson, your runaway nigger Jim is down here two mile below Pikesville, and Mr. Phelps has got him and he will give him up for the reward if you send.   Huck Finn.

I felt good and all washed clean of sin for the first time I had ever felt so in my life, and I knowed I could pray now. But I didn't do it straight off, but laid the paper down and set there thinking — thinking how good it was all this happened so, and how near I come to being lost and going to hell. And went on thinking. And got to thinking over our trip down the river; and I see Jim before me all the time: in the day and in the night-time, sometimes moonlight, sometimes storms, and we a-floating along, talking and singing and laughing. But somehow I couldn't seem to strike no places to harden me against him, but only the other kind. I'd see him standing my watch on top of his'n, 'stead of calling me, so I could go on sleeping; and see him how glad he was when I come back out of the fog; and when I come to him again in the swamp, up there where the feud was; and such-like times; and would always call me honey, and pet me, and do everything he could think of for me, and how good he always was; and at last I struck the time I saved him by telling the men we had smallpox aboard, and he was so grateful, and said I was the best friend old Jim ever had in the world, and the *only* one he's got now; and then I happened to look around and see that paper.

It was a close place. I took it up, and held it in my hand. I was a-trembling, because I'd got to decide, forever, betwixt two things, and I knowed it. I studied a minute, sort of holding my breath, and then says to myself:

"All right, then, I'll *go* to hell" — and tore it up.

It was awful thoughts and awful words, but they was said. And I let them stay said; and never thought no more about reforming. I shoved the whole thing out of my head, and said I would take up wickedness again, which was in my line, being brung up to it, and the other warn't. And for a starter I would go to work and steal Jim out of slavery again; and if I could think up anything worse, I would do that, too; because as long as I was in, and in for good, I might as well go the whole hog.

MEN, MACHINES, AND MORALITY

JONAS F. SOLTIS

By use of some fairly simple-minded contrasts between machines and men, I would like to try to present what has become for me a most perplexing problem regarding the boundaries of the sphere of morality. In a preliminary way, however, I must admit that, as I stand here before the bar of mid-twentieth–century technology, that I willingly and knowingly plead guilty to the charge of having a nineteenth-century conception of "machine." However, I beg to be excused for this "crime" because I merely wish to use the following "machine" examples to point to what I take to be some rather ordinary human assumptions about the sphere of morality which seem to be independent of any particular concept of "machine" or "Man." For example, I would expect fairly universal agreement that it makes no sense to refer to a machine as either moral or immoral. But positively, in all likelihood we would classify machines *qua* machines as nonmoral or amoral things just as we generally refrain from ascribing morality to any nonhuman thing. Of course, I do not mean to imply that a machine cannot be *used* morally or immorally. But in such cases a machine is taken to be an instrument and not an agent in the same way as a gun placed in evidence at a murder trial is not on trial for *its* life while the man who wielded it is.

If I am correct about this omission of machines from the moral sphere, then it may be instructive to compare machines with men in an attempt to isolate those characteristics which provide good reasons for calling some of the actions of one moral and the other not. Naturally, the similarities will be of less interest than the differences. Physiological machinelike descriptions of man's internal parts are not ordinarily taken to be relevant to morality. Nor, I would argue, are strict behavioristic interpretations of human behavior which seem to say, "Push this button (stimulus) and you will get this result (response)." The ideas of mechanical

Reprinted, by permission, from *Philosophy of Education 1966*, Proceedings of the Twenty-second Annual Meeting, Philosophy of Education Society, 1966, pp. 15-19.

cause and effect and automatic action seem to have little relevance to the moral sphere though both are shared in the man-machine universe of discourse. Thus, where man and machines are most similar or taken to be so, we find ourselves outside the moral sphere. But an important consideration coming out of this discussion is the clear fact that not all men's actions are within the moral sphere either (at least not those which are machinelike or mechanical) and so we can posit that the sphere of moral action for man is less than the total sphere of his actions.

But let us leave similarities and turn instead to some of the more obvious differences between men and machines which might be considered not only as distinguishing characteristics, but also as being most relevant to the moral dimension of man's activities. High on such a list, I suppose, would be "freedom," the freedom to choose alternate courses of action or, indeed, to invent or create a novel course of action. Although I am taken by this claim, I have been advised by some of my twentieth-century machine-wise colleagues that modern machines are made which have this sort of freedom and flexibility built into them. Even if I didn't believe my colleagues, I do not find it logically impossible to imagine a machine with such freedom of choice, though I would still hesitate to call such a machine, or indeed any machine for that matter, a moral agent. So, it seems that the quality of freedom of choice is at best a weakly arguable distinguishing feature and at worst, no mark at all for distinguishing between machines and men.

But there is also, of course, that whole area of humanness called the "emotions" in which Hume and others saw the spring of moral action. Included here and obviously missing from machines are human feelings such as love, desire, commitment, duty, obligation, etc. More than the fact that man has the capacity for such feeling, there is his unique (or at least claimed to be so) ability to also be conscious of such feelings. I have no friends who claim feelings or consciousness for machines, but they are so enchanted by technological progress that they are unwilling to deny the possibility of a machine being invented which did have or at least displayed the overt signs of feeling and consciousness.

I trust, however, that most of you . . . would draw the line at this point and claim feeling and consciousness as unique qualities of the human "machine" alone. Even if this were so, however,

I'm afraid that it would not bring us much closer to our goal of attempting to clearly delimit the moral sphere. For I (and I take it you recognize me as a man and not a machine) may have feelings which are nonmoral (e.g., desire for respect from my colleagues) or feelings which may be moral, immoral, or amoral (e.g., love of wife, love of another's wife, love of fresh air).

But these examples display only the feelings of love and desire; what of those more special feelings usually tied directly to morality, those of commitment, duty, and obligation which I mentioned above? Perhaps these will fare better as markers for the boundaries of the moral sphere. Concerning commitment, one might feel *committed* to a life of scholarship, but this would not be generally treated as a moral commitment. Or with "duty," may I not be in poor health and yet feel it my *duty* to come to a PES conference, even though it would seem that my absence could hardly be considered immoral? And with "obligation," may I not feel obliged to stand when guests enter a room, and though I might be considered ill-mannered if I did not do so, I doubt that for that reason alone I would be considered immoral. So the having of feelings might provide us with an opening wedge between man and machine (and note I'm only willing to say might); nevertheless, we still fall short of delimiting the moral sphere.

There are, of course, other differences between machines and men which might be pointed to, but I have little hope that they will serve us any better to limit the moral sphere. So rather, at this juncture, I think that another tactic might more profitably be adopted. Instead of seeking what is unique about man over and against some machine counterpart, I will turn to the concept of "morality" itself to see if there are certain characteristics which will serve both to delimit the moral sphere and to separate men from machines or even perhaps show us how to make moral machines.

Along this line, it is interesting to note that a writer like Hare, who carefully examines the *Language of Morals*, spends most of his time with rules, commands, and principles of a nonmoral sort (e.g., "Shut the door") so that he may avoid the emotive quality of moral language. The point of interest for us here, however, is not his strategy but the assumption he makes which most of us would also adhere to — that some rules, commands, and principles are moral and some nonmoral. In what remains . . . I will question this assumption by asking straightforwardly, "What makes a moral rule a *moral* rule?"

I think that we can all grant with Hare and other examiners of the *form* of moral language that there is no difference in form between the rule "Do not walk on the grass" and the generally recognized moral rule "Do not commit adultery." If there is a difference, one would expect instead to find it in the *subject matter* and not in the form of the rule or command.

A number of candidates to discern moral from nonmoral subject matter in such contexts comes immediately to mind, but I think we will find that they will fall short of the mark of delimiting the moral sphere. Before examining these ideas, one ground rule (a logical and nonmoral one) must be made clear, however. It would seem to me, at least, to be most improper to attempt to identify the moral sphere by pointing to those things (subject matters) which are already assumed to be moral. By that I mean that we cannot assume any *particular* substantive ethic and still impartially and objectively seek out the logical characteristics of rules which provide them with membership in the moral sphere, for by positing a particular substantive ethic, we already limit the moral sphere to whatever touches that ethic and all else falls outside of it. The problem I seek solution for, then, is not what is "moral" assuming a particular ethic, but rather what, if anything, allows one to claim a rule is a moral rule without assuming some particular ethic. In a way this problem may be similar to the one faced by the anthropologist in the field who wishes to observe a culture and to report on its various institutions without allowing his views of his particular society, particular theological beliefs, or particular morality to color his picture. In simple form, then, the ground rule I will operate on will be: *Do not count as a characteristic of the subject matter of a rule that which assumes some particular ethical view.* In a sense, all that I'm saying is that I would hope it to be possible to objectively set down a criterion for moral rules which will do the job of separating moral from nonmoral rules generally for any society, time, or place.

Having said this, I do not see any fault with counting as counter examples the general ideas we all hold in this time and place concerning certain substantive ethical positions. For as counter examples, their singular force against any universal criterion proposed is enough to deny the universal claimed.

But enough preliminaries; let us begin to test some idea. Let us assume that to be moral the subject matter of any rule must refer to human conduct. Then a rule whose subject matter refers to adulterous human conduct would have to be judged a moral rule while rules of algebra would be nonmoral. But alas, so also would a rule have to be judged moral by this criterion which referred to the human conduct of walking on the grass or standing when guests enter the room.

Obviously, the catch-all mark of "pertaining to human conduct" is too broad, for it takes in any and every rule regarding human action from rules about walking on the grass or sipping one's soup to rules governing incest and murder. But there may be a partial clue in these simple examples, for in walking on the grass or in sipping one's soup, there is human conduct in relation to some *thing* (grass and soup) whereas in the case of incest and murder, there is a rule governing a relation between human and human and not between a human and a thing. Without stretching too far, we could even bring suicide into this human relations area and so needn't even worry about self-related acts.

So our next candidate for a limiting criterion then could be given in some such form as the following: "To be judged a *moral* rule, the subject matter of the rule must deal with human conduct *as it relates to self or others.*" Although we have already seen the advantages of this added feature, it is unfortunate that it comes up short in such instances as rules which govern a game like football (with its rule about body contact with an opponent after the whistle has blown a play dead). Considering football players as subhuman will hardly get us out of this difficulty for we still have the rule governing human conduct between humans which says, "Stand whenever a guest or guests enter the room" (totally unnecessary if your guest is a machine, of course). Thus the limiting notion of human conduct and human relations in the purely human sphere is also too broad a criterion.

But surely there must be some prime candidate which I may have overlooked. Perhaps we could try some such as "The subject matter of a moral rule must be understood as *God-given,*" but again obviously this would be of no aid in an atheistic society unless we would wish to deny the existence of moral rules in such a society, and that hardly seems proper. Even the idea of a rule whose underlying principle is humanity and respect of person is of no help if we allow that standing when a guest enters a room or tipping one's hat to a lady is based on the principle of respect for person or humanness.

Perhaps the time has come to seek the advice of an expert. William Frankena, the respected contemporary moral philosopher, has faced this very problem himself in his recent clear and readable little book, *Ethics*. There he also sees the need to distinguish between the nonmoral and the moral, but instead of looking at the subject matter of rules, as we have, he turns understandably to the identification of the different *objects* of moral and nonmoral values. Values ascribed to "people, groups, traits, dispositions, emotions, motives, and intentions" mark moral values for Frankena while valuations of "experiences and forms of government . . ." (p. 48) belong to the nonmoral sphere of valuation. To take his list, it certainly seems that he is at least half (that may be too generous, one-quarter) right. In a moral sense we may judge *people* or *groups* as honest and hold morally dear the *trait* or *disposition* of honesty. The *emotion* of love for fellow man may be considered moral as may also be the *motive* of altruism or the *intent* of justice.

But, although an *experience* (as Frankena's object of nonmoral value) may be judged nonmorally as good in the sense of aesthetically pleasing or a *form of government* good in the sense of efficiency and flexibility, these same nonmoral objects are likely candidates for the moral sphere. For instance, when we call democracy good we may very well mean morally good, the morally right form of government for man, or when we call communism evil we may very well mean morally evil, the immoral subjugation of man. Similarly experiences may be moral or immoral as the law regarding "carnal experience of a minor" swiftly attests. So it seems at minimum that Frankena's candidates for exclusion from the moral sphere may on occasion enter into it.

But what of the true members, the first list of objects of moral values? Do they enjoy complete and unstinting membership? It hardly seems so. People may be judged good as, for instance, I might judge one of you to be a good scholar whose scholarship and person as a scholar I value highly while your morality makes me blush. Groups obviously come in for similar treatment, but what of things like Frankena's "traits, dispositions, emotions, motives, and intentions"? We may call the "trait" of patience a "virtue," but do we consider it a moral virtue? Even if we do, what of the trait of stubbornness? — it hardly seems to be a prime candidate for immorality! Having the disposition "to appreciate music" or "to be a pleasant person" seems equally nonmoral. The emotion of fear of God or spiders may also be quite nonmoral just as the motive or intention of the mountain climber to reach the top seems outside moral calculations while still able to be considered by some as a very "good" motive.

So it seems that even our expert Frankena fails us in that his objects of moral and nonmoral values seem to be quite interchangeable and hence hardly will do as boundary markers for the sphere of morality. We could go to other experts, but again I suspect we have little hope for success. What then is the upshot of this discussion which gets nowhere? I can only answer for myself. In very personal terms, I can testify that I have wrestled with this problem well beyond the few ideas and examples I have offered to you here, and I find myself forced to reach the conclusion that unless some specific ethic is assumed, there seems to be no way to tell a moral rule or value from a nonmoral rule or value.

Although I suspect that many of you . . . are quite eager to dissolve my problem with your wisdom or even with some simple idea I've overlooked, I feel obliged to go on just a bit more to indicate what I think this conclusion has to say to philosophers of education (just on the thin possibility that it may be a proper conclusion).

Although philosophers of education are noted for riding quite different and odd-looking horses, many have not been shy when it comes to mounting that pure white steed called "moral education" and galloping full speed into the forest of "prescriptions" and "programs" in search of the Promised Land of the Good Life and a Better World. Although I thus seem to caricature this enterprise and although I would expect to find few of you . . . with this particular bent, I think we can all agree that the contemporary world we live in could well profit from better moral training of the young and also that the possibility of such training is not totally eliminated from the realm of public education or from the concerns of philosophers of education.

But the conclusion I've drawn from my search for the clear boundary markers for the sphere of morality (namely, that unless some specific ethic is assumed, it is most difficult if not impossible to define such limits) leads me to suggest caution when approaching arguments or programs set forth as moral education. For if one argues for the need for moral education without assuming any particular ethic in his argument, then we are being given a rather empty, guideline-less sphere of action either to accept or reject. On the other hand, we may be faced with an argument or program for moral education in *general* which does assume an ethic in *particular,* and then we should be aware of the two choices which confront us and not think we only have one. That is, we may accept the idea of the need for moral education while rejecting or accepting the particular brand of moral education being offered.

I would go one step further and say that any argument or program for moral education is empty unless it *does* assume some particular ethic and then if it does, the fruitful point of contact for either acceptance or rejection is with regard to the assessment of the particular ethic involved and *not* with the general notion of moral education itself. Too many good men and good arguments, I fear, have been sidetracked by not focusing on the most relevant issue of the particular ethic involved in some brand of moral education being advocated. Who in his right mind could be against either mother or morals? It is only when we get down to the brass tacks of *which* mother and *which* morals that we have a legitimate focus for philosophical debates and judgments.

Quite obviously, we have moved in a very short time far from the initial comparison between machines and man to moral education and have not solved the thematic problem of this paper regarding the limits of the sphere of morality. If you will excuse the pun, however, I think there is a "moral" here. Even when philosophers fail to answer their unanswerable questions, what they do do may make the question clearer and may even make alternatives for practical action more easily discernible. To see that arguments for moral education *generally* are empty and that the real heart of the issue is in hidden particular ethical systems is, for me at least, an advance of sorts. More broadly, I am even led to wonder if we in the twentieth century haven't taken the sphere of morals to be too narrow and strayed from that ancient Greek notion of the full and complete "Good Life."

But that is another question hardly to be tackled at this point. Instead, I close with the invitation to you to help me solve my problem and to think about the essence of morality in objective logical terms and not, as I'm afraid we're all accustomed to, in personal, subjective, and particular terms.

TEACHING AND TELLING

ISRAEL SCHEFFLER

. . . To teach Y that one ought to be honest is thus not merely to try to get Y to be honest; it is also to try to get Y to be honest out of conviction.

The distinction here discussed is one of special importance to moral education. There are types of conduct or "patterns of action" that we want pupils to acquire, and concerning which we do not particularly care what rationales they adopt or even if they adopt any at all. Such, for example, are minimal forms of courtesy. There are sorts of conduct that we unhesitatingly support by reference to self-interest, for example, safety practices, preparation for some vocation. Moral conduct, on the other hand, is, in one important sense of the term, not merely behavior according to some independently specified norm, nor even such behavior governed by any rationale supporting the norm. Its rationale must, in a certain sense, be "objective," "impartial," or "disinterested" in its support of the norm. What this means is notoriously difficult to characterize, but it is reflected in the general and impersonal language of moral judgment (e.g., "ought") which is normally used to express some rationales but not others. The rationale of a man's moral conduct, we may perhaps say, needs to be expressible by him in the language of moral judgment.[38]

One example may suffice to illustrate the point. Three people may all have learned to be honest, yet the first may be unreflectively honest because he has been reared in a protected environment where the option of acting dishonestly has never been allowed to present itself, the second may be honest because he believes honesty to be essential for advancement in his vocation or because he finds dishonesty emotionally taxing, while the third

Reprinted, by permission, from *The Language of Education* (Springfield, Ill.: Charles C. Thomas, 1960).

[38] An important paper, to which I am indebted for its treatment of these and related issues, is W. K. Frankena, "Toward a Philosophy of Moral Education," *Harvard Educational Review*, XXVIII, no. 4 (Fall, 1958): 300-312.

may be honest because he believes that one ought to be honest. The behavior of the first two conforms to the norm of honesty, but can hardly be characterized as moral (or immoral) conduct, in the sense of the term we have here been considering.

If moral conduct is our goal in moral education, we are, in effect, striving to achieve not alone the acquisition of norms of a given sort in practice, but the reflective support of norms of this sort in an "objective" or "impartial" manner. To teach honesty as if it were a kind of safety rule or a conventional form of courtesy may effectively accomplish the first aim without in the least furthering the second. It cannot, on the other hand, be denied that a serious attempt to accomplish the second may delay and even impede the achievement of the first. (To encourage a *reflective and impartial* critique of norms may lead to a rejection of *our* norms.) We may, as teachers, try to further both aims by subjecting the very norms we are concerned with under the first aim to the sort of reflective scrutiny we encourage under the second.

REASON AND HABIT:
THE PARADOX OF MORAL EDUCATION

RICHARD S. PETERS

. . . The problem of moral education, then, and indeed of education in general, is this: how can the necessary habits of behavior and the deep-rooted assumptions of the "literature" of various forms of good activities be acquired in a way which does not stultify the development of a rational code or the mastery of the "language" of activities at a later stage?

I am assuming, by the way, like Aristotle, that children gradually acquire these desirable forms of life by some on-the-spot apprenticeship system. I am also assuming something about the factor which I previously picked out when I stressed the spontaneous enjoyment that goes with such a form of life. Spinoza put this in a very general way when he declared that "Blessedness is not the reward of right living; it is the right living itself; nor should we rejoice in it because we restrain our desires, but, on the contrary, it is because we rejoice in it that we restrain them."[3] In the jargon of modern psychology this is to say that a rational code and worthwhile activities are intrinsically, not extrinsically, motivated.

Now education, at any rate at later levels, consists largely in initiating people into this form of life — in getting others on the inside of activities so that they practice them simply for the intrinsic satisfactions that they contain and for no end which is extrinsic to them. That is why one gets so impatient with the endless talk about the aims of education and the modern tendency to speak about education in the economic jargon of "investment" and "commodity." No one, of course, would deny that many skills and much information have to be passed on to sustain and increase productivity in an industrial society; it is also the case that if money has to be raised from hard-headed businessmen or from an over-taxed and materialistically minded public, the instrumental

---

Reprinted, by permission, from W. R. Nibbitt (ed.), *Moral Education in a Changing Society* (London: Faber and Faber, 1963), pp. 46-65, with slight revisions by the author.

[3] Spinoza, *Ethics,* Part V, Prop. XLII.

aspects of what goes on in schools and universities may have to be stressed. But anyone who reflects must ask questions about the point of keeping the wheels of industry turning. And the answer is not simply that it is necessary for survival or "living"— whatever that means. It is necessary for the maintenance and extension of a civilized life whose distinctive outlook and activities are those which are passed on in schools and universities. In such institutions there is no absolute distinction between teacher and learner. It is a matter of degree of skill, knowledge, insight, and experience within a common form of life. So there is an important sense in which "life," by which is usually meant that which goes on outside the classroom, is for the sake of education, not education for life. . . .

Now anyone who has managed to get on the inside of what is passed on in schools and universities, such as science, music, art, carpentry, literature, history, and athletics, will regard it as somehow ridiculous to be asked what the point of his activity is. The mastery of the "language" carries with it its own delights, or "intrinsic motivation," to use the jargon. But for a person on the *outside* it may be difficult to see what point there is in the activity in question. Hence the incredulity of the uninitiated when confronted with the rhapsodies of the mountain-climber, musician, or golfer. *Children* are to a large extent in the position of such outsiders. The problem is to introduce them to a civilized outlook and activities in such a way that they can get on the inside of those for which they have aptitude.

The same sort of problem can be posed in the case of their attitude to rules of conduct. Is it the case that children have to be lured by irrelevant incentives or goaded by commands so that they acquire the basic habits of conduct and the "literature" of the various activities without which they cannot emerge to the later stage? Is it the case that we have to use such irrelevant "extrinsic" techniques to get children going so that eventually they can take over for themselves, without needing any longer such extrinsic incentives or goads? Or does the use of such extrinsic techniques militate against intelligent, spontaneous, and intrinsically directed behavior later on?

It might be argued, for instance, that the various maturation levels bring with them the possibility of a variety of intrinsic motivations falling under concepts such as competence,[4] mastery, and curiosity. Then there is the ubiquitous role of love and trust; for psychoanalysts such as Bowlby suggest that the existence of a good relationship of love and trust between parent and child during the early years is a *necessary condition* for the formation of any enduring and consistent moral habits.[5] Whether love, the withdrawal of love, approval and disapproval, constitute extrinsic or intrinsic motivations in respect to the development of habits is too complicated a question to consider here. Nevertheless it may well be that the use of such intrinsic as distinct from extrinsic motivations may be crucial in determining the type of habits that are formed. For the formation of *some* types of habit may not necessarily militate against adaptability and spontaneous enjoyment. However, it is often thought that, because of the very nature of habits, dwelling in the courtyard of Habit incapacitates a man for life in the palace of Reason. I now propose to show both why this need not be the case and why people can be led to think that it must be the case. . . .

. . . The formation of sound moral habits in respect of, for instance, what I have called basic moral rules might well be a necessary condition of rational morality. It can, however, seem to be antagonistic to rational morality because of an interesting sort of conceptual confusion and because of the development, through a variety of causes, of specific types of habit. I will deal first with the conceptual issue and then proceed to the more empirical one.

What, then, do we mean by "habits" and is there any necessary contradiction in stressing the importance of habit in moral matters while, at the same time, stressing the intelligent adaptability which is usually associated with reason, together with the spontaneous enjoyment associated with civilized activities? . . .

When we describe an action as a "habit" we suggest, first of all, that the man has done this very thing before and that he will probably do it again. We are postulating a tendency to act in this way. "Habit" also carries with it the suggestion not only of repetition but also of the ability to carry out the action in ques-

---

[4] See, for instance, R. White, "Competence and the Psychosexual Stages of Development," in *Nebraska Symposium on Motivation 1960.*

[5] See R. S. Peters, "Moral Education and the Psychology of Character," *Philosophy* (January, 1962).

tion "automatically." A man can automatically stir his tea or puff his pipe while discussing the latest developments in Cuba. . . . The art of living consists to a large extent in reducing most things that have to be done to habit; for then the mind is set free to pay attention to things that are interesting, novel, and worthwhile. . . .

What are the implications of this analysis for the development of adaptability which is the hallmark of skilled and civilized activities? What we call a skill presupposes a number of component habits. A fielder at cricket, for instance, may be very skillful and show great intelligence in running a man out by throwing the ball to the bowler rather than to the wicket-keeper. But to do this he would have to bend down, pick the ball up, and contort his body with his eye partly on the ball and partly on the position of the batsmen. But unless these component actions were more or less habits he would not be able to concentrate on using them in the service of the higher strategy of the game. But — and this is the important point — all these component actions would have to be capable of being performed with a degree of plasticity to permit coordination in a wide variety of very different over-all actions. The concept of "action" is "open-ended" in many dimensions. We could describe the man as moving his arm, as throwing the ball at the wicket, or throwing it at the bowler's end, or as running the batsman out, depending on the aspect under which the fielder conceived what he was doing. In what we call "mechanical" actions a man will always conceive the movements as leading up in a stereotyped way to a narrowly conceived end. In intelligent actions the component actions are conceived of as variable and adaptable in the light of some more generally conceived end. The teachers who have taught me most about golf and about philosophy are those who have insisted on conveying an over-all picture of the performance as a whole in which the particular moves have to be practiced under the aspect of some wider conception, instead of concentrating either on drilling me in moves which are conceived in a very limited way or going simply for the over-all picture without bothering about practicing the component moves.

Now the type of habits which would count as moral habits *must* be exhibited in a wide range of actions in so far as actions are thought to be constituted by the sorts of movements of the body that are usually associated with skills. Consider, for instance, the range of such actions that can fall under the concept of theft or malice. What makes an action a case of theft is that it must be conceived of as involving appropriating, without permission, something that belongs to someone else. A child, strictly speaking, cannot be guilty of theft, who has not developed the concept of himself as distinct from others, of property, of the granting of permission, etc. It takes a long time to develop such concepts. In the early years, therefore, parents may think that they are teaching their children not to steal, whereas in fact they are doing no such thing. They may be teaching the child something else, e.g., to inhibit actions of which authority figures disapprove, or to inhibit a narrowly conceived range of movements. At the toilet training stage, for instance, children may pick up very generalized and often unintelligent habits — e.g., punctilious conformity to rules, unwillingness to part with anything that is theirs. But this is not what the parents were trying to teach them. For the children probably lack the concepts which are necessary for understanding what the parents *think* that they are teaching them, namely the rule of cleanliness. To learn to act on rules forbidding theft, lying, breaking promises, etc. is necessarily an open-ended business requiring intelligence and a high degree of social sophistication. For the child has to learn to see that a vast range of very different actions and performances can fall under a highly abstract rule which makes them all examples of a type of action. If the child has really learned to act on a rule, it is difficult to see how he could have accomplished this without insight and intelligence. He might be drilled or forced to act in *accordance with* a rule; but that is quite different from learning to act *on* a rule.

So it seems as if the paradox of moral education is resolved. For there is no *necessary* contradiction between the use of intelligence and the formation of habits. How then does the antithesis between the two, which is frequently made, come about? Partly, I think, through the existence of certain explanatory expressions such as "out of habit," and partly because of certain empirical facts about a special class of habits.

Let us take the point about explanatory expressions first. In explaining particular actions or courses of action we often use the phrases "out of habit," "through force of habit," or "that is a matter of sheer habit." This type of phrase does not simply suggest that what the man is doing is a habit in the sense that he has a tendency to do this sort of thing and that he can do it automatically. It also implies that in this case:

(1) The man has no reason for doing it which would render the action other than one conceived in a limited way. He could, of course, be raising his arm to attract someone's notice. He might indeed produce such a reason for doing it if asked. But to say that he raised his arm on this occasion "out of habit" or through "force of habit" is to deny that, on this occasion, such a reason, which he might have, was *his* reason. Raising his arm *simpliciter,* we are saying, is just the sort of thing that he tends to do.

(2) The clash with the idea of spontaneity, which is also often associated with "habit," comes in also because to say that a man cleans his teeth or washes up "out of habit" or "through force of habit" is to exclude the possibility that there is any enjoyment in it for him, that he is doing it for pleasure, for what he sees in it as distinct from what he sees it leading on to. It is, in other words, to rule out intrinsic motivation. It is to explain what he does, roughly speaking, in terms of the law of exercise, and to rule out any variant of the law of effect. . . .

Given, then, that the explanation "out of habit" or "from force of habit" rules out the possibility of a further extrinsic end by reference to which an action could be deemed to be intelligent and given that "out of habit" also rules out explanations in terms of pleasure, enjoyment, or any kind of intrinsic motivation, it is obvious enough why the intelligent adaptability of a rational code as well as spontaneous delight in practicing it and in pursuing worthwhile activities are in stark opposition to things that are done "out of habit." But, as I have tried to show, they are not so opposed to habits as mere descriptions of types of action. Habits need not be exercised out of force of habit.

The fact, however, that they very often *are* brings me to my empirical point, which is that there is a great number of things which we do, in fact, do out of habit, and this is essential if our minds are to be set free to attend to other things. . . . It is also the case that in some people whom, in extreme cases, we describe as compulsives, the force of habit is so strong that it militates against intelligent performance and disrupts the rest of man's life.

Tidiness and cleanliness are in general sound moral habits because they save time and health and permit efficient and intelligent performance of countless other things. But if a women is so obsessed with them that she tries to impress the stamp of the operating theater on the nursery and bedroom of young children, she may well have reached the point where her habits disrupt not only her domestic bliss but also her own capacity for intelligent adaptation and for enjoyment of things that are worth enjoying.

And so we stand at the door of the nursery which is the gateway to moral education. For it is here, in all probability, that the pattern of character-traits and the manner of exercising them is laid down. It is here that habits are first formed in a manner which may lead to the development of compulsives, obsessives, Puritans, and impractical ideologues. To explain how this probably happens would involve a careful examination of cognitive development and the role of extrinsic and intrinsic motivation in childhood. I could not begin to tackle this vast subject in this paper. I have only tried to explain and to resolve the *theoretical* paradox of moral education, not to develop a positive theory of rational child-rearing.

Aristotle put the matter very well when he said: "But the virtues we get by first exercising them, as also happens in the case of the arts as well. For the things we have to learn before we can do them, we learn by doing them, e.g., men become builders by building and lyre players by playing the lyre; so do we become just by doing just acts, temperate by doing temperate acts, brave by doing brave acts. . . . It makes no small difference then, whether we form habits of one kind or another from our very youth; it makes a great difference or rather all the difference. . . ."[6]

But from the point of view of moral education it makes all the difference, too, at what age and in what manner such habits are formed, especially under what aspect particular acts are taught. For it is only if habits are developed in a certain kind of way that the paradox of moral education can be avoided in practice. This is a matter about which psychologists and practical teachers will have much more to say than philosophers. For I have only tried

---

[6] Aristotle, *Nichomachean Ethics,* Bk. II, Chapters 3, 4.

to resolve the theoretical paradox of moral education in a theoretical manner.

Bacon once said that the discourse of philosophers is like the stars; it sheds little light because it is so high. But when it is brought nearer the earth, as I hope it has been in this paper, it still can only shed light on where empirical research needs to be done and where practical judgments have to be made. It is no substitute for either.

THE TWO MORALITIES OF THE CHILD

JEAN PIAGET

§ 6. *Conclusions.* — The analysis of the child's moral judgments has led us perforce to the discussion of the great problem of the relations of social life to the rational consciousness. The conclusion we came to was that the morality prescribed for the individual by society is not homogeneous because society itself is not just one thing. Society is the sum of social relations, and among these relations we can distinguish two extreme types: relations of constraint, whose characteristic is to impose upon the individual from outside a system of rules with obligatory content, and relations of cooperation, whose characteristic is to create within people's minds the consciousness of ideal norms at the back of all rules. Arising from the ties of authority and unilateral respect, the relations of constraint therefore characterize most of the features of society as it exists, and in particular the relations of the child to its adult surrounding. Defined by equality and mutual respect, the relations of cooperation, on the contrary, constitute an equilibrial limit rather than a static system. Constraint, the source of duty and heteronomy, cannot, therefore, be reduced to the good and to autonomous rationality, which are the fruits of reciprocity, although the actual evolution of the relations of constraint tends to bring these nearer to cooperation.

In spite of our wish to confine the discussion to the problems connected with child psychology, the reader will not have failed to recognize the affinity of these results with those of the historical or logico-sociological analyses carried out by M. Brunschvicg and M. Lalande. *Le progrès de la conscience dans la philosophie occidentale* is the widest and the most subtle demonstration of the fact that there exists in European thought a law in the evolution of moral judgments which is analogous to the law by which psychology watches the effects throughout the development of the individual. Now to indulge in philosophic inquiry is simply to take

Reprinted, by permission, from *The Moral Judgement of the Child,* trans. Marjorie Gaboin (London: Routledge and Kegan Paul, 1932; New York: Collier, 1962), pp. 401-414.

increasing cognizance of the currents of thought which enter into and sustain the states of society itself. What the philosopher does is not so much to create something new as to reflect the elaborations of the human mind. It is therefore of the utmost significance that the critical analysis of history of which M. Brunschvicg has put to fresh use should have succeeded in bringing to light in the evolution of Western philosophic thought the gradual victory of the norms of reciprocity over those of social conformism.

As to M. Lalande, what he says on "la Dissolution," as also on the social character of logical norms, has shown more than any other work on the subject the duality that lies hidden in the word "social." There are, M. Lalande tells us, two societies: existing or organized society, whose constant feature is the constraint which it exercises upon individual minds, and there is the ideal or assimilative society, which is defined by the progressive identification of people's minds with one another. The reader will recognize here the same distinction as we have been led to observe between the relations of authority and the relations of equality.

Some of M. Lalande's minor contentions would, indeed, stand in the way of our complete agreement with his ideas taken as a whole. It does not seem to us at all certain, for example, that "evolution" in the sense of progressive organization is necessarily bound up with a society based on constraint. The passage from the homogeneous to the heterogeneous which M. Lalande agrees with Spencer in taking as the mark of evolution leads no doubt to social differentiation. But this differentiation is precisely, as the sociologists have pointed out, the condition of a break with the conformity due to constraint, and consequently the condition of personal liberation. Moral equality is not the result of an advance toward homogeneity, assuming that agreement can be reached on the meaning of this word, but of a mobility which is a function of differentiation. The more differentiated the society, the better can its members alter their situation in accordance with their aptitudes, the greater will be the opportunity for intellectual and moral cooperation. We cannot, therefore, take the identification of minds, which, for M. Lalande, is the supreme norm, to be the same thing as cooperation. Without attempting to evaluate this "vector," and limiting ourselves to the mere description of psychological facts, what the morality of the good seems to us to achieve is reciprocity rather than identification. The morality of the autonomous conscience does not tend to subject each personality to rules that have a common content: it simply obliges individuals to place themselves in reciprocal relationship with each other without letting the laws of perspective resultant upon this reciprocity destroy their individual points of view.

But what do these minor discrepancies matter since it is thanks to M. Lalande's teaching that we are able to dissociate what the sociologists have so often tended to confuse? And above all, what do the concepts that are used in the interpretation of the facts matter, so long as the method employed is the same? For in the work of M. Lalande we have an example of that rare thing — research on the evolution of norms conducted well within the limits of the psycho-sociological method. Without in any way neglecting the demands of rationality, this great logician has been able to discern in intellectual and moral assimilation processes admitting of analysis in terms of social psychology while implying by their very "direction" the existence of ideal norms immanent in the human spirit.

This concordance of our results with those of historico-critical or logico-sociological analysis brings us to a second point: the parallelism existing between moral and intellectual development. Everyone is aware of the kinship between logical and ethical norms. Logic is the morality of thought just as morality is the logic of action. Nearly all contemporary theories agree in recognizing the existence of this parallelism — from the a priori view which regards pure reason as the arbiter both of theoretical reflection and daily practice, to the sociological theories of knowledge and of ethical values. It is therefore in no way surprising that the analysis of child thought should bring to the fore certain particular aspects of this general phenomenon.[1]

One may say, to begin with, that in a certain sense neither logical nor moral norms are innate in the individual mind. We can find, no doubt, even before language, all the elements of rationality and morality. Thus sensori-motor intelligence gives rise

---

[1] We have further developed this point at the Ninth International Congress of Psychology which met at New Haven (U.S.A.). See *Ninth International Congress of Psychology, Proceedings and Papers*, p. 339.

to operations of assimilation and construction, in which it is not hard to see the functional equivalent of the logic of classes and of relations. Similarly the child's behavior toward persons shows signs from the first of those sympathetic tendencies and affective reactions in which one can easily see the raw material of all subsequent moral behavior. But an intelligent act can only be called logical and a good-hearted impulse moral from the moment that certain norms impress a given structure and rules of equilibrium upon this material. Logic is not co-extensive with intelligence, but consists of the sum-total of rules of control which intelligence makes use of for its own direction. Morality plays a similar part with regard to the affective life. Now there is nothing that allows us to affirm the existence of such norms in the pre-social behavior occurring before the appearance of language. The control characteristic of sensori-motor intelligence is of external origin: it is things themselves that constrain the organism to select which steps it will take; the initial intellectual activity does actively seek for truth. Similarly, it is persons external to him who canalize the child's elementary feelings; those feelings do not tend to regulate themselves from within.

This does not mean that everything in the a priori view is to be rejected. Of course the a priori never manifests itself in the form of ready-made innate mechanisms. The a priori is the obligatory element, and the necessary connections only impose themselves little by little, as evolution proceeds. It is at the end of knowledge and not in its beginnings that the mind becomes conscious of the laws immanent to it. Yet to speak of directed evolution and asymptotic advance toward a necessary ideal is to recognize the existence of a something which acts from the first in the direction of this evolution. But under what form does this "something" present itself? Under the form of a structure that straightway organizes the contents of consciousness, or under the form of a functional law of equilibrium, unconscious as yet because the mind has not yet achieved this equilibrium, and to be manifested only in and through the multitudinous structures that are to appear later? There seems to us to be no doubt about the answer. There is in the very functioning of sensori-motor operations a search for coherence and organization. Alongside, therefore, of the incoherence that characterizes the successive steps taken by elementary intelligence we must admit the existence of an ideal equilibrium, indefinable as structure but implied in the functioning that is at work. Such is the a priori: it is neither a principle from which concrete actions can be deduced nor a structure of which the mind can become conscious as such, but it is a sum-total of functional relations implying the distinction between the existing states of disequilibrium and an ideal equilibrium yet to be realized.

How then will the mind extract norms in the true sense from this functional equilibrium? It will form structures by means of an adequate conscious realization (*prise de conscience*). To ensure that the functional search for organization exhibited by the initial sensori-motor and affective activity gives rise to rules of organization properly so called, it is sufficient that the mind should become conscious of this search and of the laws governing it, thus translating into structure what till then had been function and nothing more.

But this coming into consciousness or conscious realization is not a simple operation and is bound up with a whole set of psychological conditions. It is here that psycho-sociological research becomes indispensable to the theory of norms and that the genetic parallelism existing between the formation of the logical and of the moral consciousness can be observed.

In the first place it should be noticed that the individual is not capable of achieving this conscious realization by himself, and consequently does not straight away succeed in establishing norms properly so called. It is in this sense that reason in its double aspect, both logical and moral, is a collective product. This does not mean that society has conjured up rationality out of the void, nor that there does not exist a spirit of humanity that is superior to society because dwelling both within the individual and the social group. It means that social life is necessary if the individual is to become conscious of the functioning of his own mind and thus to transform into norms properly so called the simple functional equilibria immanent to all mental and even all vital activity.

For the individual, left to himself, remains egocentric. By which we mean simply this — Just as at first the mind, before it can dissociate what belongs to objective laws from what is bound up with the sum of subjective conditions, confuses itself with the universe, so does the individual begin by understanding and feeling everything through the medium of himself before distinguishing what belongs to things and other people from what is the result of his own particular intellectual and affective perspective. At this stage, therefore, the individual cannot be conscious of his own thought, since consciousness of self implies a perpetual comparison of the self with other people. Thus from the logical point of view egocentrism would seem to involve a sort of alogicality, such that sometimes affectivity gains the ascendant over objectivity, and sometimes the relations arising from personal activity prove stronger than the relations that are independent of the self. And from the moral point of view, egocentrism involves a sort of anomy such that tenderness and disinterestedness can go hand in hand with a naïve selfishness and yet the child not feel spontaneously himself to be better in one case than the other. Just as the ideas which enter his mind appear from the first in the form of beliefs and not of hypotheses requiring verification, so do the feelings that arise in the child's consciousness appear to him from the first as having value and not as having to be submitted to some ulterior evaluation. It is only through contact with the judgments and evaluations of others that this intellectual and affective anomy will gradually yield to the pressure of collective logical and moral laws.

In the second place, the relations of constraint and unilateral respect which are spontaneously established between child and adult contribute to the formation of a first type of logical and moral control. But this control is insufficient of itself to eliminate childish egocentrism. From the intellectual point of view this respect of the child for the adult gives rise to an "annunciatory" conception of truth: the mind stops affirming what it likes to affirm and falls in with the opinion of those around it. This gives birth to a distinction which is equivalent to that of truth and falsehood: some affirmations are recognized as valid while others are not. But it goes without saying that although this distinction marks an important advance as compared to the anomy of egocentric thought, it is none the less irrational in principle. For if we are to speak of truth as rational, it is not sufficient that the contents of one's statements should conform with reality: reason must have taken active steps to obtain these contents and reason must be in a position to control the agreement or disagreement of these statements with reality. Now, in the case under discussion, reason is still very far removed from this autonomy: truth means whatever conforms with the spoken word of the adult. Whether the child has himself discovered the propositions which he asks the adult to sanction with his authority, or whether he merely repeats what the adult has said, in both cases there is intellectual constraint put upon an inferior by a superior, and therefore heteronomy. Thus, far from checking childish egocentrism at its source, such a submission tends on the contrary partly to consolidate the mental habits characteristic of egocentrism. Just as, if left to himself, the child believes every idea that enters his head instead of regarding it as a hypothesis to be verified, so the child who is submissive to the word of his parents believes without question everything he is told, instead of perceiving the element of uncertainty and search in adult thought. The self's good pleasure is simply replaced by the good pleasure of a supreme authority. There is progress here, no doubt, since such a transference accustoms the mind to look for a common truth, but this progress is big with danger if the supreme authority be not in its turn criticized in the name of reason. Now, criticism is born of discussion, and discussion is only possible among equals: cooperation alone will therefore accomplish what intellectual constraint failed to bring about. And indeed we constantly have occasion throughout our schools to notice the combined effects of this constraint and of intellectual egocentrism. What is "verbalism," for example, if not the joint result of oral authority and the syncretism peculiar to the egocentric language of the child? In short, in order to really socialize the child, cooperation is necessary, for it alone will succeed in delivering him from the mystical power of the word of the adult.

An exact counterpart of these findings about intellectual constraint is supplied by the observations on the effect of moral constraint contained in the present book. Just as the child believes in the adult's omniscience so also does he unquestioningly believe in the absolute value of the imperatives he receives. This result of unilateral respect is of great practical value, for it is in this way that there is formed an elementary sense of duty and the first normative control of which the child is capable. But it seemed to us clear that this acquisition was not sufficient to form true morality. For conduct to be characterized as moral there must be something more than an outward agreement between its content and that of the commonly accepted rules: it is also requisite that the mind should tend toward morality as to an autonomous good and should itself be capable of appreciating the value of the rules that are proposed to it. Now in the case under discussion, the good is simply what is in conformity with heteronomous commands. And as in the case of intellectual development, moral constraint has the effect of partly consolidating the habits characteristic of egocentrism. Even when the child's behavior is not just a calculated attempt to reconcile his individual interest with the letter of the law, one can observe . . . a curious mixture of respect for the law and of caprice in its application. The law is still external to the mind, which cannot therefore be transformed by it. Besides, since he regards the adult as the source of the law, the child is only raising up the will of the adult to the rank of the supreme good after having previously accorded this rank to the various dictates of his own desires. An advance, no doubt, but again an advance charged with doubtful consequences if cooperation does not come and establish norms sufficiently independent to subject even the respect due to the adult to this inner ideal. And indeed so long as unilateral respect is alone at work, we see a "moral realism" developing which is the equivalent of "verbal realism." Resting in part on the externality of rules, such a realism is also kept going by all the other forms of realism peculiar to the egocentric mentality of the child. Only cooperation will correct this attitude, thus showing that in the moral sphere, as in matters of intelligence, it plays a liberating and a constructive role.

Hence a third analogy between moral and intellectual evolution: cooperation alone leads to autonomy. With regard to logic, cooperation is at first a source of criticism; thanks to the mutual control which it introduces, it suppresses both the spontaneous conviction that characterizes egocentrism and the blind faith in adult authority. Thus, discussion gives rise to reflection and objective verification. But through this very fact cooperation becomes the source of constructive values. It leads to the recognition of the principles of formal logic in so far as these normative laws are necessary to common search for truth. It leads, above all, to a conscious realization of the logic of relations, since reciprocity on the intellectual plane necessarily involves the elaboration of those laws of perspective which we find in the operations distinctive of systems of relations.

In the same way, with regard to moral realities, cooperation is at first the source of criticism and individualism. For by comparing his own private motives with the rules adopted by each and sundry, the individual is led to judge objectively the acts and commands of other people, including adults. Whence the decline of unilateral respect and the primacy of personal judgment. But in consequence of this, cooperation suppresses both egocentrism and moral realism, and thus achieves an interiorization of rules. A new morality follows upon that of pure duty. Heteronomy steps aside to make way for a consciousness of good, of which the autonomy results from the acceptance of the norms of reciprocity. Obedience withdraws in favor of the idea of justice and of mutual service, now the source of all the obligations which till then had been imposed as incomprehensible commands. In a word, cooperation on the moral plane brings about transformations exactly parallel to those of which we have just been recalling the existence in the intellectual domain.

Is there any need, by way of conclusion, to point to the educational consequences of such observations? If education claims to be the direct application of what we know about child psychology, it would not be necessary. It is obvious that our results are as unfavorable to the method of authority as to purely individualistic methods. It is . . . absurd and even immoral to wish to impose upon the child a fully worked out system of discipline when the social life of children amongst themselves is sufficiently developed to give rise to a discipline infinitely nearer to that inner submission which is the mark of adult morality. It is idle, again, to try and transform the child's mind from outside, when his own taste for active research and his desire for cooperation suffice to ensure a normal intellectual development. The adult must therefore be a collaborator and not a master, from this double point of view, moral and rational. But conversely, it would be unwise to rely upon biological "nature" alone to ensure the dual progress of conscience and intelligence, when we realize to what extent all moral as all logical norms are the result of cooperation. Let us therefore try to create in the school a place where individual experimentation and reflection carried out in common come to each other's aid and balance one another.

If, then, we had to choose from among the totality of existing educational systems those which would best correspond with our psychological results, we would turn our methods in the direction of what has been called "Group Work" and "Self-government."[2] Advocated by Dewey, Sanderson, Cousinet, and by most of the promoters of the "Activity School," the method of work by groups consists in allowing the children to follow their pursuits in common, either in organized "teams" or simply according to their spontaneous groupings. Traditional schools, whose ideal has gradually come to be the preparation of pupils for competitive examinations rather than for life, have found themselves obliged to shut the child up in work that is strictly individual: the class listens in common, but the pupils do their homework separately. This procedure, which helps more than all the family situations put together to reinforce the child's spontaneous egocentrism, seems to be contrary to the most obvious requirements of intellectual and moral development. This is the state of things which the method of work in groups is intended to correct. Cooperation is promoted to the rank of a factor essential to intellectual progress. It need hardly be said that this innovation assumes value only to the extent that the initiative is left to the children in the actual conduct of their work. Social life is here a complement of individual "activity" (in contrast to the passive repetition which characterizes the method of teaching by books), and it would have no meaning in the school except in relation to the renovation of the teaching itself.

As for self-government, the fine works of F. W. Foerster . . . and Ad. Ferrière[3] have rendered unnecessary the task of reminding our readers of its principles. M. Ferrière in particular has described with great care and with that proselytizing fervor which characterizes all his educational works the various modes of gov-

---

[2] We refer the reader, on this point, to our "Rapport sur les procédés de l'Education morale," read at the Fifth International Congress on Moral Education in Paris, 1930.

[3] Ad. Ferrière, *L'autonomie des écoliers* (Coll. des Actualités pédag. Delachaux et Niestlé).

ernment of children by themselves. It is hard to read his book without being filled both with the hope of seeing the experiments he analyzes carried out more generally, and with the satisfaction at finding in the principles that characterize children's republics what we already know, thanks to the psycho-sociological study of the moral life.

As to F. W. Foerster, his moral pedagogy is still in our opinion too much tinged with the cult of authority or unilateral respect, and, above all, too much attached to the idea of expiatory punishment. But this makes the preoccupation with autonomy and self-government, which appears in the rest of his work, the more significant.

But pedagogy is very far from being a mere application of psychological knowledge. Apart from the question of the aims of education, it is obvious that even with regard to technical methods it is for experiment alone and not deduction to show us whether methods such as that of work in groups and of self-government are of any real value. For, after all, it is one thing to prove that cooperation in the play and spontaneous social life of children brings about certain moral effects, and another to establish the fact that this cooperation can be universally applied as a method of education. This last point is one which only experimental education can settle. Educational experiment, on condition that it be scientifically controlled, is certainly more instructive for psychology than any amount of laboratory experiments, and because of this experimental pedagogy might perhaps be incorporated into the body of the psycho-sociological disciplines. But the type of experiment which such research would require can only be conducted by teachers or by the combined efforts of practical workers and educational psychologists. And it is not in our power to deduce the results to which this would lead.

CAUSES AND MORALITY

RICHARD S. PETERS

. . . I have concentrated so far on half-truths from Freud and Marx which have led people to think that if causes can be found for their actions, then their responsibility for them is diminished. I wish here to discuss the relevance of the theories of Freud and Marx to morality; for there is a very widespread view that we are not responsible in our dealings with each other for the standards which we observe — or fail to observe. Freud and Marx, it is argued, have shown that these are the product either of our social class or of our childhood conditioning.

On the face of it there is nothing very novel or surprising in this suggestion. Standards must be passed on somehow. What more natural than that we should pick up the standards of our associates or parents? A middle-class man, who has been to a public school, will find it difficult to disregard the emphasis on fair play, loyalty to the side, honesty, and courage. From his parents, too, he will have learned that he must not steal, cheat, or be cruel to cats. Freud's theory that such standards are "introjected," that the nagging of conscience is the forbidding voice of the father, seems no more than an elaboration of the obvious. Clearly, traditions cannot be handed on without some sort of mechanism; they do not float from man to man like threads of gossamer.

The theory becomes much less obvious if it is thought to apply to moral standards; for by morality, as distinct from tradition or custom, I do not mean just doing the "done" thing — what our parents or associates have told us. I mean conforming to standards which we have thought about before accepting them as our own. . . . A reasoned decision not to smoke, because of its demonstrated effects, is different from an irrational objection to smoking, handed on from father to son. Freud's theory of conscience, which he called the "super-ego," seems to account for the stage when children feel irrational guilt about breaking rules that are exter-

Reprinted, by permission, from *Authority, Responsibility, and Education* (London: George Allen and Unwin, 1963; New York: Paul S. Eriksson, 1963), pp. 71-79.

nally imposed and whose validity they do not question. None of us altogether lose our childhood attitude to rules. But if by moral standards we mean those that we adopt because we see the point of them rather than merely as a result of our upbringing or class, it should follow that the causal theories of Marx and Freud do not in any way undermine our responsibility for them. After all, if a belief has good grounds to support it, there is little point in speculating about its causes. The wrongness of breaking promises is unaffected by the fact that our feeling of guilt about breaking them may have causes. Indeed it would be surprising if it had not. The point is whether, whatever our parents say, it is wrong to break promises. We, as moral beings, have to decide and stand by our decision. That is where our responsibility comes in. If there are, in general, good reasons for keeping promises — as there obviously are — and someone suggests that our duty to keep them was drummed into us at a public school or at our mother's knee, the appropriate answer is: "So what?" or "How thoughtful of them."

But the matter is not as simple as this. If Freud and Marx had provided merely a rather labored glimpse into the obvious origins of customary conduct, they would not have done so much to encourage the belief that we are not responsible for our standards. They were both well aware that men develop arguments and systems of thought to justify their conduct and they sometimes use the words "ideology" and "rationalization"[1] to describe such arguments. Both these terms made, as it were, double-barrelled suggestions; for they implied that there was something suspect about the justification, and that this could be detected by looking at the causal realities beneath the appearances. It was significant, Marx thought, that the Puritan gave religious reasons for adopting the virtues of thrift, hard work, enterprise, and respect for property — all of which were essential for furthering his economic interests. The liberal, too, extolled liberty; like John Stuart Mill he might

[1] Before his death Ernest Jones wrote to me pointing out that Freud, so far as he knew, had not used the term "rationalization." I replied that what he said about "idealization" in his *Group Psychology and the Analysis of the Ego* showed at least that he had the concept even if he did not use the term. Jones, of course, was quite right, for he himself introduced the term in his *Rationalization in Everyday Life* in 1908.

even write an impassioned and elaborate defense of it. But, said Marx, these arguments were a facade which hid the economic necessity of the exploiting class to be unhampered in their economic expansion. The liberal was not necessarily a hypocrite — merely the victim of economic forces which he could neither understand nor control.

Freud had a similar view of the contrast between the facade and the reality, namely, man's primary necessity to defend himself against threats from his own insistent wishes. To satisfy these — even to voice them — might call down disapproval, punishment, or worse upon his head. So he dealt with them by taking into himself his parents' prohibitions: what Freud called a reaction-formation. Or he might rationalize his conduct, compromise with these dangerous wishes by satisfying them under the cloak of socially acceptable reasons. Justice, said Freud, is such an excuse. We defend our social arrangements by stressing the importance of fair shares for all. But, so Freud claimed, underlying this type of justification is the insistence that, as we cannot get all we want for ourselves, others shall not have more than we do. More obvious examples, perhaps, would be that of the schoolmaster who cloaks his sadism with the theory that corporal punishment usually has beneficial effects; or the claim often imputed to Henry VIII that he was only interested in producing an heir; or the plaintive cry of the girl in trouble: "He seduced me."

These theories imply that justifications are merely excuses for what we are going to do anyway. This sort of explanation, or exposure, of people's protestations is, no doubt, often relevant and salutary. But the mistake is to assume that it is always relevant. Of course people are *sometimes* obsessed or driven by hidden fears and wishes to adopt various beliefs. But it only seems relevant to probe into these causes when they hold their beliefs against all the evidence — like the obsessive who believes that his hands are dirty — or when they cling passionately to beliefs for which no reason could possibly be produced. The causes of a belief must be distinguished from its grounds; and it seems only relevant to speculate about causes when there are no grounds.

Indeed a very strong case can be made for saying that typical Freudian explanations are not of human *actions,* of what human beings do deliberately, knowing what they are doing and for which they can give reasons. Freud's brilliant discoveries were not of the causes of *actions* like signing contracts or hitting mashie-niblick shots; rather they were of things that *happen* to a man like dreams, hysteria, and slips of the tongue or pen. If a man has a reason for what he does which is convincing, like a chess-player who takes a bishop in order to checkmate the king, or a golfer who takes a wedge to pitch over a bunker and stop the ball dead on the green, there is no need for a special explanation in terms of unconscious wishes. It is only when he is not acting with reason at all (as in his dreams), or when he makes a slip in some performance (as in slips of the tongue, hand, or memory), or when there is something *phony* about the reason which he gives for what he is doing, that Freud's special explanations seem relevant.[2]

We have, as a matter of fact, plenty of common-sense tests for deciding whether a person is merely giving a rationalization, or whether his standards are an ideology — to use the Marxist jargon. We confront him with arguments. If it could be shown for instance, in the case of corporal punishment, that in general little benefit to the boy resulted, and if the schoolmaster still advocated corporal punishment as a panacea for childhood aberrations, we would begin to say that his reasons were, in fact, rationalizations. It would be obvious that considerations which were logically relevant to his belief in no way affected his belief. Here, as in the cases in my last talk of impelling causes, we are dealing with exceptional cases, with unalterable beliefs which are the products of certain sorts of causes. But it would be logically absurd to say that all beliefs were of this sort, that all principles were ideologies, all reasons rationalizations. For then this sort of distinction itself would never have application. It is only because people sometimes give genuine reasons for their beliefs, because they are sometimes prepared to change them in the light of logically relevant considerations, that there is point in talking of rationalizations — and of reasons. Terms like "rationalization" and "ideology," which cast aspersions on beliefs, are verbal parasites. They only flourish because common experience has provided hosts in the form of rational beliefs and genuine principles.

---

[2] For elaboration of this point of view see . . . my *The Concept of Motivation* (London: Kegan Paul, 1958), Chapter 3.

And just as in my last talk I showed that the mere production of causes by itself never establishes that a man is not responsible for his actions, so also it is obvious that the mere production of causes is never sufficient in itself to cast aspersions on a belief. A story from Arthur Koestler sums up my point rather neatly: Pythagoras, it is supposed, was drawing triangles in the sand. A friend came up and sat by him and Pythagoras said: "I don't know why I keep on drawing these triangles. They worry me and fascinate me." His friend asked shrewdly: "What is your relationship like with your wife?" Pythagoras looked a bit downcast and mumbled that he feared her affections were straying. "Aha!" said his friend: "I now see why you can't keep your mind off those triangles." "I suppose you are right," said Pythagoras. He then got up and did nothing further about developing his theorem! Many a decent man has wanted to do something worthwhile but has had his confidence undermined by irrelevant remarks like "You only do it because you unconsciously need approval" — as if his unconscious had anything to do with the worthwhileness of what he intended.

Yet, as a matter of fact, I think that the last thing that Freud or Marx intended was to undermine morality or to suggest that men can never take responsibility for their standards. Both were rather puritanical men, demanding an unusually high standard of integrity from their colleagues and from themselves. They both shared the scientific humanism of the nineteenth century and thought that men could be freed, to a certain extent, from the forces which worked beneath the surface by coming to understand them. As Freud put it: "We have no other means of controlling our instincts than our intelligence."

Marx was opposed mainly to moralizing rather than to morality. He thought that preaching was not simply an ineffective way of dealing with evils but was a substitute for doing something about them. He distrusted the moral indignation of the bourgeois reformer, for he thought that his moralizing was a way of delaying the inevitable overthrow of bourgeois society. Doing something about evils meant, for Marx, understanding their economic causes and working to shorten and lessen the agony of an age that was passing. He believed ardently in the genuine principles of equality and fraternity which could flourish only when the system of exploitation of man by man had been replaced by the classless society. Admittedly, he was rather hazy about the distinction between ideologies and genuine principles. He assumed some sort of connection between genuine principles and the practical scientific outlook, but he was not at all clear about what this connection was.

Freud was equally unclear in his conception of what he called "the psychological ideal — the primacy of the intelligence." Like Marx he thought that he could help people to shake off their servitude to the dark forces which possessed them by introducing them to the reality beneath the appearances. But he never worked out the precise relationship between this "education to reality" and morality. Indeed, in a letter to a friend he confessed that he could subscribe to the maxim that "what is moral is self-evident." "I believe," he said, "that in a sense of justice and consideration for others, in disliking making others suffer or taking advantage of them, I can measure myself with the best people I have known." People who say that moral principles are self-evident often mean that no further reasons can be given for them. But perhaps they sometimes mean that the reasons for them are so obvious that they hardly need mentioning. Freud probably fell in this second category; for he stated that there were such good reasons for behaving decently that it was a pity to rest morality on a religious basis. In his view, there were not such good reasons for belief in God, and if people got wise to this and thought also that decency depended on a belief in God, they would — mistakenly — throw morality overboard with their religion.

Freud believed, above all things, in integrity and intelligence. His aim in analysis was not to deprive people of standards or to explain them away, but to bring people to choose their own. By revealing the infantile sources of many of the demands people made on themselves and on others, he was able to help them to stand on their own feet and to take responsibility for their own lives. The burden of the message of both Marx and Freud was that a man who understands the causes of social evils and personal predicaments is in a position to do something about them. Understanding paves the way for action as well as for sympathy. Neither of them would have had much sympathy for those who, understanding such causes, merely look back in anger.

ON EDUCATION AND MORALS

R. W. SLEEPER

According to Plato, Socrates used to go around Athens asking the question "Can virtue be taught?" It puzzled him that, if virtue can indeed be taught, there existed no learned specialists in the "subject matters" of prudence, temperance, fortitude, and justice. And, from what we know of the Athens of his time, it would seem that Socrates' question was very much in order. As it turned out, the question was judged to be subversive as well as puzzling and, in condemning the man that asked it, the citizens of Athens demonstrated how dangerous it can be for a teacher to question the morals of the community at large.

The depressing regularity with which this "demonstration" has been repeated throughout the generations since Socrates is not, however, the subject of this essay. Rather, I shall attempt a philosophical diagnosis of why such incidents occur at all, an analysis of why it is that teachers are so often held to blame for "corrupting the youth of the city," why they are expected to "teach" a morality which they are not encouraged or even permitted to question, why it is that the teaching and learning of morals is so persistently treated as categorically a completely different business from the teaching and learning of matters of fact. The key question in this cluster of problems, I shall argue, lies in the relative positions assigned to "facts" and to "values" in the conceptual schemes with which we operate. When it is assumed that "facts" and "values" occupy two entirely different ontological levels, it follows that knowledge of "facts" and knowledge of "values" must be categorically different kinds of knowledge as well. And from this it follows that the teaching and learning of "facts" is a categorically different process from that involved in the teaching and learning of "values." But the assumption that "facts" and "values" do occupy entirely different ontological levels, that because of this difference in status different cognitive processes and conceptual structures are required, this seems to me to be de-

Reprinted, by permission, from *Studies in Philosophy and Education*, VI, no. 3 (Summer, 1968): 231-248.

monstrably false. It rests, in a phrase made popular by Gilbert Ryle, on a "category mistake."[1]

But here I must enter a warning. Because I shall contend that there is no *ontological disjunction* between facts and values, it does not follow that there is *no difference* at all between them. Nor do I wish to claim that coming to know a fact is, in every case, to come to know a value, or that knowing the difference between right and wrong is, in every way, the same as knowing the facts. For there *are* differences here. They are differences that are preserved in the structure of our natural languages, in what linguistic analysts sometimes call the "depth grammar" which we employ in moral discourse and in our talk about "purely factual" matters. But they are differences that neither language nor the "depth grammar" itself is responsible for; these are but tokens of different sorts of experience, of different ways of experiencing things, of dealing with them, of acting on and towards them.

But what *is* the difference? What *is*, after all, the crucial difference between experiencing a fact and experiencing the difference between right and wrong? Not the worst clue to this is perhaps contained in Ryle's remark that ". . . children have to be taught the difference between right and wrong, but we know in our bones that this teaching is not a species of either factual or technical instruction."[2] For he goes on to suggest that we can come to see what sort of knowing is involved in morals if we carefully consider the difference between knowing how to play tennis, for example, and having acquired a taste for it. Or by comparing the learning of all the facts about the Lake District from a geographer and a botanist with the love for it that we may learn from Wordsworth. "Learning to enjoy, to love, or to admire is not acquiring a skill or a parcel of information. Nonetheless it *is* learning."[3] And, elaborating on this, Ryle goes on to show that

[1] The phrase was used in Ryle's *Concept of Mind* (London: Hutchinson's University Library, 1949), to indicate the *faux pas* involved in conceiving "body" and "mind" as distinct ontological "substances." Its use here, in a different context, seems appropriate to my argument.

[2] "On Forgetting the Difference between Right and Wrong," in A. I. Melden (ed.), *Essays in Moral Philosophy* (Seattle: University of Washington Press, 1958), p. 153.

[3] *Ibid.*

he can account for this learning without recourse to an ontological disjunction between facts and values, without committing that sort of "category mistake." For he argues that coming to enjoy, to love, to admire is not something that one comes to *after* one has learned some skill, *after* one has learned some body of facts. It is, rather, a part of what "coming to know" means. Enjoying, loving, admiring thus may be seen as the *exercise* of knowledge and not its effect — or, at least, it may be in those cases where enjoying, loving, and admiring come into being *along with* knowledge and are not generated independently. And if a critic should object that what is *knowledge,* what is *learned,* must be either a piece of information or a technique, that learning to enjoy, love, or admire is none of these, Ryle judges that the critic begs the question. For the question is, in part, why must it be either one or the other?

But here Ryle is himself inconclusive. For enjoying, loving, and admiring can be "learned" and yet remain short of "knowledge." They may, as the ethical emotivists have urged, be understood to be merely the expressions of "attitudes" and not "knowing" at all. And it is easy to see how a family, a group, or a community could "teach" children what to enjoy, love, or admire, how persons can be trained and constrained to adopt and express as their own attitudes of approval and disapproval. Aristotle, in defining virtue as the "habit of right action," knew how large a role is played in morals by attitudes and emotions. But he made room for "intellectual virtue" as well, room for *knowing* the difference between right and wrong as well as for *choosing* good and avoiding evil. In the end, even the purest of our modern ethical emotivists — A. J. Ayer, for example, and C. L. Stevenson — are aware that facts and our knowledge of them, our beliefs about them, are reflected in our moral attitudes. And so, like Aristotle, they find a way to make their "so-called noncognitive theory of ethics" more cognitive than it seems.[4]

What bothers Ryle, though, is not so much that learning to enjoy, love, or admire may be the simple result of a process of conditioning, of "inculcating" tastes and attitudes. For it may also

---

[4] See my article "Noncognitivist Ethics May Not Be What It Seems," *Studies in Philosophy and Education,* III (Spring, 1964): 200-214.

be the result of a "higher" and "purer" form of learning, a process in which *genuine* knowledge plays a part and is not displaced by mere "habit formation." But what kind of knowledge is it? G. E. Moore, when faced with this problem, chose to think of knowledge of a moral sort as "intuitive"— meaning thereby to indicate and express his conviction that the experience of the difference between right and wrong is unique and irreducible to other kinds of experience. "Good," he argued, is a "simple indefinable quality." And to think that it could be defined or described in factual terms is what Moore called the "Naturalistic Fallacy." And it is because of this "fallacy," which Ryle is at such evident pains to avoid committing, that his own conclusions are left in mid-air. If he is to avoid the "Naturalistic Fallacy," he must carefully distinguish among "knowing the difference between right and wrong" and "knowing how" and "knowing that."[5] But, as is evident, he also wants to avoid the "intuitionist" response adopted by Moore. So he is left with the claim that moral knowing is *really* knowing, no question of it is allowed to shake his claim, but yet he is unable to say much of anything very clear or very convincing about it.

But why should Ryle have such fear of the "Naturalistic Fallacy" at all? The question gives us pause. Once upon a time the "Naturalistic Fallacy" was held up as a virtually infallible dogma of moral philosophy. Like the assumption that "facts" and "values" occupy different levels on the ontological scale, and for similar and sometimes identical reasons, the putative "fallacy" of the "Naturalistic Fallacy" seemed to be invulnerable to attack. But no longer is this the case. Like many an old dogma it appears to be dying the death of a thousand qualifications. Why so? Why does what once seemed to be the "fallacy" of ethical naturalism now no longer seem to be the "fallacy" it once was? These are questions so important that no clear answer to the questions before us can be reached short of resolving them. For if the "Naturalistic Fallacy" is a fallacy indeed, there would be little point pursuing a theory which sees values as facts and which denies that there is a radical ontological disjunction between them.

[5] See Ryle, *The Concept of Mind,* pp. 27ff.

What Was the "Naturalistic Fallacy"?

In dealing with questions like these it is helpful to recall some bits of intellectual history. What *was* the "Naturalistic Fallacy"? Through what stages did it pass on the way to oblivion? As in the case of both God and Mark Twain, we run the risk of writing a premature obituary — of exaggerating a death which is not yet final. My own feeling is, however, that if the "Naturalistic Fallacy" is not already dead, it is at least dying. It is not too early to start preparing an obituary notice.

One thing at least is clear. The "Naturalistic Fallacy" has had a distinguished parentage; its God-parents and sponsors have been drawn from the ranks of our most honored philosophers. As I have already suggested, its conception was by Socrates (whether by accident or "planned parenthood"). Its actual birth was delayed, however, until the days of Hume and Kant.[6] After a somewhat less protracted youth, during which the Utilitarians proceeded in blissful ignorance of its existence, it was baptized by Prichard, confirmed by G. E. Moore, and made a naturalized citizen of this country by Frankena in his now classic paper, "The Naturalistic Fallacy."[7] In its early years it seemed clear that the putative fallacy to which the dogma pointed was the fairly simple one of deriving ethical conclusions from nonethical premises. We cannot, the dogma said, derive normative conclusions from non-normative premise-sets by any of the standard rules of logic.[8]

[6] Although it is generally thought that both Hume and Kant rejected the deducibility of value propositions from factual ones on epistemological grounds, it is clear that neither rejected the possibility of moral *knowledge*. The basis for Kant's contention that moral knowledge is possible is well known, though generally rejected. It is thought to be too patently "metaphysical." It is less well known that Hume accepted ethics as an "empirical science." Yet, I take it, this has been convincingly shown to be the case. (Cf. Capaldi's conclusion that "In place of a normative conception, Hume holds that ethics is an empirical science." N. Capaldi, "Hume's Rejection of 'Ought' as a Moral Category," *Journal of Philosophy*, LXIII (1966).)

[7] W. K. Frankena, "The Naturalistic Fallacy," reprinted in W. Sellars and J. Hospers (eds.), *Readings in Ethical Theory* (New York: Appleton-Century-Crofts, 1952). This is the *locus classicus* and gives the earlier history.

[8] For a succinct and convincing critique of this "derivationist" form of the "Naturalistic Fallacy," see J. F. Lange, "The Logic of Derivationist Versions of the Naturalistic Fallacy," *Ratio*, VIII (1965). I have been

Now, for my own part, I have no desire to question the standard rules of logic. For, if they are not as final as they might be (at least in the logic books with which I am familiar), there is no need to question them in order to make the point that I wish to make. It is simply that the question of the *cognitivity* of morals is surely well outside the domain to which such rules apply. If the only form of the "Naturalistic Fallacy" is the fallacy of deriving by logical rules what those rules prohibit, then to employ it as an argument against *all* forms of ethical naturalism is surely *non ad rem*. It appears to succeed only because it misrepresents the issue. This is a point which would, of course, be conceded by G. E. Moore and by any other deontologist. For what they uphold is indeed that values are *knowable,* but not knowable in the same way as facts are, that normative concepts are in no way completely analyzable into descriptive ones. For it was Moore who taught us to think that we know values — or, at least, the meaning of the word "good" — by a direct "intuition" in much the same way as we come to know the meaning of the word "yellow." Accordingly, Moore did not advance the "derivationist" form of the "Naturalistic Fallacy" argument. What counted with Moore, what bothered him throughout his life, was the fact that he could not "say," "say exactly," or "define" what it is that makes predicates of value different from other predicates.[9] Long after he had written in *Principia Ethica* that he could not see how predicates of value could be given an analysis into other predicates, he was still trying to see why they couldn't. Far from being satisfied with an "intuitionist" solution to the whole problem of how it is that we know the meaning of "good," how it is that we know the difference between right and wrong, Moore became more and more convinced that "intuition" is just the label that we give to our *failure* to find a solution. It merely signals the difficulty and does not resolve it. When Moore wrote his essay on the "Conception of Intrinsic Values," of course, he was still defending the

greatly helped in my own thinking by this and by another article by the same colleague: "R. M. Hare's Reformulation of the Open Question," *Mind,* LXXV (1966).

[9] See John Wisdom's account of the development of Moore's thought on the subject in *Paradox and Discovery* (Oxford: Basil Blackwell, 1966), pp. 148ff.

view that value predicates cannot be analyzed into naturalistic ones. There is a difference. He says that he *sees* the difference, but that he "cannot see *what* it is."[10] It is this difficulty that leads him to consider the possibility that the meaning of such words as "good" is "self-evident" and that what they represent can only be known "intuitively," that there is something "intrinsic" about values.

John Wisdom has suggested that the difficulty that Moore was up against was not so much that he couldn't *see* the difference as that he couldn't *say* what the difference is.[11] And I think that Wisdom is right. For we all *do* know that there is a difference between right and wrong, that some things are good and others not. And in knowing this we *see* a difference and we see *what* the difference is. But we *do* have difficulty in *saying* what it is that we see and know. And because we do have this difficulty, we have also the difficulty that we cannot say just how it is that predicates of value are different from others. So we say, perhaps, that predicates of value are arrived at "intuitively" while the others are not. But when faced with a difficulty like this isn't it just an evasion of the issue to claim that what we cannot define is "indefinable," that what we cannot find an analysis for is "unanalyzable"? It is in this sense that Moore saw the doctrine of "intuitionism" that he himself had advocated as begging the question.

Now it sometimes happens that when someone says that he cannot explain just what it is that he means, that he cannot "define" or say something "exactly," that he has nevertheless made it perfectly clear what he has in mind. We all acknowledge cases like this and give our assent to those who say "I don't know how to put it in words, but you know what I mean," or when we agree with someone who adds to his inexact expression the words "you know what I mean." The fact that we do not always do so, or that we sometimes do so without really knowing, only shows that we sometimes do, that sometimes we really *do know*. We know the difference between agreeing and not agreeing. And there are other cases where someone who has been trying to make something clear that he has in mind gives up too soon, for ex-

---

[10] *Ibid.*, p. 157 (Wisdom quoting Moore).
[11] *Ibid.*, p. 157.

ample, cases where he stops trying to get across his meaning by giving instances of the sort of thing he is thinking about. In these cases it may not be that "words fail us"; it may be we who are at fault. Perhaps we have not tried hard enough or gone far enough with our examples and illustrations.

And there is a third sort of case, perhaps more rarely encountered than either of these sorts, where the speaker is prevented from saying what it is that he has in mind by some rule of language or grammar. Having accepted some prohibitive stipulation prevents him from saying what he would otherwise have said or, at least, inhibits his utterance. Admittedly, the common man does not often accede to such prohibitions for we find him saying such things as "It is a fact that robbery is wrong" and "The fact is that we ought not to lie to each other." For if the common man were aware of the logical rules against saying such things, and if he accepted them as binding, he might feel inhibited in ways that he does not. Or he might *not* feel inhibited at all. He might go right on insisting that he meant what he said. Why, after all, should he feel bound by the rules of logic? Why should he feel an *obligation* not to say what he means?

There is a form of the "Naturalistic Fallacy" argument which depends, I think, on just such stipulative prohibitions being accepted as binding. It is the form in which it is stipulated that a sentence cannot both describe something which is a matter of fact and commend it.[12] This seems to be, as Professor Lange and others have pointed out, an incomparably powerful form of the argument which shows the fallacy involved in thinking that we can somehow give an analysis of value predicates by others. In this form of the argument it is not just said that "good," whatever it is taken to be, is not *yet* analyzed into nonnormative terms. It is said that it *cannot* be. There is just one trouble with this argument, invulnerable though it may be. And that is that it wins its invulnerability at the cost of emptiness. For it is emptiness to maintain that any evidence that could possibly falsify an assertion can be ruled out by the assertion itself and to maintain, at

[12] Cf. Richard Mervin Hare's argument in *The Language of Morals* (Oxford: Clarendon Press, 1952), pp. 92, 93, and Lange's criticism of it in the article cited in note 8.

the same time, that one is asserting something meaningful about the empirical world. It is useless to hold that what can and cannot be done with descriptive predicates is a matter over which we can legislate by logical stipulations and definitions. It has been wisely said that "Whether or not axiological predicates can be defined in terms of descriptive expressions is not a question to be decided by stipulations concerning value-words and descriptive expressions, but by an investigation of what are acceptably understood to be value and descriptive expressions, and the relationships which obtain among them."[13]

This is, of course, a version of the "Naturalistic Fallacy" argument which never appealed to Moore. For he tried and tried again to find out what it was that the common man meant when he said that something was "good" or that one "ought" to do something. He never maintained that value predicates *cannot* be analyzed into naturalistic ones. He only wanted to be *shown* that they could; the questions he asked remained *open* ones. But ethical naturalists and others who wish to maintain that there really *is* a kind of moral knowing which is not just "intuition" and is like, if not *just* like, factual knowing, should not think that they have yet made their case. For it is still necessary to show how it is that we *do* know the difference between right and wrong, how it is that "good" can be given a descriptive analysis. For if this cannot be done it is hard to see how it can be maintained that there is a fallacy in the "Naturalistic Fallacy" argument. If this cannot be done, our obituary notice will indeed have been premature.

The Epistemology of Morals

If G. E. Moore did much to lend authority to the belief that there is, after all, a fallacy involved in thinking that we could know what the word "good" means in the same way that we know the meaning of descriptive terms, he also did much to reinforce our faith in the common man's way of reckoning. Wittgenstein did even more. For what Wittgenstein suggested is that the problems of philosophers are often nothing but pseudoproblems. And

[13] Lange, "Hare's Reformulation of the Open Question," p. 245.

yet it is not the case that, to paraphrase Pope's couplet on Newton, "Meaning and meaning's laws lay hid in night. God said, 'Let Ludwig be,' and all was light." For Wittgenstein and his followers often gave the impression that if the language of philosophers is sometimes obscure, the language of the common man is always clear. We may, as Ryle has said, "know in our bones" that teaching the young the difference between right and wrong is not just a matter of factual or technical instruction. But what does the expression of the common man mean? How does he use the expression "know in my bones" in such a way that we know what he means? Ordinary language too needs analysis. And more.

For my own part, I am impressed with Peter Strawson's way of putting the matter. Pushing for the conception of what he calls "descriptive metaphysics," he argues that the analysis of ordinary language is — up to a point — an effective way of revealing our conceptual structures, the structures of experience:

> But the discriminations we can make, and the connections that we can establish, in this way, are not general enough and not far-reaching enough to meet the full metaphysical demand for understanding. For when we ask how we use this or that expression, our answers, however revealing at a certain level, are apt to assume, and not expose, those general elements of structure which the metaphysician wants revealed. The structure he seeks does not readily display itself on the surface of language, but lies submerged. He must abandon his only sure guide when the guide cannot take him as far as he wishes to go.[14]

Now it is not my purpose here to explicate Strawson's metaphysics, nor do I feel especially qualified to do so. But I do wish to draw attention to a basic distinction which Strawson makes and to make use of a fundamental connection which he establishes. The distinction is between the logical grounds for predicates of two types: M-predicates and P-predicates. M-predicates describe features characteristic of material entities. P-predicates describe features characteristic of persons. The two, Strawson claims, cannot be collapsed into each other. The grounds for P-predicates are not the same as those for M-predicates. This leads to the conclusion that the concept of a person is "logically primitive."

[14] P. F. Strawson, *Individuals* (London: Methuen, 1959), pp. 9-10.

The connection that Strawson establishes is between the concept of a person and that of actions of the sort which he speaks of as being "in accordance with a common human nature."[15] They will include predicates like "is smiling," "is thinking hard," "loves horses," "believes in God," and so on. It is at first tempting to think that ascriptions of first- and third-person predicates differ in some important way which might prevent us from ascribing to others what we readily ascribe to ourselves. And we might think that predicates which we ascribe to others need some different logical foundation from those we ascribe to ourselves. With P-predicates this is not the case. Though we are inclined to say that "feelings can be felt but not observed, and behavior can be observed but not felt," and we oscillate between philosophical skepticism and philosophical behaviorism, this will not do at all. For it can clearly be shown that even with P-predicates such as "is depressed," the ascribed depression is what it is, is one and the same thing, which is observed and not felt by the ascriber and felt but not observed by the person to whom it is ascribed. Strawson reminds us that what can be observed can also be faked or disguised, but also that there can be self-deception about what is felt. Yet he insists that to refuse to accept that first- and third-person P-predicates may refer to the *same thing*, despite the fact that the empirical bases may be different, is to refuse to accept the structure of the language in which we talk about such things as "depression" and all that P-predicates ascribe. And more. To refuse is to reject the *experience* of being both self-ascribers and other-ascribers. It is to open oneself to hopeless muddles in trying to understand what is meant when a person says "I am depressed" and another says of him "He is depressed."

There is, of course, a difference between having a logical basis for ascribing to others what we ascribe to ourselves and having an empirical warrant for doing so. The language structure supplies the former but not the latter. Ascriptions such as those for which we employ P-predicates require empirical evidence, whether we are ascribing to ourselves or to others. It is evidence, we might say, that you are depressed, that your actions are listless, you show no interest in things that usually amuse you and annoyance at things that you usually tolerate. And it is evidence that I am depressed that I feel listless, can take no interest in the things that usually amuse me and feel annoyance at things that I usually tolerate. I cannot be sure that you are depressed. You might be dissembling, disguising what it is that you really feel. But then again, I cannot be sure that I am really depressed. Perhaps I am dissembling too, hiding from myself my true feelings. But these considerations, while they serve to caution us against too facile ascriptions, do not detract from our willingness to make ascriptions at all. This language game is played!

And a moral lurks within this fact, I think, and one which hardly can be concealed. Consider the matter again. What is it that we know when we know another person? A fact, of course, or a lot of them. And more. We know each other as intending beings, as acting and doing things, as purposeful in our behavior. We know ourselves as such. We share, as Strawson says, a "common human nature." If we can know this much, we can know all that is required for knowing the difference between right and wrong, for knowing the meaning of "good." It was Aristotle who said that "Every art or applied science and every systematic investigation, and similarly every action and choice seem to aim at some good; the good, therefore, has been well defined as that at which all things aim." In these opening lines of the *Nichomachean Ethics,* Aristotle was setting forth all that he thought that he really needed to ground his analysis of predicates of value into naturalistic ones. For "good" means that at which all things aim and aims are facts that can be described.

We are put off, of course, by the consideration that aims are sometimes difficult to describe. We call them ideals and distinguish them from facts. Describing an ideal, we say, is describing something which is merely possible. An ideal is not what is the case but what "might be" and, if we are prescribing an ideal or commending it, we may add that it "ought" to be the case. What puts us off in Aristotle's way of doing ethics is that he "*de*scribes" what he also "*pre*scribes" when he "*a*scribes" to all things their aim at the "good." What a muddle! But look again. Is there, perhaps, in this seeming welter of confusion a pattern hidden? Is there a structure here which the surface grammar conceals?

Ascribing, Describing, Prescribing

In John Wisdom's recently published *Paradox and Discovery* there is given an impressive account of a feature of Wittgenstein's philosophical technique. The thing that Wisdom tries to bring out about the technique is that Wittgenstein again and again warned us against thinking that the meaning of a word is always an object. Perhaps it never is! In any case we need to be on guard against that habit of "abstract" thought which often, if not always, misleads us by inducing us to seek clarity through definitions instead of through concrete cases. Subscribing to this, Wisdom says:

> I believe that if, faced with the extraordinary pronouncements of metaphysicians, we avoid asking them to define their terms, but instead press them to present us with instances of what they refer to contrasted with instances of what they do not refer to, then their pronouncements will no longer appear either as obvious falsehoods or mysterious truths or pretentious nonsense, but often as confusingly presented attempts to bring before our attention certain not fully recognized and yet familiar features of how in the end the questions of different types are met. These are features without which the questions or statements of the type in question would not be themselves. And they are features which can seldom or never be safely or vividly brought to mind by the use of general terms.[16]

And he goes on to say that what Wittgenstein claimed was that "too often when what we need is to come down toward the concrete, we don't, and that this especially hinders our philosophy, our metaphysics."

For my own part, I wish that this message had been a bit more briefly stated so that I could have it engraved on a plaque and put on my classroom wall. It might do, of course, to substitute Husserl's more economical battle-cry — "To the things themselves!" — but I wouldn't want my analytically minded students to think that I am pushing phenomenological existentialism!

Well, what does happen when we try to bring such concepts of philosophy as "ascribing," "describing," and "prescribing" down to the concrete? In the first place it becomes clear that the meaning of the words we employ in doing these things, in performing these actions, is *context-dependent*. The familiar predicate "is

[16] Wisdom, *op. cit.*, pp. 101-102.

depressed" may be a simple ascription to another of what I am familiar with in myself. But if I am asked to describe a patient in a psychiatrist's waiting-room I may use the same predicate, not so much ascribing to another what I am familiar with in myself, but what I observe. Or I may utter the predicate as a complaint about myself or as a plea for help for another about whom I am concerned, not so much ascribing or describing as entering a moral claim, prescribing. It has often been noticed that value predicates are ambiguous in this way, that they are "multi-functional." The predicate "is good" can ascribe, describe, and prescribe depending upon the context in which it is used. So much would be acknowledged by all those who have argued for "noncognitivism" in ethics as well as by the "cognitivists." What is it, then, that separates them?

The answer that I wish to propose is not a new one. And yet I put it forward cautiously for it has often been rejected. It is that descriptive predicates are, in fact, the only "moral" ones. That what we have been led to look for as the meaning of a value predicate is an "object" of some sort, or a "quality." In searching for such "normative" entities we have drawn a blank. And so we divide. Some, the ethical "naturalists" and "cognitiv-ists" among us, contend that knowing the meaning of "good" is the same as knowing what it is that the word designates. We commit the putative "Naturalistic Fallacy" by reducing the mean-ing of value predicates to others. Appalled by this fallacy, the others take up the noncognitivist position. But if we do not think that the meaning of "good" is an object or a quality such that it constitutes a "normative" entity, if we look instead at the way in which descriptive predicates function in concrete situations, we may see that every descriptive predicate has, *in use,* a claiming function. By that I mean to say that every factual assertion made in actual use, in a situation where it is *working* and not just idling, makes a claim to be observed, taken into account. It is this trait of facts, that in asserting them we respond to and express their claim-possessing character, that shows how it is that we can know the difference between right and wrong. For there are, I think, no *de jure* entities or qualities *as such.* It in only in the *abstract* that a statement of fact does not embody a moral claim. But, it should be remembered, there are no facts in the abstract. For it is their peculiarity to exist only in the concrete.

Let us suppose that it is a verified fact that it is raining outside. In what sense, you may ask, does this fact exert a moral claim? In this sense: you ask me what the weather is like outside, I know that it is raining. Do I have a moral obligation to you? I do. You have made a claim upon me. The fact has a claim on me. I do my moral duty and tell you that it is raining outside. I have, in responding to your claim, ascribed to you the right to an answer. I might not have done if circumstances were such that I thought that some fateful harm might come to you if I responded truthfully, but that would have been my response to other facts and their claims. As it is, I have ascribed to you the right of a truthful answer, for I am a metaphysical sort of person (the only kind there is) who is both a self-ascriber and an other-ascriber. We have, as Strawson has said, a "common human nature." But more. I have responded to your claim by giving a description. I am a describer as well as an ascriber. And yet more. I have prescribed your obligation to the fact that I have described. Language has not been idling. A language game has been played.

Trivial, you say. Yes, but of such trivial things the world is made. And it is, in the end, a moral world. There is another context from that in which I have been quoting him in which Strawson has this to say: "It is a condition of the existence of any form of social organization, of any human community, that certain expectations of behaviour on the part of its members should be pretty regularly fulfilled: that some duties, one might say, should be performed, some obligations acknowledged, some rules observed."[17] A true description of what is the case, you may say, but it begs the question. For while these expectations are facts, is it not that what is expected is not a fact but a value? When the members of a community prescribe for each other the minimal rules and duties, are they describing merely facts? Or are they laying down the norms and standards, referring not to what is the case but what ought to be? My answer is that when the members

[17] P. F. Strawson, "Social Morality and the Individual Ideal," in I. T. Ramsey (ed.), *Christian Ethics and Contemporary Philosophy* (London: Student Christian Movement Press, 1966), p. 284.

of a community prescribe for each other the rules and duties of minimal behavior they are describing what they take to be the facts about a community, the facts without which a community would not be what it is. Of course they may be mistaken: a rule which seems to be necessary may not be. But in that case a mistake about the facts has been made, not just a mistake about a norm or an ideal. You may say that "facts," then, are nothing but values in disguise, that I have begged the question again. But I should say that there is no disguise at all. In coming to know the facts that make a community what it is and not another thing, we have truly come to know the difference between right and wrong, we have truly come to know something of what "good" means.

And yet there is more. For "good" means not just minimal morality but maximal too. And it is truly the case that what is minimal is not also maximal. The failure to notice this is what makes the case of the "sociocultural relativists" — the followers of William Graham Sumner — go wrong. Yet the function of minimal morality provides us at least with a start on the road to the highest good. It introduces us to knowledge of such matters of fact as "conscientiousness," "obligation," and "duty" in a concrete and realistic way. "These notions," says Strawson, "have been treated almost entirely abstractly in moral philosophy in the recent past, with the result that they have come to seem to be meaningless survivals of discarded ideas about the government of the universe. But as most ordinarily employed I do not think they are that at all."[18] In knowing what the facts are, what claims are made upon us, we come to know — in ways which are, perhaps, primitive but for which there is no need to apologize — the difference between right and wrong. If there is more to the highest "good" than this, it is at least continuous with it.

There are those instances where we want to condemn the ways of the society in which we live, to defy its sanctions, to stand up in righteous indignation against the rules, to act in civil disobedience. And there *are* those cases where we want to claim that we know where our community, our culture, our nation has gone wrong, where it has gone right. There *is* a sense in which we want

[18] *Ibid.*, p. 287.

to claim that our moral knowledge transcends the given morality of our situation. But it is important that these claims have about them the air of humility. For, as Aristotle used to remind us, we can expect of any knowledge only that degree of accuracy and precision which the facts permit. The more complex the facts are and the more varied, the greater will be our uncertainty. But the very tentativeness with which we must hold these transcendent ideals has its moral advantages. For it is only in the case of fixed ideals that toleration of difference is lacking. With fallibility admitted there is ever room for the richness and diversity, not only of personal ideals, but of social and political ideals as well. The holder of the cognitive view of morality, far from being committed to a single-minded vision of what is right for all men, becomes the natural enemy of all those who would fix a closed conception of the ideal upon the common human nature which he shares. To hold that virtue can be taught is not to be, *ex hypothesi,* an enemy of the "open society."

One last observation before I summarize. If there is any point in the view that I have here been advocating, the view which takes it that predicates of value are analyzable into predicates of fact *in working situations,* it is not the point that there is nothing "emotive," "attitudinal," or "dispositional" about our moral expressions. What I have been insisting on is that no matter how expressive our moral language is of how we feel, of our attitudes and dispositions, no matter how much so-called "noncognitive" meaning we pack into it, our *moral language is essentially descriptive.* It tells us something about the world as about ourselves. It is a blunder, I think, to say that we have no way of knowing the world as we know ourselves. And it is this blunder that causes us to think that we are all, by force of metaphysical necessity, alienated from each other, that we are alienated from the "objective" world by the metaphysical prison of our "subjectivity."

It is because of this mistake that we are led to think that the only possibility of generating a moral order in the world will be through the generalization of the moral law within until it becomes the moral law without. In *Freedom and Reason,* a book which I much admire though it seems to make the mistake to which I refer, Professor Hare concedes that his thesis of "universal prescriptivism" requires a basis in descriptive knowledge — we would not know what to prescribe or if it would be universalized without such factual knowledge — but he insists that there is another "essential element in the meaning of moral judgments . . . the prescriptive," and he takes it that it is this element which ultimately prevents the success of the sort of theory which I have been proposing. For, he argues, no merely factual knowledge can function prescriptively.[19] But is that enough to account for the actual force of moral obligation? My own answer should be clear by now. It is that no mere universal prescription is binding in a moral sense, not only unless we decide to accept it, but also unless it contains a claim upon our decision — the sort of claim that arises from the working conditions of the situation in which we find ourselves. I find Professor Ramsey, whose close association with Hare has given him a rare insight into the way Hare's mind works, worth quoting on the point: "Let it be granted that no one can say, 'You ought to do x' or 'It was good of you to do y' without indulging in some description. Further, Hare has shown how both assertions, being moral judgments, must be prescriptive and universalysable. But without in any way denying those important analytical insights, my point is that something more remains to be said, viz. that both judgments *presuppose* that x and y are *claim-possessing* circumstances, whose claims I acknowledge in making the moral judgments that I do."[20] In my own way, for purposes quite different from those of Ramsey, I have been harping away at the same point.

I have argued that knowing the difference between right and wrong is wholly empirical. In order to do this I have tried to show what the common man, perhaps, would think is quite unnecessary. I have had to show that moral judgments are not unlike those that we call factual. I have said that factual claims are moral under working conditions though they may lack this trait when language is idling. I have claimed that knowing the

[19] R. M. Hare, *Freedom and Reason* (Oxford: Clarendon Press, 1963), p. 191, also p. 21.
[20] Ian T. Ramsey, "The Autonomy of Ethics," in I. T. Ramsey (ed.), *Christian Ethics and Contemporary Philosophy* (London: Student Christian Movement Press, 1966), p. 162.

difference between right and wrong is not knowing any distinctively moral entity like the "Moral Law Above" but that it is, instead, entirely a matter of knowing all that we can possibly know of the facts in the case. And among these facts, I have argued, it is important to include knowledge of other persons as of ourselves. For if it is difficult to know another person, to know what the other person demands of us by virtue simply of being another person and quite independently of the claims that he may articulate, it is nevertheless required of us that we do so. It is required by the facts of the case, by the fact that there are, in any human society, certain minimum obligations which must be borne out as the factual conditions upon which that society depends. We come to know the difference between right and wrong in this concrete and empirical way.

So "facts" and "values" are not two distinct and separated types of "entity," occupying distinct and separate levels on the ontological "scale." If we are sometimes persuaded that they are, it may well be because we rightly think that the minimal conditions of society are not also the expressions of our highest moral ideals. But the highest of moral ideals must be continuous with the minimal conditions, the knowing of what ideals to choose must be continuous with knowing what minimal conditions are necessary. For the achievement of the highest of moral ideals is dependent upon the most mundane of facts. It is the facts themselves, in the end, that will determine which of all possible worlds is indeed "the best." So the teaching and learning of values is not a categorically different process from the teaching and learning of facts.

But we must not be misled into thinking that the minimal conditions of our social existence are fixed and invariable, that because they are "matters of fact" they are beyond dispute and argument. For even the minimal conditions may vary from group to group, from place to place, and from time to time. And it is a feature of what moral individuals are, a fact of what makes up a person, that his moral perceptions and aspirations may exceed those of his group, his place, his time. Although, as Scripture says, "We are all members of one another," there is no reason to suppose that there is any fixed road to salvation: "In my Father's house are many mansions: if it were not so, I would have told you." The predicate is descriptive. It expresses what is so as a matter of fact. It is also an expression of an ideal. And so are the predicates which describe the ways of love as various and infinite. But to go on this way would be to talk moral theology.

MORAL AUTONOMY AND REASONABLENESS

THOMAS D. PERRY

When we try to understand moral reasoning, I think we always have to remember that it is a method of justifying our *autonomous* moral judgments that we are after. As a way of introducing a discussion of such reasoning, let me therefore briefly point out how the obstacles in the path of ethical method — the all too familiar reasons why it seems impossible to give valid and complete justifications for our moral judgments — are closely bound up with our personal autonomy in making such judgments.

People who have the concept of autonomous morality (many adults and adolescents in our culture, and in various other cultures as far as I know) often want to make, and do make, "autonomous moral judgments." That is, they evaluate their own and other people's character and behavior quite independently of the authority of any person or group who would claim to prescribe to them the correct principles or standards for such evaluations or to tell them what judgment to make on a particular occasion. We who make autonomous judgments often accept the principles that our neighbors or elders prescribe to us, but we do so on our own authority, and we reserve the right to qualify or reject any principle, rule, or standard (for short, any "norm") that we sincerely find repugnant, whether generally or in some particular application. And in the rules of ethical discourse, we accord the same right to others; we recognize their right to challenge and reject any norm that we may happen to find acceptable but which they do not. Twentieth-century ethics begins with G. E. Moore's noticing this aspect of moral talk. The norm that is announced in any "naturalistic definition" of an "ethical term" can always be disputed without linguistic error. One therefore cannot show that one's judgment is morally correct merely by pointing out that it follows deductively from such and such matters of fact and such and such a naturalistic definition or other norm that one accepts. One cannot successfully justify it either to others or to oneself in

Reprinted, by permission, from *Journal of Philosophy,* LXV, no. 13 (June, 1968): 383-400.

that way. For in autonomous morality we not only claim the right
to judge for ourselves; we also have the responsibility to judge
soundly or correctly. The mere fact that one does find such and
such a norm acceptable is obviously no guarantee that one has
done the latter.

In heteronomous and other norm-hypothetical evaluations, matters are far different. There we can hold that, *granting* such and
such a customary moral norm (or some norm prescribed by a
political or religious authority, or perhaps some norm we have
merely postulated or stipulated) and granting that it is the controlling norm for a given case or question (there could be a conflict of such norms), then the correct judgment to make in that
case is thus and so. In a practical syllogism or instance of "normative reasoning," as I will prefer to call it, we can simply deduce
such a judgment from pertinent facts plus the norm, and this
counts as a complete and valid justification of our judgment, provided we have shown that the factual premise is true. Of course,
following customary morality or carrying out the general orders of
a "moral superior" have difficulties of their own. We may be in
doubt about what the customary norm for the present case is; or
our knowledge of our orders may be deficient, however slavishly
we may intend to follow them; and in any event there will often
be problems of interpretation. But we do not have the mysterious
task of explaining how nonevaluative facts can even be conceived
to justify an evaluation in which the very claim put forth precludes the identification of a normative major premise that will
give us passage from "is" to "ought," from a pure fact to an evaluative conclusion about some particular action, for example. In
autonomous judgment, on the other hand, that is just the sort of
claim that is put forth. If we imagine that we might construct a
deductive justification for our autonomous judgments by going on
to give an ethical justification of an appropriate normative premise,
as well as an empirical or logical justification of the nonnormative premise, we are met with the familiar and apparently conclusive objection that we would then either be led into an infinite
regress in normative reasoning or have to stop somewhere and
merely stipulate an ultimate form, thus defeating our very purpose.

Ethical naturalists would try to cure this trouble by recognizing
some ultimate moral standard or principle as *the* norm for ethics,

usually claiming to find it presupposed by existing institutions or discourse, and sometimes forthrightly suggesting that it be legislated. But this either ignores or abolishes autonomous judgment, depending on whether it is offered as a reportive or reconstructive account of ethics. For in autonomous judgment we reserve the right to reject the ultimate norm itself, be it some principle of general utility or of victory for the master race, or whatever. Even if we are inclined to accept the principle of utility in one of its formulations, we still reserve the right to make an exception to it by rejecting any rule or particular evaluation which, in conjunction with the facts, it might entail, if we find such rule or evaluation repulsive.

Those who would try to avoid the difficulties of ethical naturalism by replacing ultimate standards or principles with special "rules of inference" for ethics are met with a well-known objection which can also be seen to rest on our moral autonomy. Any general authorization to accept factual statements of such and such a kind about objects of moral evaluation as sufficient, if true, to establish such and such an evaluation of such objects, will itself be a substantive moral principle. Hence it will be challengeable in autonomous morality. Hence any justification made in reliance upon it could not be valid and complete.

But could we not show that a moral judgment is objectively sound not in the sense that it is true, i.e., correct as against its contraries and for anyone, but rather in the sense that its author reasonably makes such judgment or holds such moral opinion? It would be his judgment *act* that would primarily be justified, because he had gone about forming his opinion reasonably or in accordance with a "morally reasonable" procedure binding on everyone. The *content* of his judgment would be justified only by derivation from that fact, and it would not necessarily be the judgment that others would reasonably make on the same subject, although they very well might, and his reasonableness would no doubt have persuasive weight for others if it were made known to them. At first sight, such a suggestion seems implausible because we hate to give up the notion of moral truth. Nevertheless, I think this is the approach that will lead us out of our difficulty. I believe that if we follow up this suggestion and stick to it in our attempt to work out the method of justification for autonomous morality, we will find that we can make better sense of ethics than by any other means. I think we will end by seeing that the demand for truth in morals is easily dispensable, and in fact a nuisance of which we can easily rid ourselves. We will not merely see that in "sacrificing" it we purchase an important reconciliation of other ideas and gain a method of ethics. Unless I am mistaken, we will also finally come to appreciate that it is hardly to be considered a sacrifice at all. This is what I hope to show.

I

Recalling that the reason why we cannot infer moral truths from nonevaluative truths is that the major premise or inference rule required for this purpose will be a moral principle which itself must be shown to be true, let us notice that this premise or rule would only have to be shown to be "reasonably held" if we were going to show that our moral conclusion is reasonably held on the basis of the nonevaluative facts we cite for its support. And this notion of a moral principle reasonably held is not so very hard to explain and apply. It may have difficulties of detail, but we know what we mean by it; it is not essentially obscure, like the notion of a true or universally valid principle. Thus it seems very natural and true to say that a person holds such and such a principle reasonably if he has thought about it carefully, has considered alternative principles with an open mind, has informed himself with some care about relevant facts, e.g., the likely consequences to himself and others of adhering to this principle or to some alternative, and has considered these things disinterestedly and in a normal state of mind. Now these conditions, traditionally collected under the rubric of "the moral point of view," are notoriously difficult to specify and apply as a test of moral truth. But it will be seen in a moment, I think, how they are quite manageable as a test of reasonableness.

This gives us the beginning of a theory of moral reasoning. But it can certainly be no more than a beginning if our account is to ring true as an analysis of how people actually reflect and argue in morals when they would be conceded to be doing so cogently (whatever the proper grounds for the concession might turn out to be). For it is clear that in moral reasoning we do *not* simply adopt norms and then apply them mechanically to cases whose descriptions instantiate them. No doubt we do this in answering many moral questions, but it is certainly false that we always do it. We sometimes add new qualifications or exceptions to norms that may have previously seemed eminently reasonable as they stand; even more commonly, we find ourselves having to choose between conflicting principles which have no recognized exceptions that would exclude their application to the instant case. On rare occasions we change our norms more radically, as when a certain rule we once accepted no longer seems reasonable at all. Rather than simply *applying* antecedent standards or rules to a moral problem that confronts us, we use these to organize our evaluative reflection about it, to remind ourselves that we almost certainly will want to pay attention to these and these factual aspects as morally significant, and to help ourselves dispose expeditiously of many "easy" moral questions (those in which but one accepted norm seems to apply, and no fact is brought to our attention that we feel has such countervailing weight as to require a new exception to the norm).

It seems clear, therefore, that the primary focus of attention in moral reasoning — the first parameter of judgment, as it were — is the concrete situation and problem, not the rule or principle under which we range it. It is our judgment of the concrete case that determines what rule we will accept for disposing of it, and not the reverse, even though antecedently accepted rules do figure as aids to (not ineluctable premises for) that judgment. But notice how easy it is to complicate our initial account of reasonable decision making to allow for this. Such a role for norms is just what one would expect in autonomous morality, where we reserve the right to qualify or reject any principle or standard or rule whatever if we should be repelled by the thought of applying it to some question to which it logically does apply. And when we realize that it is our moral autonomy which determines such a role for antecedently accepted norms, we avoid a misinterpretation that is otherwise suggested by the very convenience of norms for making the bulk of our unproblematic evaluations. Because we very often can simply instantiate them and because our moral life would be chaotic if we could not, it may seem that norms are somehow of controlling or undeniable authority, like the norms that were given to us by our parents before we had the concept of autonomous morality. But in fact we reserve the right to reject any norm in application to any case where it would seem to give a morally wrong result.

In this way we are not only able to avail ourselves of recognized exceptions to customary norms and to make new exceptions to them or reject them outright; we can also do the same with norms that we have adopted or would adopt from the moral point of view. Such a norm may have seemed entirely acceptable when taken in the abstract, but we may find ourselves unwilling to apply it to the problem confronting us when we consider *that problem* from the moral point of view. Thus the normative major premise of our syllogism must be reasonably held not merely in the abstract, but also and especially when considered in connection with the matter we are presently judging. And this strongly suggests that the whole syllogism must be viewed as the *result* of moral reasoning (decision making) rather than as the form of that reasoning; it is the way we formulate the outcome of our reflection on and judgment of the concrete case.

How is it the result? How are we to make sense of this notion of "judgment" in the concrete case? Do we have to say that it is a matter of intuiting "ethical qualities" or apprehending "synthetic entailments" of ethical by nonethical truths? Clearly we do not have to trouble ourselves with either of these famous but obscure theories when we recall that judging rightly, according to our view, is deciding reasonably. There is no mystery about it. It is simply a matter of reaching an evaluation in the concrete case from the moral point of view. That is, if we inform ourselves adequately about *this* moral question — for example, the question of how some particular person in a concrete situation should act or should have acted — and if we decide the question with attention to the relevant facts about this person and his situation, and do so disinterestedly and calmly, etc., then our judgment is reasonably made and held, and otherwise it is not. Let us briefly consider these several conditions.

First, what facts have to be taken into account if the person is to be reasonably well informed? Well, most obviously, any fact that is made deductively relevant for the evaluation of the object of judgment by a norm which he regards as acceptable or plausible — not necessarily *after* full and disinterested reflection. Also, and in view of the social setting of ethical judgment and discourse, he should pay attention to any fact similarly made relevant by a norm which anyone else is known to regard as acceptable or plausible or which "reasonable" inquiry would disclose. And it seems that the referential meaning of this latter evaluative term could also be established from the social setting of ethics, at least well enough for practical purposes. Thus we see how norms pick out relevant facts; but facts also pick out relevant norms. If a certain fact strikes us as plainly relevant to the evaluation of a certain action or course of conduct, we may stop and reflect on just how it is relevant, to what evaluative result it tends. In answering (and generalizing our answer) we spell out a norm, a norm with which that fact may have been "laden" in its normal expression, e.g., the norm conventionally attaching to the role we ascribe to someone (being a "father," for instance), or a norm entering into the concept of some action that we attribute to someone ("promising," for instance). But all relevant norms will not be found in such mixed fact-norm expressions; nor are we confronted with "is-ought" entailments when they are found there, for these norms too are challengable.

What about the "normal state of mind" in which we should form our judgment? Here it seems that we could make a fairly extensive list of necessary conditions: that a person should not be depressed or intoxicated or exhausted or distracted or mentally ill, etc. While there is no complete list of necessary conditions that can be given to specify this customary procedural norm, it seems that we know well enough what we mean by a psychological condition that would be an abnormal one for judging reasonably in morals.

And what about the "disinterestedness" of our judgment? This means, I think, that it should be "impartial" and "generalizable." That is, we must be willing to make the same judgment in response to a question like the present one no matter who might be involved in it, *so long as the morally relevant facts remained the same.* And we must feel that our judgment would be the right one to make about this matter or any other matter similar to it *in all relevant respects.* Now, it seems impossible to specify the meaning of these emphasized phrases for the purposes of a method of truth. Different moral agents or judges might very well disagree as to which facts are morally relevant. And since in autonomous morality there can be no canonical set of relevance-giving norms, there is no point at which one can say that all relevant considerations have been taken into account and assigned their correct relative importance, in order for the correct judgment to be deduced from the facts and the controlling norms. But in a method of the sort we are discussing, there is no such problem. Here we can say that the relevant facts for the purposes of the impartiality and generalizability of our judgment are simply those facts which have struck us as salient and have in fact had some "weight," i.e., have made a difference for our evaluation, as we considered the matter from the moral point of view. Incidentally, although these last two requirements may at first seem inconsistent with our freedom to amend and reject norms that we have previously accepted, a moment's thought will show that they are not. Of course, if a person seems to reject his own moral precedents quite frequently and lightheartedly, this is strong evidence that he is not taking the moral point of view, i.e., making impartial and generalizable judgments. But it can and sometimes does happen that we are forced to qualify or reject an earlier evaluation if we are to make an honest judgment on the present occassion.

A statement of the fact(s) we hold to be of controlling weight or importance, coupled with a general normative statement assigning such and such an evaluative consequence to that sort of fact or facts, would thus give us our premises for a deductive argument of the sort mentioned before: one in which our judgment would be entailed by true facts and a moral principle reasonably held. And now it is obvious, I think, how the whole of such an argument is only the product, or statement of the result, of the actual process of moral reasoning or decision making. Rather than being deductive in character, that process is more one of *selecting* premises, i.e., facts and evaluative responses that one *decides* are of greatest importance. And it is done by taking thought in a way that is appropriate to making an "ethical" decision or judgment. The justification of our decision or judgment as morally reasonable lies just in the fact that we did take thought in that way.

What then is the point of giving one's "justifying reasons," of stating those controlling or outstanding facts and offering them to another person as the reasons or ground of one's judgment? I think we have to understand that in giving moral reasons a person invites his interlocutor to look at the matter in the ethical way himself and see whether these same facts will not also cause him to make the same judgment.

Here, then, is a summary of our account of moral reasoning:

(1) The logical relevance of a factual reason to a certain moral conclusion consists in its entailment of that conclusion when taken in conjunction with some general norm.

(2) In reasonable reflection on and judgment of a moral question, one (a) surveys the facts that (together with norms people might variously regard as plausible) entail this or that moral evaluation in response to such question, and then (b) decides in a disinterested way which of these fact-norm combinations are indeed plausible and significant and which one, finally, is of dominant or controlling weight or importance.

(3) The latter fact is the reason one gives in justifying the *content* of one's judgment to another. One may also spell out the associated norm by which it does entail one's judgment, but this is quite commonly left unexpressed as obvious. It is also common to acknowledge any countervailing facts that one considers to be significant but outweighed by the reason given.

(4) One's judgment is in fact reasonable if those reasons and that conclusion have been selected in the manner indicated in (2).

(5) There are thus two distinct senses of "to justify" involved in our account: (a) to cite facts as having controlling weight to influence the content of moral judgment in such and such a way when they are considered from the moral point of view, and (b) to show that a person has formed his judgment from the moral point of view.

(6) There are also two distinct ways or senses in which facts are "morally relevant" to a certain moral question. (a) They entail some evaluative response to that question when taken in conjunction with norms that *someone* regards as plausible. Hence they should be taken into account in one's "survey of the relevant facts." (b) They entail some evaluative response when taken in

conjunction with norms that the author of the judgment finally regards as plausible (but not necessarily controlling) in connection with that moral question. Hence they may be cited either as controlling facts or acknowledged as countervailing facts, as in (3) above; and they are the facts that are relevant for the purposes of the impartiality and generalizability requirements.

II

There will be space for only a few brief illustrations to show that this conception of ethical method matches up well with familiar modes of reflection and discourse in morals. I will also try to answer the most obvious objection that will certainly be made to it.

Take the case of a man who makes a promise to do something and then fails or refuses to do it. If that were a description of all the relevant factual aspects of the matter, almost anyone would judge that the man ought to keep his promise, or that it was wrong of him not to keep it. Obviously, this is because we accept the norm that it is wrong to break one's promise; and it normally would be superfluous to articulate this norm. Such judgment is of course entailed by that norm and the fact that he promised. But suppose the man is ill, and that it would cause him distress or risk aggravating his illness if he were to do what he promised, say, to make a speech at some meeting. Then almost anyone would hold that it is all right for him to break his promise, because we accept the normative statement that it is all right to break one's promise, or at any rate promises of that sort, in order to protect one's health. Thus we have one plausible norm-fact combination or set of premises outweighing another. But how are we to know that these are all the facts that need to be considered? Well, just a little familiarity with the man and his circumstances, and with the promisee and his circumstances, might well give us practical assurance that no other facts will be salient or of important weight. For instance, we may learn that the promisee, a dinner chairman, is having trouble getting another speaker on short notice; or that the promissor will now have the opportunity to spend one of his rare evenings at home with his family. If these seem to be the sort of evaluatively significant facts that can be further adduced, we may well conclude that they will not affect our judgment either way. All we would need to say then is that the man's action was not wrong because, although he had promised to make the speech, his health would not permit it.[1] Here we have an acknowledgment of a countervailing fact, both relevant norms remaining tacit. On the basis of all the factual inquiry that the question could be held to require if we were to be reasonably well informed of the facts, our judgment would be an eminently reasonable one. Obviously it would be no less reasonable if, by some unlikely series of coincidences that no one could have been expected to anticipate or inquire into, his going to make the speech would have resulted in some great good to many other people and only small discomfort to himself. Thus a limit to inquiry is possible under this theory, as indeed we normally assume in actual moral practice and discourse, whereas it seems to be impossible under a method of moral truth.

Suppose we add a few more facts that might influence one's judgment in view of norms reasonably held. Let us suppose that the man decides that it is his duty to speak at the meeting, a science convention, in spite of a very grave illness. He thinks he has made an important discovery but is now too weak to prepare an adequate report of it, and he fears that this may be his only chance to disclose it informally to competent people. One might well agree with him that it is his duty to do what he promised, although it would not be the promise but something else that was the basis of his duty. At least one might easily agree that this is a reasonable judgment on *his* part, given his well-known dedication to science. But his wife, although fully aware of these circumstances, concludes that it is by no means his duty; she feels that he would be fully justified in trying to prolong his life by avoiding this severe tax on his strength, with the hope of still being able to make his disclosure at a later date. Assuming that her judgment is disinterested, it might easily be a reasonable one. Thus contrary judgments may be equally justified.

We have just seen how facts whose relevance depends on norms one concedes to be plausible or morally acceptable may nevertheless be outweighed or discounted. But we have said that a rea-

---

[1] I have expanded an example of Stevenson's; see *Ethics and Language* (New Haven, Conn.: Yale University Press, 1948), p. 126.

sonable survey of the facts will also involve our attending to matters which others regard as relevant but which we may or may not finally regard as relevant ourselves. That is, in taking the moral point of view we may or may not finally agree that the norms on which such facts would depend for their logical relevance are morally plausible. This may sound complicated but it need not be, as the following statement will illustrate: "I admit that school desegregation would promote social intimacy between members of different races. But it would help to lessen the educational disadvantages now borne by the minority race. Moreover, the whole ideal of racial exclusiveness is bad for the very reason, among others, that it perpetuates these disadvantages." Here, both norm 1 (that intimacy between the races should be avoided) and norm 2 (that a minority race should not be placed at an educational disadvantage, and any such existing disadvantages should be removed) are initially taken into account. But then facts whose relevance depends on norm 2 are cited for the rejection of norm 1, and with it the relevance of facts that depend upon it for their relevance.

Supposing that we have explained how a person's judgment can be a reasonable one for *him* to make, is this what is meant by saying that a moral judgment is sound or justified? It will be objected that a person's judgment could be justified in our sense (b) and yet be morally objectionable or outrageous. There is nothing in our method that will certainly prevent a person from reaching absurd or shocking judgments if he is only eccentric enough psychologically. My answer to this is, first, that if a person does offer a judgment and reasons for it which, it seems, no informed and disinterested person would offer, it may well be that he has not in fact satisfied the conditions of our method. It might be possible to determine whether he has or not; and in any case if he has not, then he poses no problem for our theory. If he has, then we must indeed regard him as a very eccentric person. But what of it? The objection that his judgment is "morally absurd" only takes one's own moral opinion as the absolute standard for judging others'; or at least it assumes that there is some method of certifying moral truth, and that its results are, or would be, so and so. Neither assumption has the slightest warrant. If a person had formed his moral opinion in accordance with our method, it would be quite *unreasonable* for anyone to say that it was an absurd or outrageous opinion. On the other hand, the more people did use this method the greater would be the likelihood that their substantive evaluations would tend to agree. At least it is plausible to think so, and surely this would be so among people of similar cultural experience and moral traditions. And no other method of forming and testing our autonomous moral judgments would seem quite so likely to have such a tendency. Moreover, even when people did arrive at contrary results by using this method, there would seem to be a good chance of their preserving a measure of mutual respect and understanding if each knew that the other had made up his mind in this way. Indeed, there would probably be a better chance than in almost any other situation one could imagine.

Let us intentionally take a difficult example, one that will embarrass our theory if any plausible example will. It just may be plausible that *some* people born and raised in the United States, particularly in the South, could disinterestedly and in full awareness of relevant facts and the interests of everybody concerned, judge that racial segregation ought to be preserved, that it is morally wrong to require or permit desegregation. (I do not believe that millions who still favor segregation have reached or could have reached this position via our method.) Now, much as one might regret that a person should hold such a view, especially a disinterested and informed person, I think it would be quite unreasonable to say that he is objectively or substantively wrong, and "obviously so." It would be unreasonable because there does not seem to be a single fact or inference of any kind that one could advance to show that he is "objectively and substantively wrong." All we could say is that a careful examination of the salient facts leads us to make a judgment contrary to his. We might well be amazed that he could persist in his attitude while actually viewing the question disinterestedly and in full awareness of the interests and desires of everyone concerned, and of the effects of segregation as they are now understood by competent students, and of all other plainly relevant facts. But notice that even in such a case ethical disagreement does not necessarily entail a blank wall of mutual hostility, as other "noncognitivist" theories often conclude.

For despite our amazement and disappointment, we could not have utter contempt for someone who was willing to test his moral opinions in the way we have described. One could hardly call the man a contemptible racist, although he would certainly be a product of racism. We might regret that our civilization has been the kind to produce this sort of civilized person, but he would be civilized in a very important sense.

If anyone wants to insist that such a person's judgment is not a reasonable one, let him explain how to show (or even what it means to say) that the man's judgment is false or interpersonally invalid in autonomous morality. It seems quite clear that the best we could hope to give is a fairly strong empirical argument that *no* one could in fact arrive at or retain that view under our method. This may be true, and of course one hopes it is.

III

Can it be shown that this *is* the proper method of ethics? In order to show this, it seems that there are at least two main hurdles one would have to jump. First, since I have eradicated the notion of moral truth, I will be accused of making as radical a change in moral conceptions as ethical naturalism makes, although a different one. Second, how can *any* method for autonomous morality be consistently laid down or identified? Won't the methodic norm for ethics be itself a challengeable moral prescription? I will try to explain why I think the answer to the latter question is No, and I will conclude by showing that the first accusation is also mistaken.

It will be helpful at first to try to conceive of ethical discourse as having some social function that will justify the method set forth in sections I and II, although we will later on dispense with this speculation. The sense of "function" we will use is one that has emerged in the philosophy of biology and social science and has been discussed by others in connection with "the function of ethics."[2] This is the sense in which to say that some organ or

[2] See, e.g., Ernest Nagel, *The Structure of Science* (New York: Harcourt, Brace and World, 1961), pp. 520-535, esp. pp. 525f.; and also part 1 of Chapter 12. Cf. also R. B. Brandt, *Ethical Theory* (Englewood Cliffs, N.J.: Prentice-Hall, 1959), pp. 255-258.

activity has function F means that there is some system S such that F is a necessary condition for the existence of S, or for the maintenance of S in some certain state, often a state of "health." Thus it is a fact that the function of the heart is to pump blood. A given organ or activity can of course have more than one function in this sense, and with respect to more than one system.

Let us sketch an empirical hypothesis about the function of ethics, using the foregoing sense of "function." Let us suppose that ethical reflection and discourse have the function of producing agreement, or at least favorable conditions for the occurrence of agreement, among people who engage in such discourse. That this is the direct "job" of ethics may gain some initial plausibility from the intuitive conception of ethical reasonableness that we have just sketched. Let us suppose, further, that a group of people cannot continue to exist (nonpathologically or at all) as a "society" unless there is maintained among them a certain minimum level of agreement in moral evaluations. So that our hypothesis may be more than a tautology (see Nagel), we shall not make it definitive of "society" or "healthy society" that this level be maintained. We shall assume that there are other necessary conditions of the existence and health of a society besides this one. Now (to continue the guess) ethical reflection and discourse act to maintain the necessary level of consensus by causing people to have disinterested and informed views and to communicate them to one another with supporting reasons. As I remarked before, no other method would seem so likely as the method of sections I and II to promote moral agreement; and it seems plausible that the widespread practice of such a method would be the most likely means of attaining and sustaining a given level or extent of agreement among the members of society generally. For when people take a *disinterested* stance, and base their judgments on (by and large) the same body of relevant facts, the two greatest obstacles to agreement are overcome: personal interest and ignorance. The *communication* of our judgments and reasons, moreover, provides important favoring conditions for agreement. It is then more likely that we will structure moral problems similarly, and no doubt there is an important factor of nonlogical persuasion in such communications. Without ethical discourse, we would probably not develop enough of the same evaluations to enable us to live together and cooperate, at least in any satisfactory and viable way. For, of course, disinterested moral views can vary on given substantive issues (consider the status of women in different moral traditions, to take a single example). That a group of people should happen to live together according to one style or pattern rather than some other is no doubt both a result and a cause of their having similar disinterested opinions on moral questions.

Obviously this sketch would need to be specified in various ways. For instance, one would need to propose suitable, nonquestion-begging definitions of "society" and "ethics" or "ethical reflection and discourse." One would need to specify clearly the state G of society that ethics operates to maintain. *What* level and degree of agreement? And what do "level" and "degree" mean here? And how is failure to maintain this level or degree related to a pathological condition of society? And what pathological condition? Shall our hypothesis apply to all societies or only to certain types of society or subsociety, for example those in which people *commonly* make autonomous moral judgments? These and other questions would no doubt have to be answered if one were to try to devise a hypothesis that was both testable and worth testing. My purpose is not to do that, but merely to spell out a *conceivable* procedure under which the method sketched in the last two sections could be shown to be the correct way to form and offer reasons for one's autonomous moral judgments. That procedure is to find the function of the activity known as ethics (if it has a function) through empirical research and then to determine how such activity must be carried on if it is to fulfill that function. In order to illustrate this procedure, I have made a broad guess as to what the outcome of applying it would be. This guess, to sum it up, is as follows. First, there is a certain activity (A) in which people make autonomous evaluations and identify them in one way or another as "ethical" evaluations and give reasons to one another for holding them. Second, this activity has the function (F) of producing agreement among people in those evaluations. Now the condition of A requisite for the occurrence of F to the extent necessary to maintain state G (such and such a level of moral agreement among people generally) which is in turn requisite for the existence of the society (S) is as follows. A must be carried on in the manner indicated in sections I and II above, by the people constituting *S* to the extent *E*. In other words, unless the individuals of a certain aggregation of people make disinterested and informed moral evaluations and propose them to one another as acceptable in the light of salient facts and unless they do this frequently and commonly enough, "social" life breaks down or does not begin in that group.

Now suppose an investigation were made of such a hypothesis and it were overwhelmingly confirmed. It seems that we would then have found out the purpose or point of ethics, and could say what it was in a true nonethical statement. The direct "natural purpose" or function of ethical reflection and discourse would be to produce agreement in our autonomous moral evaluations, while the indirect purpose would be to maintain state *G*, just as the direct function of the heart is to pump blood "in order that" certain physiological states may be maintained. And it seems that we could then affirm that the method given in sections I and II is the proper method of ethics without making an ethical statement. To be sure, we would be making an evaluative statement, but not one the making and defending of which would tend to maintain *G*. The proper method of defending our statement, indeed, would not be at all like the method whose employment operates to sustain *G*. We would not appeal to the moral point of view and try to explicate reasonable norms and relevant facts and the rest of it, to show the reasonableness of our statement. On the contrary, we would employ a certain type of normative reasoning and actually show its truth. We would argue that, *granting* the desirability of *G*, this is the correct way to form and defend our moral judgments. We would cite the evidence which shows that it is only through the widespread use of such method that *G* is likely to be secured. We would not have to say, "One ought to pursue *G*," or "*G* is intrinsically desirable." And even if we were to say such things, it is clear that we would not and could not be making *ethical* statements. If we said "One ought to pursue *G*," we might possibly mean that we ought to pursue *G* if we want to attain some other end whose attainment *G* makes possible, e.g., the existence of our society; and if we said "*G* is intrinsically desirable," we might possibly mean just that we enthusiastically endorse or desire *G*. But more than likely we would be confusedly trying to make ethical statements and failing. Once the lesson of our new empirical knowledge of the game of ethics had sunk in, however, we would no doubt come to appreciate the futility and pointlessness of such attempts and simply stop making them.

It may seem that this is not correct, and that someone could still make an issue of G, and hence of our method, by challenging or denouncing them in ethical terms. But logically no one could do this, since ethical terms would have no cognitive significance and would derive their only function and meaning as justifiably predicable terms from that very method or practice. That is, in using such terms, what we would be claiming is precisely that we had followed that method or satisfied the rule of that practice, with such and such an evaluative response resulting. Thus it would be nonsense to say that the method of sections I and II is ethically wrong, for example, because this would amount to invoking and rejecting it in the same breath. To be sure, as matters actually stand it does *seem* as though we can use ethical terms to evaluate any human activity whatever, and this may very well be so; but it is a point that runs to the empirical plausibility of the hypothesis, not to the logic of the situation that would be disclosed if the hypothesis were found to be in all probability true. In that situation, to sum it up, we could give valid and complete arguments to justify the moral reasonableness of our judgments, because

(1) we could actually carry through the method of reasonableness in forming our judgments;

(2) we could justify these judgments in sense (b) by showing that we had in fact carried that method through;

(3) that method itself does not constitute a challengeable moral principle because it assigns no evaluative consequence to any fact; and

(4) that method could not otherwise be challenged for its moral justification because it would be constitutive of the concept of moral justification.

Now, to be sure, people might eventually decide to abolish or change this game, this social art whose rule had thus been made clear. But no single prophet or eccentric moralist would have the jurisdiction or influence to do this. He could not reject the method of ethics in an ethical judgment. The best he could manage, if he were clearheaded, would be to avoid inconsistency by announcing that he refuses to play this game and resolves hereafter to use this evaluative terminology in his own way, a way which he would have to explain to us if he wanted us to understand him. He might announce, for example, that when he says G is undesirable, or that it is wrong to follow the method of ethics, he just means that he personally finds G distasteful, or perhaps that he likes some condition H much better, and G hinders H.

IV

Taken as a whole, the foregoing hypothesis is not very plausible, both for the reason mentioned in the preceding paragraph and for other reasons one could mention. But worse yet, there is something fishy after all in this use of the idea of a function. In the case of the heart, we naturally tend to assume that state G is a certain "normal" state, e.g., the state of the body in which it is able to do very much more work than can the body of a heart patient who is barely able to hold his head up. But we can say that if G' is the state in which the patient has just that much strength and no more, then it is a fact that his heart has function F' (pumping blood, but poorly relative to G) in the sense that F' is a necessary condition to maintain G' in S. This is just as much a fact as that the heart has function F, i.e., pumping blood well relative to G. And so even if the hypothesis sketched in section III were true, we could not really conclude that the method of sections I and II is the right way to engage in the activity of ethics, for that might have no better standing as a fact than if someone were to say that such and such another method (e.g., forming our judgments disinterestedly but with no factual inquiry or reflection) is right because ethics would sustain such and such another condition of society if it were generally done that way.

What is the point, then, of this armchair anthropology? Its point is that it shows us how to make sense of ethics. It gives us a model for constructing a valid and completable method of testing and justifying moral judgments *without any radical change in the ordinary concept of an autonomous moral judgment,* such as that made by ethical naturalism, *and without any other radical conceptual change.* I think this can be seen as follows.

(1) People could *decide* what end they want to further through the practice of making autonomous moral judgments and engaging in justificatory discourse concerning them. This goal might be regarded as necessary for the "health" of "society," but this is optional. In establishing a literal purpose for ethics, we would avoid all the problems about the existence and identification of a "natural purpose" that were just mentioned. *G* would be identified beyond doubt. (How people could be induced to make such a decision, and what events would constitute or signify the decision, are questions I shall not discuss.)

(2) People could then adopt a procedure for making and defending autonomous moral judgments that would be most likely to further that end or purpose if it were commonly followed. This would be a matter for empirical inquiry and judgment.

(3) The procedure adopted, however, would have to be morally neutral in the sense that it could not entail or constitute a substantive moral norm, i.e., a principle, standard, or rule that assigns determinate valuative consequences to determinate matters of fact. This would impose a restriction on the sorts of goals that could be chosen under (1).

(4) A logical situation similar to that described in items (1) through (4) of the last paragraph of the preceding section would then obtain. We would have a valid and completable method of justifying autonomous moral judgments.

(5) My own candidate for the function or direct job of ethics (*F*) is that it produce or at least favor the occurrence of agreement among people in their autonomous moral judgments and that it foster mutual respect when they disagree. And my candidate for the goal or purpose of ethics (*G*) is that it maximize the amount of such agreement and mutual respect among people generally. I submit that the method of sections I and II would have that direct effect, and is the method most likely to further that purpose. That much of the hypothesis sketched in section III I propose quite seriously.

(6) Unless I am mistaken, people often do carry on ethical reflection and discourse at least roughly as described in sections I and II, but they do not clearly realize that the main point of moral discourse is that just proposed. I believe this is because they con-

fusedly hang onto the demand for moral truth, not realizing that it is proper only to heteronomous morality.

There is certainly some reshaping of concepts involved in this proposal, but I think we can see now that the clarification attained is well worth it and that the cost is indeed slight in itself. We have revised the confused notion of objectivity in autonomous morality so as to exclude the demand for truth, i.e., unique interpersonal correctness of content in moral judgments. This demand is undeniably present in the common notion of moral objectivity. It is just the conceptual element that precludes the justification of autonomous judgments even as it reinforces our demand for such justifications. But when we see this and when we see how it is possible to get along without this element, we cease to cherish it. Since it is utterly obscure how an autonomous moral judgment could be shown to be uniquely and interpersonally correct in content, it is incredible that this notion of moral truth has any application at all. I think we will hardly have any urge to retain it once we are quite clear that it is the notion of truth in *autonomous* morality that we are talking about, and that there is another perfectly clear and useful sense of objectivity and rationality available there.

EPILOGUE

Enter the Prophet. We hear him repudiating and condemning this goal for ethics (or whatever goal the people of our society or the world have set up satisfying the foregoing requirements). Is he making an ethical statement and thereby showing that the method thus obtained is not valid and completable? What shall we say about him now? Only this: he is not playing our game. He is not making an ethical statement that is permissible under the rules of ethical discourse as they have now been clearly worked out. No doubt he is making an ethical statement of the *old* sort. No doubt it did not then seem to be an abuse of language to say such a thing, and therefore was not. And in a way it still is not, for the Prophet does not have to play our game. He is still raising an ethical issue in the old sense. But who should care? The old sense seems to have been (remediable) nonsense.

INDEX